Campaigns and Elections

Campaigns
and Elections

A Reader in Modern
American Politics

Edited by

Larry J. Sabato
University of Virginia

Scott, Foresman/Little, Brown Series in Political Science

Scott, Foresman and Company

Glenview, Illinois   Boston   London

LIBRARY OF CONGRESS
Library of Congress Cataloging-in-Publication Data

Campaigns and elections : a reader in modern American politics /
    editor, Larry J. Sabato.
        p.   cm.
    Edited articles which originally appeared in Campaigns and
elections magazine.
    Includes index.
    ISBN 0-673-39912-5
    1. Electioneering— United States.   2. Campaign management—United
States.   I. Sabato, Larry.
JK2281.C35   1989
324.973'09—dc19   88-15507
                                                                   CIP

1 2 3 4 5 6 7 8 9 10 — MVN — 94 93 92 91 90 89 88

Printed in the United States of America

TEXT CREDITS

Portions of Articles 1, 11, and 13 are drawn from *The Rise of Political Consultants:
New Ways of Winning Elections* by Larry J. Sabato (Copyright © 1981 by Larry J.
Sabato) and are used by permission of Basic Books, Inc., Publishers, New York.

Copyrighted material appearing in Jonathan Robbin's article, "Geodemographics:
The New Magic" is reprinted from the Spring 1980 edition of *Campaigns and Elections*
magazine by permission of *Campaigns and Elections* and Claritas Corporation.

Portions of Chapter 18 have been extracted from *PAC Power: Inside the World
of Political Action Committees*, by Larry J. Sabato, with the permission of W. W. Norton
& Company, Inc. Copyright © 1985, 1984 by Larry J. Sabato.

ART CREDITS

Photographs for Articles 2 and 26 Courtesy of the Smithsonian Institution,
Washington, D.C.

To Professor Stanley Kelley, Jr.,
with gratitude and admiration

Foreword

In 1948, Harry S. Truman defeated Thomas E. Dewey in the campaign for president of the United States. It was a major upset, for just about everyone had predicted a Dewey victory.

While I was only peripherally involved in campaign politics at the time, I was much involved with then-new electronic computers. I felt that a business approach to campaign politics would some day be adopted by campaign strategists. I used my research laboratory's calculators to "target" some local elections successfully and started building files on the "technology" of the electoral campaign process.

Thirty-two years later my campaign technology files were huge, and following my success with *Mergers & Acquisitions* magazine, I launched *Campaigns & Elections* magazine, which has been well received.

The exciting thing about *Campaigns & Elections* is that it has helped to open up the political campaign process. The material in *Campaigns & Elections* can potentially aid anyone in running for office. A campaigner with a home computer can buy a list of voters in the morning and can solicit votes and money in the afternoon. To win, however, candidates and staffers must learn what works and what doesn't. *Campaigns & Elections* contributors have tried to tell readers why they lost as well as why they won.

During the first years of *Campaigns & Elections* we published some 150 pieces. Larry Sabato and I, with the help of David Beiler, former *Campaigns & Elections* editor, reviewed them, and for this book selected those we believe best demonstrate that the political campaign process is both art and science—with a good measure of fun and games thrown in.

One idea behind this volume is to help readers understand the political campaign process that seems to cause discomfort and confusion to so many. In my fifty years in Washington, I've known hundreds of politicians. Ninety-nine percent were and are honest. They run honest campaigns and are honestly elected. Most are also very hardworking—both in running physically exhausting campaigns and in serving in office after the election.

You may ask why they give up promising careers in law or business with only a fair chance of getting elected the first time out. The romance, honor, and joy of service to one's community, state, or nation is the answer. To be on the inside and to play a part in molding the future is thrilling. I hope many readers will sense this thrill as they read this volume, and by better understanding the election process, will be willing to get involved themselves.

Stanley Foster Reed
Founder and Former Publisher,
Campaigns & Elections

Note: For information about *Campaigns & Elections* magazine, write 1835 K Street, N.W., Suite 403, Washington, D.C. 20006.

Preface

The campaign craft is in many respects a subterranean enterprise, obscured by a focus on personalities—the candidate's, the family's, and the political consultant's. What attention is received by the craft's specialties—the new campaign technologies such as media advertising, polling, and direct mail—is mixed; they are simultaneously glorified and damned in the popular press, praised for their mystical contribution to a candidate's election, and lamented for bold deceptions and the depersonalization of politics they represent.

This collection, primarily utilizing articles that have appeared in *Campaigns & Elections* magazine, examines some of the technologies that engender such awe and scorn. The authors of the various articles comprising this anthology have attempted to explain and analyze the techniques of modern politics for laymen and professionals alike, under the guidance of former magazine publisher Stanley Foster Reed. I have edited the volume with the hope that concerned citizens and students just beginning their study of politics will find it as useful as novice campaign staffers and candidates.

I wish to thank Stanley Foster Reed for enlisting me to undertake this project, David Beiler for his skillful research assistance, Beth Dougherty for her careful proofreading, Pierce McCleskey for another outstanding job of indexing, and Mildred and Weldon Cooper for their usual sustenance. My editor, John Covell, and his able assistant, Yvonne Mottershead, have made my association with Scott, Foresman and Company a pleasant and productive one. Finally, my thanks are due to Virginia Shine and her assistant, Paul Santoro, who efficiently supervised the production of this book.

This volume is warmly dedicated to Professor Stanley Kelley, Jr., of Princeton University, who first introduced me (and hundreds of other eager students over the years) to the world of political consultants. I remember not just Professor Kelley's ground-breaking research in the field but also the thoughtful and concerned attention he showered on each of his students—an example that should serve as a model for aspiring teachers everywhere.

Larry J. Sabato
Charlottesville, Virginia

Contents

Campaigns and Elections

Part One

Introduction

Magic . . . or Blue Smoke and Mirrors?

Reflections on the New Campaign Technology and the Political Consultant Trade

Larry J. Sabato

It was 1936, and Republican presidential nominee Alfred M. Landon had a revealing brush with the new campaign technology of public opinion polling, then in its infancy. The *Literary Digest* had taken a poll by mailing a sample presidential ballot to ten million Americans, and the returns suggested a stunning upset was in the making: Landon would handily defeat President Franklin D. Roosevelt.[1] As Landon later recalled it, the poll was the "one time in that 1936 campaign when I thought I might beat Roosevelt. For an hour or so that night, I could see myself in the White House."[2] The technology failed Landon mainly by an extreme oversampling of wealthy Republican-leaning citizens—and the voters failed him, too, as FDR won one of the greatest landslides in presidential history.

Polling has become far more sophisticated in the decades since, and other technologies, from media advertising to direct mail, have been invented and refined. Yet the technologies still often fail candidates and campaigns;

the political consultants who develop and master the technologies frequently make mistakes in judgment that startle amateurs; and despite popular lore and journalistic legend, few candidates can truly be said to be creations of their clever consultants and dazzling campaign techniques.

This is partly because politics always has been (and always will be) far more art than science, not subject to precise manipulation or formulaic computation. *In the end, in most cases, the candidate himself or herself wins or loses the race; his or her abilities, qualifications, communications skills, and weaknesses have far more impact on the shape of the vote than all consultants and technologies combined.* This simple truth is both warmly reassuring and remarkably overlooked by election analysts and reporters who are seemingly mesmerized by the exorbitant claims of consultants and the flashy computer lights of their technologies.

The voter deserves much of the credit for whatever encouragement we can draw from this candidate-centered view of politics. Most of the electorate want to take the real measure of the people seeking their vote, and they retain

---

[1] Larry J. Sabato, *The Rise of Political Consultants: New Ways of Winning Elections* (New York: Basic Books, 1981), p. 69.

[2] As quoted in *Washington Post*, 13 October, 1987, p. A6.

a healthy skepticism about the techniques of running for office. Political cartoonist Tom Toles suggested as much when he depicted the seven preparatory steps the modern candidate takes: (1) set out to discover what voters want; (2) poll extensively; (3) study demographic trends; (4) prepare sophisticated interpretation of in-depth voter interviews; (5) analyze results; (6) discover that what voters want is a candidate who doesn't need to do steps 1 through 5; (7) pretend you didn't. The chastened politician tells his assembled throng, "I follow my conscience."[3]

Having opened this book by debunking its subject, I hasten to add that consultants and new campaign technologies *can* contribute a great deal to campaigns. The consultants (or the best of them) add a lifetime of experience in politics spanning hundreds of separate campaigns, which produces the instinctive judgment and informed guessing that help to chart a campaign's course. The technologies confer efficiency and knowledge, above all. They make it possible for campaigns to make the best use of limited resources, to transfer information to voters in appealing and potentially effective ways, and to provide vital data about the preferences of individual voters and the collective electorate. All of this comes at a high price, of course; campaign techniques can be enormously expensive (though in the politician's view, the most costly campaign is the one that is lost).

The emphasis in this reader is necessarily on the substance of the technologies that have transformed the ways modern campaigns are waged. The rest of Part One contains an introductory piece on candidate imagery through American history and an article for novice candidates on "getting started." Part Two will review new applications of some old campaign techniques, including computerized opposition research, press release writing, speechwriting, door-to-door campaigning,

paid canvassing, and special event fundraising. Then, Part Three discusses advanced campaign technologies, especially television and radio advertising, polling, voter registration, direct mail, telemarketing, elaborate voter identification and targeting schemes, and political action committee (PAC) fundraising.

Finally, eight case studies are presented, featuring the new technologies at work on the campaign trail. Among the diverse cases analyzed are the 1987 Kentucky governor's race that propelled an unknown into the statehouse, a mayor's race in Charlotte where a microcomputer helped a black candidate win, initiative campaigns on nuclear power in Washington State and gun control in California, the 1984 U.S. Senate race in North Carolina where independent PACs aided Senator Jesse Helms's reelection, registration drive politics in Chicago, and the election of a tribal chairman among the Navajo Indians.

The concluding article in this volume on "the first media campaign," written by the Smithsonian Institution's Keith Melder, places the new campaign technology in proper historical perspective. Melder's look back at the 1840 presidential campaign is chock full of analogies to present-day electoral practices—a sobering reminder of the unchanging essence of American politics and a cautionary tale of the enduring dangers in technique-laden campaigns.

This is intended to be a reader not so much for the politically sophisticated as for the novice, not just a "how-to" volume but an examination that mixes enthusiasm for the wonders of the consultant trade with skepticism about many contemporary campaign technologies—the combination of emotions most likely, in this editor's opinion, to produce real enlightenment about the ways and means of modern American election techniques.[4]

---

[3]From 1987 cartoon by Tom Toles, copyrighted by *The Buffalo News*.

[4]Some of these introductory remarks are excerpted from a paper written for a colloquium on political campaign technology held February 2, 1988, in Washington, D.C., and sponsored by the Annenberg Washington Program on Communications Policy Studies.

Larry J. Sabato

Creating Candidate Imagery:
The Man on Horseback

Keith Melder

Image-making was a fixture of American politics long before the television age, as Keith Melder shows in this article. At least since the advent of full-fledged party politics in the 1830s, candidates and their managers have vigorously sought to shape the public's view of each election's personalities and issues. While television makes image-making easier in some respects, instant mass communications—monitored by a vigilant press and opposition—make it much more difficult for candidates to lie blatantly and to create images for themselves out of whole cloth. Similarly, as Melder illustrates, the candidates of old were packaged and managed more completely and simplistically—and in some cases more misleadingly—than any modern-day political consultant could possibly engineer.

Modern interpretations of political campaigning associate the concept of images in politics with television and political advertising. Historically, however, we can trace the exploitation of public images back to the earliest days of American politics—to the time of George Washington.

The Founding Fathers had no acquaintance with the idea of political imagery, or at least they had no thought of using the word *image* in association with political power. Nevertheless they well knew the most powerful candidate imagery in American history. The very foundation of national survival in the era of the Constitution rested on the image of authority and unity embodied in George Washington. Washington, the unanimous and only possible choice as first president,

Keith Melder is a curator in the Division of Political History in the National Museum of American History of the Smithsonian Institution.

possessed a larger-than-life image understood by his contemporaries. He would probably have used the term "reputation" instead, but in essence his fellow-revolutionaries had contrived an image for him, making him a monument in his own lifetime.

What is a political image? In his book *The Image*, significantly subtitled *Or What Happened to the American Dream*, Daniel J. Boorstin identifies certain characteristics of the image: It is "synthetic" or contrived, constructed to achieve certain goals. It is "believable," appealing to the common sense and values of its audience; it is "passive," "vivid and concrete," "simplified," and "ambiguous." Images offer materials from which their observers supply interpretations and draw conclusions.

Political images are specialized applications of image-making. They serve as devices of shorthand identification, distortion, appeal, and illusion—inevitable elements of modern political persuasion. Like language itself, images create a symbolic universe. In the world of commerce, they are fabricated in order to produce results in the marketplace. Similarly, political images are most effectively applied in that marketplace of politics, campaigns, and elections.

Looking again at George Washington's political image, we can see a model, a standard against which the projections of other candidates could be measured. Washington was first a hero, a gallant military leader, a Cincinnatus who left his plow in order to save the republic. Distant and disinterested, he occupied a pedestal of honor, elevated above his contemporaries, a symbol of the nation itself. In time, regard for his exploits grew to the point that he was thought of as a superman, almost godlike.

In the years after Washington's death, his image enlarged. An extensive and fascinating mythology grew up around the story of his life. The Federalist Party identified itself with his goals and personality, founding political clubs known as Washington Benevolent Societies to perpetuate and take advantage of his memory. Other partisan groups and candidates used the Washington image to promote themselves. Political devices produced in favor of such disparate candidates as Zachary Taylor, William Jennings Bryan, and Douglas MacArthur exploited the Washington image. The mythic qualities of Washington imagery are integral parts of American historical and political culture.

During the quarter century after Washington's death, with the ascendency of presidents from the Virginia dynasty, presidential imagery became subdued. Contests of this period left few reminders of such campaign devices.

The conquering commoner

The next great surge of political image-making appeared with Andrew Jackson in 1824. Widely known and already popular as the Hero of New Orleans because of his great victory over the British forces in the War of

Grand in Peace, Brave in War,
Lovingly in the Hearts of His Countrymen.

First in Peace, First in War,
First in the Hearts of His Countrymen.

As this folding handbill would indicate, the managers of William Jennings Bryan went to extraordinary lengths to associate their candidate with the Washington image.

Keith Melder

1812, Jackson was a ready-made image candidate when he decided to run for president. Combining the heroic demeanor and military prowess of a Washington with new rustic elements of the western frontier, Jackson projected a powerful image of romantic energy and authority. His nicknames—the Old Hero, Hero of New Orleans, Old Hickory, and others—all reflected his manliness and bravery. A host of devices from hickory poles to campaign songs, ceramic ware, and campaign novelties promoted the Hero's powerful reputation.

The theme of presenting the candidate as rustic hero developed still further in the Whig campaign of 1840. As we will discuss in a later article in this reader, the Whig Party settled on a central image of their candidate, associating him with the log cabin and hard cider. Whig partisans organized in all the states to promote the images of William Henry Harrison and his running mate—"Tippecanoe and Tyler Too." Harrison was portrayed in thousands of campaign items as a simple farmer living in a log cabin, comforted by his ever-present hard cider barrel. With latchstring always out, the mythological Harrison was ready to welcome all visitors to his cabin, whether notable or ordinary, with plain frontier hospitality.

Not only a man of the people, the hard cider candidate was depicted as a victorious and brave military leader, a hero worshipped by his men. Stories of his success in battle, published endlessly and celebrated in song and slogan, recalled Harrison's decisive martial leadership. Harrison was also one of the first presidential contenders to have his likeness widely distributed across the nation in prints, ribbons, and other devices.

Several of Harrison's successors also attempted to delight and capture the attention of the public by projecting positive images. Henry Clay ran in 1844 with several image clusters, mainly adhering to the rustic pattern established by Jackson and Harrison. He called himself the "farmer of Ashland," the "mill boy," and "gallant Harry of the West," suggesting his rural origins, even though, like Jackson, he was a wealthy planter and slave owner.

But Clay's most vivid appeal came with the nickname "the old coon," which was translated into "that same old coon," symbolized by the depiction of a raccoon on many campaign devices representing Clay. The coonskin, like the log cabin, stood for rural simplicity and a homespun personality. Clay's opponent, Democrat James K. Polk, posed as "young hickory," the strong inheritor of Jackson's mantle.

Hail hero

Several hero–candidates appeared during the 1840s and 1850s. In 1848 the Whigs nominated a professional soldier who had never voted in a presidential election. Zachary

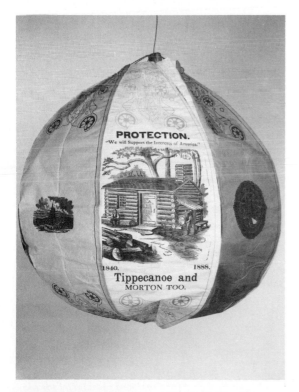

Benjamin Harrison tried to evoke the spirit of his grandfather's fabulously successful image campaign of two generations before.

Taylor, a victorious general in the War with Mexico nicknamed "Old Rough and Ready," had few qualifications as a candidate except for his heroic image. Praised and paraded as a noble military leader who could take charge of the nation, he won the race for the presidency. Four years later the Whigs, divided and nearly defunct, nominated another professional general, Winfield Scott, who fulfilled the requirements of martial heroism. Unfortunately nicknamed "Old Fuss and Feathers," General Scott was not a winner in the presidential sweepstakes.

Between 1852 and 1856 the unlucky Whigs disintegrated. Many reorganized with other opponents of the Democrats to form a new "Republican Party" opposed to the spread of slavery. Campaigning with such slogans as "free speech, free soil, free labor, free men," the Republicans ran their first presidential nominee in 1856, one John C. Fremont. Not a general, but a hero nevertheless, Fremont had won fame as an explorer of the American West. His exploits were presented to the public through his image as "the pathfinder."

Political leaders clearly recognized the advantage of running hero-candidates for the presidency. Their reputations for bravery provided ready-made fame and images akin to that of Washington. At a time when parties might not agree on all issues and public policies, hero–candidates provided a positive image around which all could rally.

Imagery on the offense

At about the same time that image candidates became popular, party organizers developed negative-image campaigns aimed at the opposition. In the election of 1828 both candidates, Andrew Jackson and John Quincy Adams, were dragged down by negative "mudslinging." Jackson was hit with accusations of being a would-be emperor, murderer, duelist, and adulterer, among other things; Adams was tagged as a monarchist, procurer, and an effete snob. Jackson's successor, Martin Van Buren, had to run against charges that

he was a corset-wearing dandy and an unscrupulous political schemer. Opponents accused him of misusing public funds to live in high style, drinking champagne from golden goblets in the White House.

"Honest Abe, railsplitter"

Abraham Lincoln, the second Republican nominee, was an image candidate both in the partisan sense that he was the focus of a positive appeal and in the neutral sense that his public identity was established in the course of the campaign. Comparatively obscure in the spring of 1860, Lincoln had to be promoted vigorously following his convention victory.

Two positive attributes dominated Lincoln's political image: his integrity and his rustic Western background. The slogan "Honest

John Charles Fremont was chosen the first Republican nominee for President principally for his very marketable image. Dubbed "the pathfinder," Fremont traded heavily on his fame as an explorer of the American West.

Keith Melder

Abe" circulated widely during the contest, appearing on banners, sheet music, and in campaign publications. A variety of devices promoted Lincoln's association with the rural West. The ingenious image of Lincoln the "railsplitter," contrived at the 1860 Illinois Republican convention, evoked almost ideally the candidate's real frontier background. Simple, emotional, suggesting basic American aspirations of individual achievement, the railsplitter image surely equaled the log cabin in promotional force.

Perhaps more than any other candidate since William Henry Harrison, Lincoln had his visage projected across the land. Popular prints with Lincoln's portrait circulated everywhere, making the candidate's likeness widely available and familiar. Printmakers worked from photographs, sketches, and portraits to mass-produce likenesses of Lincoln the candidate and, later, the president. Sometimes they flattered him, sometimes they made him look homely, and they came in many different styles and price ranges.

Such prints sold by the thousands to an audience eager to learn about the appearance of this little-known prairie lawyer. Less widely distributed but available to a large public were the many photographic portraits of President Lincoln. By 1864, when he ran for reelection, Lincoln must have known that most Americans were familiar with his somewhat ungainly yet reassuring looks.

Crowning the crusaders

After the Civil War, not surprisingly, the image of the general or military leader became prominent among presidential hopefuls. Lincoln's wartime Democratic opponent in 1864 was a general, George B. McClellan. Ulysses S. Grant, an able general, and an unfortunate president, traded effectively on his reputation as a military hero in running for the highest office in 1868 and 1872. Other Republicans taking advantage of their wartime military experience included Presidents James A. Garfield (1880), Benjamin Harrison (1888),

and William McKinley (1896, 1900).

Campaigning took on a distinctly military bearing during this period with uniformed marching groups and army-like discipline. Republican candidates assigned the entire Democratic Party a potent anti-image, picturing Democrats as Southern sympathizers, accusing them of being responsible for the Civil War, and "waving the bloody shirt." (The latter term originated when "Beast Ben" Butler of Massachusetts stood on the floor of the Senate waving the blood-drenched blouse of a Negro lynched by allegedly Democratic Klansmen.)

In the election of 1896, a new set of candidate and party images created a different campaign atmosphere from that of earlier contests. On both the Democratic and Republican sides, the contest was depicted as a crusade. William Jennings Bryan, the Democrat, ran as a crusader for moral righteousness, the common man, and the underdog, against the unrighteous power of gold and monopoly. Bryan, the candidate of silver, treated the coinage issue as a great moral cause. Silver coinage at a ratio of sixteen ounces of silver to one ounce of gold would overturn the "Crime of '73" which devalued silver. It would redeem the people as against the bankers and rejuvenate the depressed economy.

In contrast to Bryan's righteous revolution, Republican William McKinley conducted a moral crusade for conservatism. Billing himself as the "Advance Agent of Prosperity" during the severe depression in effect after 1893, McKinley championed the protective tariff and sound money. He openly courted the industrial labor force, arguing that ultimately the working man's wages benefited from high tariffs and a sound, gold-based money supply. Contrasting his solid secular imagery with Bryan's wild-eyed utopian visions, McKinley branded the free-trade, free-silver moralism of Bryan as un-American anarchy. In a hard-fought, expensive, unprecedented image contest, McKinley's responsible conservatism triumphed over Bryan's revolutionary zeal.

Energetic, audacious, physically aggressive, a lover of the outdoors and a firm moral leader, Theodore Roosevelt may have projected the most vivid image of any candidate in American history.

Man of action, compassion

One of the most vivid image candidates of the twentieth century was the century's first elected vice president, elevated to the highest office upon McKinley's assassination in 1901. Theodore Roosevelt (sarcastically called "that damned cowboy" by one Republican leader) came to the office by accident, but quickly became a natural and enthusiastic incumbent. His reputation as an outdoorsman stemmed in part from a youthful stint as a Western cowpuncher, reinforced by his leadership of a troop of volunteers called the "Rough Riders" in the Spanish–American War.

A colorful, outgoing, energetic president, "Teddy" Roosevelt had a genuine gift for self-created imagery. He popularized several political phrases reflecting his ebullient spirit: "Speak softly and carry a big stick—you will go far"; "muckraker," referring to journalist crusaders; "bully pulpit," use of the presidency to inspire; and "strong as a bull moose."

A related Roosevelt image was that of the Teddy Bear, derived from a 1902 incident in which the president refused to shoot a bear cub presented to him as a target. The occasion was immortalized in a newspaper cartoon by Clifford Berryman, then made tangible through the introduction of stuffed toy bears named after "Teddy" (with his permission) by the Ideal Toy Company of Brooklyn, New York.

The net impact of all these incidents and phrases produced a generally positive image for Roosevelt: energetic, audacious, physically aggressive, a lover of the outdoors, a moral leader. That he had certain less admirable attitudes and achievements did not detract much from his public image.

Other presidents since "Teddy" projected distinct yet less vital images than that of the first Roosevelt. William Howard Taft was considered a gregarious dilettante, Woodrow Wilson a somewhat detached scholar, Warren Harding an embodiment of middle America, Calvin Coolidge a taciturn Yankee, Herbert Hoover an engineering genius and efficiency

The story of Theodore Roosevelt's sparing a bear cub while hunting helped soften an overly rambunctious image. The act was immortalized with the introduction of the "Teddy Bear" by the Ideal Toy Co. The original (pictured here) was presented to Roosevelt's young son, Kermit.

Keith Melder

expert, Franklin Roosevelt an inspirational leader and friend to all, Harry Truman a plucky commoner, and Dwight Eisenhower a kindly, competent father-figure. Then came television and the rise of political consultants, inaugurating the modern age of image-making in politics.

How were these images created and propagated in contests that took place long before modern media campaigning? The ideas behind the images developed in many different ways. Heroic images emerged from military service in wartime and were embellished, sometimes almost beyond recognition. Other kinds of images often grew out of the experiences and personalities of the candidates, as for example the railsplitter candidacy of Lincoln. Some strong images, such as Harrison's log cabin, were invented almost by accident. Often, however, the circumstances of an image's origin were used creatively and were greatly enriched to enhance the office-seeker's appearance.

Although they did not call themselves public relations experts, the men who created and dispensed political imagery through most of the nineteenth and the early twentieth centuries were thorough professionals. Campaign managers, political writers, artists and cartoonists, and editors, they learned by experience how to present themselves and their candidate "products" in the most appealing manner.

As we have observed, images were conveyed through campaign devices of many varieties with varying methods, all aimed at similar purposes. The primary content of millions of mass-produced ribbons, buttons, textiles, and paper objects created a bond between the candidate and his supporters and gave his cause social credibility. Publications such as broadsides, pamphlets, newspapers, and campaign biographies developed stories and pictures that established, then reinforced certain public perceptions about the candidates. Graphics, including prints, photographs, posters, and caricatures, gave voters a feeling of personal familiarity with their proposed leaders. Long before television, other media presented vivid images to the electorate.

This brief account necessarily oversimplifies and compresses an intricate, lengthy story. The point is that candidate and presidential images have been ingredients of American politics since the earliest campaigns. Political imagery has a long if not always a distinguished history. The images we cherish grow out of our democratic faith in leaders of humble origins, close to the soil, morally sound, decisive yet fair. We support the kind of candidates who seem to represent the values we believe in.

Ultimately, whether "true" or misleading, candidate images are projections of faith and belief, not expressions of cool deliberation.

Sources

Boorstin, Daniel J. The Image, or What Happened to the American Dream. New York: Atheneum, 1962.

Brown, William Burlie. The People's Choice. The Presidential Image in the Campaign Biography. Baton Rouge, LA: Louisiana State University Press, 1960.

Fischer, Roger A., and Edmund B. Sullivan. American Political Ribbons and Ribbon Badges 1825-1981. Lincoln, MA: Quatterman Publications, 1985.

Heale, M J. The Presidential Quest: Candidates and Images in American Political Culture, 1787-1852. London and New York: Longman, 1982.

Holzer, Harold, Gabor S. Boritt, and Mark E. Neely, Jr. The Lincoln Image: Abraham Lincoln and the Popular Print. New York: Charles Scribner's Sons, 1984.

Jensen, Richard. The Winning of the Midwest: Social and Political Conflict, 1888-1896. Chicago: University of Chicago Press, 1971.

Pessen, Edward. The Log Cabin Myth: The Social Backgrounds of the Presidents. New Haven: Yale University Press, 1984.

Post, Robert C., ed. Every Four Years: The American Presidency. Washington: Smithsonian Exposition Books, 1980.

"Everyone Has to Start Somewhere": Veterans' Advice to Novice Candidates

Lorene Hanley Duquin

Running for office is one of the most difficult—and potentially rewarding—tasks anyone can decide to undertake. Especially in this age of investigative journalism and no-holds-barred campaigning, the costs of political candidacy can be high— and few office-seekers are oblivious to the dangers. Why, then, do people run? How do they become convinced that the benefits of electoral success are worth the considerable risks and sacrifices? Lorene Hanley Duquin asked these questions of a few of those who have thrown their hats into the ring and succeeded. Their answers are simple and unsurprising, yet refreshingly devoid of cynicism, and their advice may encourage others to give political candidacy a look. Expertise in politics or campaign techniques is less important than desire and hard work; after all, as Duquin explains, "Everyone has to start somewhere!"

The mighty oak was once a tiny acorn. And senators, representatives, governors, and mayors were once unknown individuals with big dreams. Some were doctors, lawyers, business managers, and teachers. Some were blue collar workers. But all had the attributes of a leader and strong ambitions that drew them into public service.

How did they get started? What made them decide to run? What have they learned in the political arena? What advice would they offer to political newcomers?

Successful elected officials from different parts of the country were asked these four questions. Their answers provide some

thoughtful and honest guidelines for anyone who has ever considered a career in public office and some sage advice on what's really important on the campaign trail.

The decision to run

Whether they were running for a seat on the local school board or for Congress, our elected officials agreed that deciding whether or not to throw the hat in the ring for the first time can be an excruciating process. On one hand, they described in abstract and ideological terms their desire to serve in public office, their strong feelings on issues, the need for good leadership in their communities, the failings of the incumbent, and the conviction that they could do a better job.

Lorene Hanley Duquin is a political writer and campaign advisor based in Williamsville, N.Y.

On the other hand, they also described the drawbacks: When running for office, candidates must have not only a strong sense of self-worth, but also the humility necessary to ask others for money and assistance. Then, there is the pain of knowing that in any campaign their good names could be dragged through the sometimes muddy political arena. They would have to sacrifice time with their families. The campaign could have a potentially disastrous effect on their careers. And worst of all, there was no guarantee that they would win.

Congressman Tom DeLay (R-Texas) was employed as an exterminator when he decided to run for office. "I was fed up with government interference in the marketplace and people's lives," he says. "I ran for a seat in the Texas state legislature in 1978 and I was the first Republican ever elected from Fort Bend County."

Tough odds. But DeLay attributes his success to giving the grueling campaign nearly all his time. "I'd advise political newcomers not to run unless they are willing to sacrifice everything to win," he says. "You must be committed or you will lose. . . . Don't take anything for granted."

Congressman Don Young (R-Alaska) agrees. "You win when you work," he says. "You lose when you don't."

Young entered politics at the local level in 1960 because he saw the "need for strong leadership" in his hometown—eight miles above the Arctic Circle. He ran for a council seat and won. Later, he was elected to the Alaska state legislature. When the legislature wasn't in session, Young worked as a riverboat captain in the summer and a fur trapper in the winter. In 1973 he won a congressional seat in a special election. "You have to have the experience of living and working close to the people you'll represent," Young says, "and you have to believe in yourself."

Congresswoman Patricia Schroeder (D-Colorado) entered the Democratic primary in 1972 seeking a place on the ballot in a Denver congressional district because of her "desire to help the less fortunate and the less powerful in society." An attorney and a law school instructor, Schroeder agonized over the question: *How can I be a congresswoman and be a mother at the same time?*

"In my brain I knew I could do it, but my gut feeling was 'There's no way you can,'" she says. Schroeder's belief in herself won out and she went on to win the Democratic primary and the general election.

"I'd tell political newcomers that with determination, spunk, and an army of volunteers, you can overcome just about anything—even a better financed opponent," she says. "If you really want to run, then do it!" [Editor's note: Schroeder may have a somewhat tempered view now, given her decision not to run for president in 1988 after months of preparations.]

If at first you don't succeed

Not everyone is successful in the first quest for public office and many have to swallow the bitter pill of defeat before they realize their goal. But the true test of a successful candidate is whether he or she can pick up the pieces after a loss, analyze the mistakes, and try again. Looking back at their own careers, several elected officials said they learned some very important lessons from lost elections.

Congressman Berkley Bedell (D-Iowa) entered public service in the early 1960s when he entered a race for a seat on the local board of education because he was "concerned about school problems." He won the election, but he never considered it a political position or himself a politician. His first love was fishing and he invented a new type of fishing leader and line that resulted in a multimillion dollar fishing tackle business. But after thirty-five years in business, his political ambitions and concerns grew. In 1972 he decided to run for Congress and lost.

"I underestimated how difficult it is to run for a national office," he says.

Two years later, with the full realization of how much time, effort, and money is needed to sway the voters, Rep. Bedell ran for Congress again. This time, he won.

"I wouldn't want to give anyone the impression that they have to have previous experience to run for a major office," he says. "Just be realistic and prepared."

Building a platform that won't wobble

Without issues, a campaign would be nothing but a personality contest. Successful candidates agreed that issues and differing opinions on how to solve problems are the meat of a campaign.

There are two kinds of issues: the ones that deal with a problem or situation in the community, and the ones that deal with the incompetence or ineffectiveness of the incumbent. Start by asking yourself what government is doing wrong. Are there any particular problems that anger or irritate you? Do you have some solutions that no one has tried yet?

Another way to learn about the important issues is to read the newspaper. Watch the letters to the editor. That's where you'll find grassroots issues beginning to take form. You could also talk to the newspaper reporter who covers the office you're seeking. Reporters have insight into how well the government is functioning.

If you're seeking a legislative position, it's a good idea to attend some sessions. Review your opponent's voting record and attendance record. Opinion polls are another way of determining the important issues as well as the strengths and weaknesses of the incumbent.

Developing strong issues is important on all levels of government, but many local campaigns are won or lost on a single issue. Here are some examples:

- In Grand Rapids, Michigan, Gerald Helmholdt, a paint and wallpaper store owner, won the mayor's seat in his first run for public office with a promise to continue the neighborhood improvement drive that he initiated as a citizen activist.
- In Sacramento, California, registered nurse, teacher, and former League of Women Voters president Anne Rudin won the mayor's seat when she opposed developers who wanted to build a stadium on land that had been zoned for farm use.
- In Hammond, Indiana, political newcomer Tom McDermott beat both the Republican and Democratic machines when he pledged to stop the deterioration of the city's fire and police protection, streets, job opportunities, and quality of life.
- In Phoenix, Arizona, Terry Goddard became the city's youngest mayor by opposing the at-large city council structure that he claimed deprived many residents of an equal voice in city government.

Former San Francisco Mayor Diane Feinstein ran successfully eight times since her first election to the County Board of Supervisors in 1969. While issues are important, she emphasizes that potential candidates must "be sure they can raise the funds to get their message out."

She also advises political newcomers to know their strengths and weaknesses, obtain professional campaign advice, develop a strategy, and make sure the campaign is managed properly. "I had wanted to run for a long time," she says, "but my life was never such that I could. In 1969 it just seemed that the time was right."

How do you recognize the right moment? The elected officials we talked to agreed that it's important to wait for the right opportunity, but warned against extended hesitation. A few advised becoming involved in your political party so you'll be "in tune with the political wavelengths." They also mentioned that once you've made political connections there's always the possibility of being appointed to a vacant seat before the term runs out, which would allow you the advantage of running as an incumbent in the next election. (The

Lorene Hanley Duquin

chances of this happening are really very slim, however.)

There were also some mavericks who advised staying away from party politics and putting together your own grassroots organization to win the primary and the general election.

Timing was an important factor for Congressman John LaFalce (D-New York). "It's important to take advantage of the right time and the right place," he says.

LaFalce was a young attorney in 1970 when an incumbent Republican state senator had become embroiled in a scandal. "I saw the opportunity for a major upset and I decided to run," LaFalce says. He won the state Senate seat in a primarily Republican district.

But just two years later, in 1972, reapportionment eliminated LaFalce's seat. Taking events in stride, he ran for the state assembly that year and won. Then, just two years later, in 1974, opportunity knocked again when the incumbent Republican congressman announced that he would not seek reelection. LaFalce threw his hat in the ring and won a congressional seat.

"From my first race, I learned that upsets are possible and that I could win an election," he says.

Georgia Governor Joe Frank Harris won his first race in a major upset victory in 1964. With the help of family and friends, he entered a race for a seat in the Georgia legislature against "a veteran legislator with many political ties and connections." At the age of twenty-eight, all Harris had to offer the voters was his desire to be of public service and the business experience he had learned in the family-owned concrete products business.

"In that first race, I learned the value of saying what you mean and meaning what you say, and the importance of carrying out your commitments and pledges—no matter what," he says. "No one should take lightly the responsibilities of public office nor should one ever believe that an office belongs to anyone other than the people themselves. When an officeholder begins to feel that the office belongs to him, not the people, that person should resign the post and pursue other interests."

Appearances can be deceiving

If there is one thing all of the successful elected officials agree upon, it is that campaigns should not be treated lightly. And while it may appear to be easy, campaigning is one of the most stressful, expensive, and exhausting things they've ever done. It takes skill and commitment. Sometimes, it takes luck. But one thing is certain: There are no magic formulas . . . no simple steps.

Ready, set, run

If you're a political newcomer and thinking about throwing your hat in the ring, now's the time to do a little soul searching. Here are some questions to ask yourself:

- Are you a good public speaker?
- Do you like meeting people?
- Can you think on your feet?
- Can you take criticism?
- Can you work under pressure?
- Can you handle frustration?
- Are you honest?
- Are you sure there are no skeletons rattling around in your closets?

If the answer to each of these questions is yes, you have some basic skills needed for becoming a candidate. But even the best candidates sometimes need a little brushing up on public speaking techniques and communication skills. If you're weak in any of these areas, plan to get help before you enter the race.

Now ask yourself:

- Can your health withstand several months of extreme stress and strain?
- Would your family support your bid for public office?

- Can you count on your friends and associates for help?
- Can you afford the time to campaign?
- What effect would a campaign have on your current job?
- Could you raise the money to properly finance a campaign?
- Are you willing to take the risk of losing?

If any of your answers is no, think twice before entering into a political race. A good candidate needs more than just good ideas. You'll need money, the support of your family and friends, time, energy, and a burning desire to win. If any of these elements is missing, you'll be entering a race with your own deck of cards stacked against you.

Now ask yourself:

- What office are you seeking? What are the duties? The salary? The length of the term?
- What special skills or abilities could you bring to the office?
- Would you be happy serving in this capacity?
- Would there be any conflict with your other interests or regular occupation?

- Could you get the endorsement of the powerbrokers in your party? If not, what are your chances of winning a primary without them?
- Do you have someone you can trust who could guide your campaign, or do you have the money to hire a professional campaign manager?
- Can this seat be won?
- Do you really want to win it?

If you can't answer all of these questions, you aren't ready to run. "Political campaigns are difficult, costly, and take a total commitment," warns former Mayor Feinstein.

On the other hand, if the time is right, the seat is winnable, and all of your answers are pointing you toward an elective office, why not go for it? "I take every opportunity to encourage good citizens to seek public office because citizens with a wide variety of interests and backgrounds are vital to the success of our democratic system," says Georgia Governor Joe Frank Harris.

Everyone has to start somewhere!

Part Two

Some Old Techniques and Some New Applications

Computerized Opposition Research:
The Instant Parry

Michael J. Bayer • Joseph Rodota

The new campaign technology is at its best when it can apply advanced techniques to a sound and tested method of competitive politics. There is no better example than opposition research: *the compilation of facts about the opposing candidate's public record and statements. Campaigns have long recognized the necessity of accurate, timely opposition research, but computer technology has now enabled strategists to take a quantum leap in producing useful information, available almost instantly.*

The state-of-the-art example is the Republican opposition research effort conducted in the 1984 presidential election, which enabled GOP operatives to uncover Democratic vulnerabilities at the push of a button. Funded by $1.1 million from the Republican National Committee, a research team spearheaded by the authors of this article built an unprecedented computerized textual database of information about Walter Mondale and the Democrats. Culled from over 400,000 documents, this database was used by the White House to prepare President Reagan and Vice President Bush for their autumn debates with Walter Mondale and Geraldine Ferraro. It also served as the centerpiece of a telecommunications network of Reagan–Bush operatives across the country, so that effective responses to Democratic charges could be made immediately while well-targeted, factual attacks could be launched whenever contradictions in the Democratic record surfaced. The 1984 Presidential Opposition Research Group was impressive indeed; it was a remarkable advance in a time-honored campaign technique that is certain to serve as the model for campaigns at all levels in the future.

Michael J. Bayer was Director of the Republican party's 1984 Presidential Opposition Research Group. Joseph Rodota was editor and principal author of Vice President Malaise, *the official 1984 Republican analysis of the Mondale record.*

Andy Warhol once said, "Art is anything you can get away with." During the 1984 primary campaign, former Vice President Walter F. Mondale appeared to have borrowed a page from the pop artist's book. In confrontations with his chief rival Gary Hart, Mondale got away with murder. A few examples:

- Mondale savaged Hart for voting against the 1979 Chrysler bail-out legislation. In Northeastern industrial towns, Mondale cited this vote as evidence of callousness toward the needs of working men and women. Hart took the bait and argued the merits of the bail-out bill. He thus drew additional attention to his anti-Chrysler vote, while winning few converts. By the time Hart aides discovered that Mondale had voted against a 1973 bill in the Senate to bail out the Lockheed corporation, the campaign debate had moved on to other issues.
- Mondale made health care policy a campaign issue when he charged that Hart had voted against a cost-containment bill and "with the hospital lobby." Hart, groping for an answer, countered with arcane comparisons of various health care proposals considered by Congress in the 1970s. He could have turned the discussion quickly to his advantage by citing Joseph Califano, President Carter's Secretary of Health, Education, and Welfare, who wrote that Hart voted *with* the Carter–Mondale administration on health care cost-containment legislation.
- In a tough fight for nuclear freeze voters, Mondale repeatedly challenged Hart's commitment to arms control. During a televised debate on the eve of the New York primary, Hart wilted under Mondale's attacks. The Colorado senator could do little more than glare at his opponent. It was clear that Mondale had studied his rival's record: The former vice president could cite Hart's votes and statements going back several years. It was just as clear that Gary Hart was not prepared to attack Walter Mondale's arms record. The debate may have turned out differently if Mondale had been challenged to defend his support for the MX missile and the B-1 bomber as vice president and U.S. senator.

What stopped Gary Hart in his march to the Democratic nomination? Fundamentally, Gary Hart's tragic flaw was that he did not know enough about Walter Mondale. Hart may have been knowledgeable about new industrial policy, military reform, and yuppies, but he possessed only a sketchy outline of Mondale's twenty-year public record and had no base of information from which to predict his opponent's next move. By contrast, Mondale understood Hart's weaknesses and executed an effective strategy. He made Gary Hart the issue, confident that Hart lacked the resources to turn the debate around. Mondale hit hard, keeping the Colorado senator on the defensive until the nomination was in the bag.

It should come as no surprise that Republican strategists observed the Democratic primary process in excruciating detail. In Mondale's success was found the secret to his undoing. For the first time in his career, Walter Mondale would be forced to confront—and run against—his own record.

Veteran Reagan speechwriter Ken Khachigian believes that campaigns are won and lost in the library. This is the story of a computerized library that helped bring down the Democratic candidate for president in 1984.

The core of the system

The Opposition Research Group was formed in February 1984. Funded with $1.1 million from the Republican National Committee, the group's first task was to gather every possible piece of information on all eight Democratic candidates then running for president. The research staff amassed a staggering amount of material. Over 2,000 sources were tapped; in the end, more than *400,000* documents were collected.

Is knowledge power? Only if it is comprehensive and accessible. The magnitude of this collection effort would have broken any traditional opposition research organization; storing the documents would have required room after room of file drawers—with no guarantee that the information would ever be retrievable in a practical sense. Only the application of computer technology could guarantee the results a national presidential campaign demanded: useful information that is instantly retrievable.

The system was built in stages during the first weeks of the campaign. The first step was to develop procedures to review the thousands of documents that had been collected. A staff of readers sifted through newspaper and magazine articles, *Congressional Record* speeches, campaign literature, broadcast transcripts and other public sources, to identify key passages. In order of priority, readers/coders looked for (1) direct quotes by the candidates; (2) quotes attributed to the candidates; and (3) quotes about the candidates by other individuals, ranging from Democratic leaders to Iowa farmers. Readers familiar with candidates and issues sifted the wheat from the chaff, selecting only the most important quotations. Quality control procedures reduced the risk that an important fact or quote would be overlooked. Key excerpts culled from primary documents became the "data" used in this computerized research system.

The data were then entered into the Republican National Committee's mainframe computer according to a hierarchical, issue-oriented dictionary with a total of over 600 individual categories. The process was evolutionary. As Democratic candidates dropped from the race, day-to-day collection and analysis of materials pertaining to that candidate were terminated and staff resources shifted to the remaining candidates. As our methods improved, resources became simultaneously focused on fewer candidates, thus ensuring that we would be at peak efficiency when only one man was left.

The system eventually grew to approximately 75,000 items, including 45,000 quotes documenting the complete career of Walter Mondale—easily the largest collection of opposition materials on a political candidate ever assembled. (The 1980 Reagan–Bush campaign based its research on approximately 6,000 items related to Jimmy Carter.) In gathering the materials, the objective was to assemble a database that was both current and comprehensive. The Mondale collection even included the law review article he had written while a student at the University of Minnesota in 1950. During the height of the campaign, the entire database was updated every twenty-four hours. The major newspapers were analyzed each morning and data entered into the computer by noon the same day.

The data were stored in a dictionary that anyone with fifteen minutes of training could use to conduct basic or advanced research. The operator responded to a series of screen prompts for subject, candidate, source, data, etc. The implications of this system were awe-inspiring: When a candidate opened his mouth, it would take just a few seconds to compare his statement with others made during the course of his career. A complete history of a candidate's statements on a specific issue could be reviewed in minutes. Charges could be researched and countered almost immediately. Opposition research resources, formerly used for next-day (or next-week) responses, could now be injected directly into minute-by-minute campaign trench warfare. A barrier in political research activities had been broken.

Linking headquarters and the field

Traditional opposition research operations are usually handicapped by inaccessibility. In most campaigns, research is performed at headquarters, where the reference library and issue analysts are located. When the candidate or surrogate is on the road, access to opposition materials is limited to what can be read over a telephone or sent via a telecopier. And the standard research effort limits the campaign in other important respects as well.

Campaign headquarters staff normally generate their own research requests, typically on topics that are national in scope and of intense concern to combatants "inside the (Washington, D.C.) beltway." Field staff need research assistance, too; but they generally require information on topics of local interest, such as the candidate's record on black lung benefits or peanut price supports. Because research resources are limited and the research staff is physically located at headquarters, requests generated there inevitably take precedence over requests from the field. The situation can degenerate rapidly. As field staff research needs are passed over, frustrated state and local campaign workers cease asking headquarters for help; they attempt to perform their own research, producing material of uneven quality and fragmenting the campaign's message. Campaigners in the field ignore orders to send primary materials to headquarters for analysis. When materials do not flow from the field to headquarters, the campaign's central reference collection becomes increasingly irrelevant.

The Opposition Research Group overcame this traditional obstacle by making its resources accessible to all elements of the campaign. An electronic communications system was developed to link fifty state party headquarters, fifty state campaign headquarters, and spokesmen in all 208 ADIs (Areas of Dominant Influence—broadcast rating markets) with Opposition Research, the Republican National Committee, and Reagan–Bush '84 headquarters. Party and campaign spokesmen had instant access to up-to-the-minute talking points, issue papers, and draft speeches for use in discussions with local media. The database itself was accessible to key campaign and party officials—even on board Air Force One and Air Force Two.

Benchmark analysis

Once the database was made comprehensive, retrievable, and accessible, a team of senior analysts was assembled. In addition to director Michael J. Bayer, the group included: Joseph Rodota, a former staff member of the Senate Republican Policy Committee; Susan Carleson, former legislative assistant to Rep. Jack Kemp (R-New York); Susan Hopkins, a former speechwriter for Housing and Urban Development Secretary Samuel Pierce; Candace L. Strother, a former White House staffer in the Office of Public Liaison; and Don Todd, former executive director of the American Conservative Union. With the assistance of a twenty-four member research and computer support staff, these analysts went to work building the case against Walter Mondale.

The first step was a crash program to generate a series of benchmark issue papers on virtually every salient public policy issue, from abortion and welfare to the space program and the Soviet arms buildup. The computerized database made otherwise daunting research projects manageable. A complete analysis of Mondale's record on defense procurement, for example, could be performed in less than two days by reviewing the contents of a dozen or so computer files. An analyst in a traditional opposition research operation would need at least a week for a similar project, with no assurances that the research was comprehensive. Within six weeks, five analysts at Opposition Research produced over 1,000 pages of benchmark analysis on Walter Mondale (as well as dozens of papers on Gary Hart who, at that time, was still within striking distance of the nomination and thus was a possible vice presidential nominee). Benchmark issue papers, typically five to thirty pages in length, discussed key aspects of the candidate's record, including outrageous statements, shifting positions, contradictions, vulnerabilities, and strengths. These papers formed the primary resource from which were developed most Reagan–Bush '84 and G.O.P. attacks on the Mondale/Democratic record.

A quantum leap in research capabilities

Once benchmark analysis was completed, the Opposition Research team tackled a wide array of campaign assignments. A review of key projects illustrates the versatility of this computer-based research system:

Michael J. Bayer • Joseph Rodota

- **Quick set-up**. Traditional opposition research operations take several weeks or months to develop reference collections on candidates. Until 1984, this was sufficient for presidential campaigns; "dark horse" presidential candidates were a rarity and the vice-presidential picks were almost never of sufficient interest to warrant an immediate, full-scale research effort. Walter Mondale, however, interviewed "nontraditional" candidates—minorities and women—for the second spot on his ticket. This heightened public attention to the selection process and required careful planning in the Republican camp. As Mondale interviewed Democrats in his North Oaks, Minnesota, home, Opposition Research developed a series of plans to assemble complete databases on each of Mondale's possible choices. Less than ten days after Mondale selected Geraldine Ferraro, Opposition Research had collected some 25,000 source materials and entered into its computer approximately 5,000 key statements documenting the public career of the congresswoman from Queens. Using this database, benchmark analysis of the Ferraro record was completed in less than three weeks.

- **Overnight analysis**. During the Democratic National Convention, key addresses by Mondale, Ferraro, Edward M. Kennedy, Gary Hart, Mario Cuomo, and Tip O'Neill were analyzed overnight by the Republican team. When Hart half-heartedly praised Mondale as a "tough competitor," a search of the computer revealed that Mondale had referred to the Colorado senator as a "cold-hearted wretch" and implied that Hart had entered politics to get away from his family. When Ted Kennedy lauded Mondale in his introduction, a few commands to the computer quickly generated a print-out listing every barb the two pols had traded since the bitter 1980 campaign. Without the aid of a computer, such detailed research and analysis would have been virtually impossible to carry out in the time allowed.

- **Publications**. As the general election campaign began, the Opposition Research Group produced *Vice President Malaise*, a 200-page book published by the Republican National Committee in August 1984. This volume, the official 1984 Republican analysis of the Mondale record, was a valuable reference tool used by Reagan–Bush '84 and Republican party officials throughout the country. Another example of the Republican's application of computer technology to political research: *Vice President Malaise* was available on floppy disks compatible with most small word processors and personal computers.

- **Pinpoint accuracy**. What did our opponent say the last time he visited St. Mary's, Ohio? This question would have stumped a traditional research system, but the Opposition Research Group's database enabled users to retrieve statements and quotes by geographic location. This added a new element to candidate and surrogate scheduling. Campaign planners could know instantly the issues their opponents were stressing (or avoiding) in a given locale. Voters could be reminded of statements the Democratic candidate had made in their city one month—or twenty years earlier.

- **Party building**. The Opposition Research Group had an extensive list of "clients" in addition to Reagan–Bush '84 and the Republican National Committee. Senator Jesse Helms, for example, tapped the Group for assistance in his race against North Carolina Governor Jim Hunt, whom he tagged "a Mondale liberal." Assistance was provided to virtually every Republican candidate interested in running against the Mondale–Ferraro ticket.

Preparing for the debates

The Opposition Reseach Group's greatest test during the campaign was the presidential and vice presidential debates. The computer-based research system was essential in projecting opponents' charges and responses; enhancing the simulation effects of debate practice sessions; spotting weaknesses and developing attack themes; and generating post-debate analysis.

In August, well before negotiations over debate format had begun, the Opposition Research Group prepared for the White House debate preparation team a 200-page briefing book that projected Mondale's attack themes and responses to a range of questions. This book containing hundreds of Mondale's actual statements was used extensively by Office of Management and Budget Director David Stockman to prepare for his role as "Mondale" in President Reagan's practice debates. Excerpts of these materials were inserted directly into the president's debate briefing books.

What subjects would Mondale be most likely to emphasize during the debates? What would he avoid? Candidates are creatures of habit. Mondale and Ferraro (and, for that matter, President Reagan and Vice President Bush) could be expected to dwell on issues and themes with which they felt most comfortable. The Opposition Research Group generated weekly breakdowns of the volume of candidate statements entered into the database, by subject. A review of the six-week period preceding the debates revealed, for example, that Mondale had not addressed the defense of Europe or our strategic relationship with Japan. Analysis of Mondale's shifts in emphasis helped White House debate strategists to use their resources and the president's time more efficiently by focusing on issues Mondale himself pressed leading up to the debates.

Opposition Research provided materials and analysis, including detailed scenarios of Democratic tactics and strategy, during preparations for both presidential debates. On several occasions, various members of the president's debate preparation team called Opposition Research analysts while a session was in progress, asking about Mondale's *exact*

phrasing of a particular charge. The analyst would search the database and find the answer within seconds—with the caller still on the line.

The Opposition Research Group and its computer system played a similar role in preparing Vice President Bush for his debate with Geraldine Ferraro. In less than a week, the group prepared a comprehensive briefing book that projected Ferraro's likely attack themes and suggested possible responses. Opposition Research analysts prepared Rep. Lynn Martin (R-Illinois) for her role as the Ferraro stand-in; the team also attended and participated in the vice president's mock debate sessions. Nearly all of the arguments and themes Ms. Ferraro used in the actual debate were expected by the vice president from his preparations.

For six months, the Opposition Research Group also met to review videotapes of Mondale, Hart, Ferraro, and other Democrats. This duty led to videotape studies of both Mondale and Ferraro. These tapes, depicting the candidates' behavior in a variety of debate situations, were also studied by the president and the vice president prior to each of the televised debates.

Following all three debates, the Opposition Research Group worked through the night preparing detailed analyses and complete transcripts. Comparisons of the candidates' debate statements with their records were performed quickly with the aid of the computer. In the first debate, for example, Walter Mondale stated that he supported the eventual repeal of tax indexing. Mondale campaign aides quickly issued a retraction, claiming that Mondale favored partial repeal of indexing in the near term, followed by a return to full indexing as the budget came into balance. The computer file of Mondale's statements on tax indexing told a different story. As far back as 1981, Mondale had consistently advocated the total repeal of income tax indexing. By October, the Opposition Research Group analysts were so familiar with the Mondale–Ferraro record that a thorough review and analysis of the debates could be completed in several hours. Research Group memoranda were of considerable value to White House, campaign, and Republican party teams at the debate sites; these spokesmen and strategists received the texts early in the morning after each debate—via electronic mail from Washington.

Secret weapon?

Post-election news reports identified the Opposition Research Group and its computer system as the Republican "secret weapon" in 1984. The label, if it applies to the operation at all, would perhaps be a better description of the role computerized opposition research will play in 1988.

Although the Mondale–Ferraro ticket pulled ahead of President Reagan and Vice President Bush in some polls after the Democratic convention, the Reagan–Bush lead remained healthy throughout the campaign. As a result, the two rival camps never engaged in the minute-by-minute "trench warfare" for which the Republican system was specifically designed.

Closer races probably lie ahead: The Republican presidential candidate in 1988 will not enjoy the benefits of incumbency—or Walter Mondale to run against.

In 1984, advanced computer technology was successfully applied to opposition research for the first time. When tomorrow's close races are fought, the technology developed this year could give some Republicans the winning edge.

The Effective Press Release:
Key to Free Media

Sallie G. Randolph

Much of the information voters receive and believe about candidates does not reach them directly from the campaigns; it is filtered through the news media. Winning the hearts and minds of voters, then, can depend in part on winning over—or at least securing the cooperation of—editors and reporters. Every candidate strives to achieve high visibility, and expensive television and radio advertisements are one vital means to accomplish the goal. But the news that papers print and television stations air generally has higher credibility with voters than the candidate-produced ads—and, best of all, it is free. Gaining this gratis access to the airwaves and news columns can be a crucial variable in determining a candidate's fate.

In this well-written instruction designed for candidates and their staffs, Sallie Randolph reveals some of the trade secrets of composing snappy, newsworthy, and accurate releases. Many recent campaigns, incidentally, have supplemented the printed press release with audio and visual "actualities"—clips of the candidate delivering the highlighted statement or speech. Whatever the format, the principles of effective care and feeding of the news media remain the same. Randolph's article gives us a glimpse of the demanding yet delicate relationship between a properly skeptical press and an attention-seeking candidate.

The press release is a vital tool for the candidate. Good ones can swing voters and votes to your side. They can influence editors to the point of endorsement. They can reward the hard work of campaign volunteers with recognition. Effective press releases can clarify issues, motivate voters, and, importantly, confound opponents.

Poor press releases can lose votes by generating sympathy for opponents. They can muddle issues, antagonize editors, and create an image unfavorable to the candidate. They can lose votes. And sometimes lose elections.

Sallie G. Randolph is a political public relations consultant and a former newspaper reporter and correspondent.

Effective press releases take only rudimentary skills to prepare. Yet very few good ones ever cross an editor's desk. In an average week, the *Arcade Herald*, a weekly newspaper in upstate New York, receives hundreds of releases. Jeffrey C. Mason, the beleaguered editor, must go through each one and decide whether or not to use it. In most cases the releases are consigned to the wastebasket. Why? Because the *Herald*, which has an average of twenty tabloid pages to fill with news and advertising each week, simply doesn't have the space, the staff, or the time to deal with this deluge.

A daily newspaper in an average U.S. city might receive as many as a thousand press releases each week, all vying for limited space and editorial attention. Many press releases are ignored, often not even read. The few that are used are heavily edited because they're so poorly prepared. Editors would welcome, and use, more well-written releases.

The essential ingredients

There are ten essential ingredients to the effective press release. Before you deliver your releases, make sure they include these important elements:

- **Purpose**. Before writing, you must know what end you wish to accomplish. Each press release should be a planned part of a campaign.
- **Targeting**. Score a bull's-eye by identifying your target audience, choosing the best newspaper to reach that audience, and tailoring your release to fit the needs of that paper.
- **A strong lead**. Whoever said "Well begun is half done" was right in the case of the press release. Sometimes, in fact, well begun is completely done.
- **News value**. Editors say that puffery is the single most common flaw in political press releases. A candidate who regularly distributes releases with little or no news value will have them routinely consigned to the round file.
- **Brevity**. You'll probably get more mileage out of releases that are short than long because you increase the chances that they will actually be read.
- **Clarity**. Help potential voters understand your message by eliminating jargon, redundancies, and clutter. Author Jan Struther once wrote, "There is no Heaven but clarity, and no Hell except confusion."
- **Accuracy**. Editors demand accuracy. Editors and voters resent being misled. Mistakes here can cost an election.
- **Timing**. To comedians, timing is of the essence. It's important to you, too. Meet deadlines to maximize your media opportunities.
- **Style**. To be successful, you must mesh your writing style with the style of the newspaper.
- **Preparation**. Proofread the damn thing. If *you* don't know English, for heaven's sake find someone who does.

Purpose

Each press release should be carefully planned before it is written and should be part of an overall campaign strategy. It should be coordinated with your other communication efforts, such as advertising, television and radio appearances, speaking engagements, and literature distribution. Whom are you trying to reach with your message? What is the message?

Once you have decided on the specific goal of a release, you are in a better position to plan the other elements and to do the actual writing. Conversely, if you have trouble identifying specific goals, it is an indication that you either need to rethink your strategy or to hire someone to do it for you. Goal-directed group efforts are always more efficient and effective than random effort.

Targeting

A good press release that reaches the wrong audience won't do your campaign any good. To be effective, press releases must be targeted.

Targeting is a two-step process. First, identify the readers you want to reach. Then, pick newspapers that serve the readership you have in mind. Circulation and market information can also be kept on a microcomputer database for easy access. If you want to announce the names of the town chairmen for your campaign, for example, find out which papers include those towns in their circulation area. You'll be sending your releases to those papers.

If you are not sure what papers serve your target audience, check at your library for a newspaper directory. The yellow pages are another good source, as are area Chamber of Commerce directories. Study the papers to determine the type of news they cover and their requirements. A good way to learn the needs of the papers is to call and ask the editors for advice. "I'm glad to spend time explaining our needs and policies," says assistant city editor Paul R. Price of the *Buffalo News*, a respected western New York daily. "If more people would call and ask questions before sending us their news, it would save everyone a lot of time."

Now target the releases to fit the papers. Readers in one community are not usually interested in who is working in distant areas. Your news must have a local slant. You might send the entire list of town chairmen to a major daily or to a regional paper. Then, break up the list geographically and send the name of each local chairman to the proper local paper.

You can target the local releases further by including more information about each chairman—information that would be unlikely to interest a daily or regional paper. Here is an opportunity to reward your workers with recognition and keep your candidate's name before the public at the same time. Include such things as biographical data and perhaps a short quote about why the local chairman supports your candidate.

Targeting is a matter of knowing whom you want your news to reach and what information the papers in your target area are likely to use. Study the papers and send them news that's on target.

A strong lead

The beginning of a press release has to accomplish three things: (1) It must get the attention of a busy editor and reader. (2) It must focus on the central point of the release. (3) It must include the necessary information for the lead to stand alone as a short article. It must do all these things in two or three sentences, without resorting to gimmickry. That's a tall order—but not impossible if you follow these tips:

- Plunge right in and start off with the most interesting or important fact. (That is rarely the name of the candidate.)
- Follow up with the rest of the five Ws— Who, What, Where, When, and Why.
- Then add supporting details, a lively quotation, or a summary.

This style of writing is called the inverted pyramid and is used by newspapers because the amount of space available for routine stories is never known until the last minute. It may be necessary for an editor to shorten a news item. The inverted pyramid style allows the editor to cut paragraphs off the bottom of the article, without compromising the overall message. Write it so that the release can be shortened to a single lead paragraph and still make sense.

Here's a good lead from a press release from New York State Assemblyman L. William Paxon:

"More of the elderly will be eligible for a partial real property tax exemption under provisions of legislation signed into law by Governor Cuomo, according to Assemblyman L. William Paxon (R-C, Akron), a supporter of the measure in the Assembly. Paxon explained that the bill establishes a sliding scale real property tax exemption at local option for some senior citizens. . . ."

Paxon's release plunges right in with the salient news, the fact that more elderly residents of New York State will now be eligible for property tax exemptions. He then works in the name of the governor and his own name, indicating that he was a supporter of the legislation. Next comes a brief summary of the major provisions of the bill, then a quote from Paxon stating why he supports it.

The release goes on to give fuller details of the new tax exemption guidelines and winds up with a final quote from Paxon. It is effective because the lead works well.

It's a common mistake in political press releases to lead with the name of the candidate, even though that is not usually the most interesting or important part of the release. Here's an example from a joint release from Erie County Executive Edward J. Rutkowski and City of Buffalo Mayor James D. Griffin:

"County Executive Edward J. Rutkowski and Mayor James D. Griffin today announced that Chairman L. Stanley Crane of U.S.-owned Conrail will address local industry represent-atives at a noon luncheon sponsored by the Western New York Transportation Council, Inc. in the Buffalo Hilton September 15. The purpose of Mr. Crane's visit will be to discuss

Conrail's future role in Buffalo as a follow-up to an April meeting in Mayor Griffin's office. . . ."

The lead manages to get in all the essential information, but not in a way that was interesting enough for the editor to use. This possible rewrite would have been far more effective:

"The future role of Conrail in Buffalo will be discussed by its chairman, E. Stanley Crane, at a noon luncheon of local industry representatives on September 15 at the Buffalo Hilton, County Executive Edward J. Rutkowski and Mayor James D. Griffin announced today. The meeting, sponsored by the Western New York Transportation Council, Inc., is a follow-up to an April session in Mayor Griffin's office on issues related to Conrail service in Buffalo."

To write a good lead, remember to condense the essential information into a single, attention-getting point. Then work in the traditional five Ws and add supporting information. Trim the length of the lead to two or three clear sentences.

News value

Press releases should always have genuine news value. Don't waste the time of editors, their readers, or your staff with puffery, gimmickry, or meaningless fluff. It helps to think in terms of news for the editor and reader rather than publicity for the candidate.

A county legislator from Erie County, New York, Thomas M. Reynolds, an appointee who ran last fall for his first full term, sent out this hard-hitting release headlined "Reynolds Blasts Phone Rate Hike."

"A New York Telephone Company plan to raise Sardinia phone rates drew a blast this week—and a promise of action—from Erie County Legislator Thomas M. Reynolds (R-Springville)."

The release continued with details of the plan, then several punchy quotes from Reynolds, who called it "outrageous" and described it as hitting "particularly hardest at those who can least afford it, the homebound, the elderly and the handicapped."

After additional quotes, Reynolds concluded, "There is no way this rate hike can be permitted to go into effect."

At first glance the release seems solid and effective, but editors and readers realize that county legislators have no control over phone rates. Reynolds was merely spouting off, and the release wasn't used by the *Herald*. In fact, the paper gave the legislator this lukewarm endorsement later in the campaign: "Since we belong to the 'If it ain't broke, don't fix it' school of politics, we see no reason for voters not to elect Reynolds to a term of his own. Though he has a tendency to seek more publicity than we think necessary, we also feel. . . ."

Reynolds won his race, but probably because he was a Republican incumbent in a solidly Republican district. His press releases didn't help him much.

What is legitimate news value? This is a judgment call, to be sure, but, in general, you should stick to hard facts about events and issues that are relevant to the office being sought. If you want to spout off in print, do it by giving a speech to a recognized local group, then reporting highlights of the speech in your press release.

Paul Price of the *Buffalo News* says that the lack of legitimate news value is the single most common flaw in political press releases. "We're just not interested in what a candidate for the city council, let's say, thinks about foreign policy. Local governing bodies are famous for passing resolutions about issues over which they have no jurisdiction."

And local editors are famous for ignoring puffery. Make sure your releases contain *real news*.

Brevity

Since space is at a premium in newspapers and since the average typewritten page translates into six to ten column inches of newspaper copy, effective press releases should be short. In fact, there are few circumstances during the typical campaign that justify a release of more than one or two pages. If you have a lot of information to convey, break it up into several short releases.

Confine releases to a single, salient point. If your candidate gives a thirty-minute speech, don't try to cover it in its entirety. Pick out the major issue and find a quotation from the speech that highlights or summarizes that issue. Lead with the quote. Add the details of who, what, where, when, and why, then follow up with one or two more quotes.

Editors love short releases. They know from experience that they are likely to be well written. Short items fit space requirements better and offer flexibility. They're faster to deal with and easier to verify. And readers are more likely to read and comprehend short articles.

To achieve brevity:

- Limit the release to a single point. After it is written, weed out every word that is unrelated to that point. Be brutal here. You can use what you cut another time.
- Examine each word and phrase with a lean eye. Substitute single words for phrases. Get rid of unnecessary adverbs and adjectives. Cut out all unnecessary sentences. This is sometimes painful for those who have been overexposed to political jargon, but it *is* possible. And it *is* effective.
- Combine sentences. Take a look at your shorter, leaner sentences. Can some of them be combined to avoid repetition? A likely candidate for combining is the nuts and bolts portion of your lead. See how many of the five Ws can be worked into a single sentence.
- Make every word work and every idea count. Your pared-down release will have cohesion and clarity. It will please editors and reach readers.

Clarity

An unclear release reduces the likelihood of reaching voters and increases your chances of being misunderstood. Muddled writing leaves a negative impression with editors and readers. Make your writing crystal clear:

- Eliminate jargon. Political catch-phrases are rampant. Why not use "now" instead of "at this point in time"?

- Use short words. The purpose of press releases is to communicate, not show off your vocabulary. Substitute short words such as "use" for longer ones such as "utilize."
- Use the active voice, not the passive. Don't write, "The economy has been ruined by the administration." Say, "The administration has ruined the economy."
- Avoid synonyms for the word "said." A simple said is less intrusive than such distracting substitutes as stated, explained, shouted, demanded, or exclaimed.

Many daily papers have a reporter verify and rewrite all press releases. If your writing is unclear, you risk having its meaning distorted when it is rewritten.

Accuracy

Press releases must be accurate on all levels. Spelling, grammar, and punctuation should be correct. Information should be clearly presented and true. Opinion should be labeled as such and attributed to the candidate or source.

Deliberate or inadvertent distortion of facts costs a candidacy credibility and, sometimes, the election, as was the case with Rex Willard, a Republican candidate who opposed the incumbent Democrat last fall for the position of Cattaraugus County, New York, Clerk.

Willard was an attractive, articulate candidate with a solid business background. He had the backing of a strong party. His opponent, although an incumbent, was a member of the county's minority party and therefore vulnerable. Willard faced an uphill, but winnable contest. Unfortunately, he chose to fight with manipulated information.

He attempted to blame incumbent Gloria Bilotta for the failure to install computer validating equipment in a branch office, even though the installation had been blocked by his own party in the county legislature. And he accused Bilotta of failing to seek the lowest price for office computers, even though she was restricted to only a single brand that was compatible with the state's computer system.

Willard's press releases and ads containing

Sallie G. Randolph

Press Release Do's and Don'ts: Tips from the Experts

Do

- Include all of the essential ingredients outlined in this article.
- Call editors for information on their requirements.
- Prepare the release carefully and professionally.
- Keep the competition of the newspapers in mind. (Alternate exclusive releases between daily papers. Remember that the main competition for many weeklies is the shopper or penny-saver type publication that is all advertising. Don't advertise in the shopper and expect the newspaper to print your press releases. Spread your advertising dollars evenly. Be fair and scrupulously honest.)
- Meet deadlines.

Don't

- Resort to gimmickry. Make sure your press releases are straightforward and businesslike.
- Expect editors to use every release you send them in the exact form you sent it. Remember, *they* make the decisions.
- Send meaningless puffery. Editors resent it.
- Complain to editors about the handling of your releases. It doesn't do any good and it might do some harm.
- Send releases to papers that don't cover the type of news you're including. Make sure news has a local slant.

---

the misleading allegations generated a flurry of angry letters to the editor. Jeff Mason of the *Arcade Herald* responded in print:

"We know of no newspaper, including the *Herald*, that has printed Mr. Willard's press releases as they were submitted. The *Herald* has either not used his press releases or has heavily reworked them to bring them into line with reality."

Willard's continued manipulation of the facts ultimately earned him this stinging rebuke in the *Herald's* endorsement of his opponent: "The advertising campaign he has waged this fall, however, has shown him to be a person who relishes in distorting the truth and who is nothing short of vicious in his description of his opponent."

To achieve accuracy in your releases:

- Stick to the facts. Don't be tempted to manufacture issues or manipulate information. The risk is too great.
- Be careful with details. Double-check spelling, punctuation, dates, places, and other information.
- Spell people's names right. Most will take the misspelling of their names as an insult.

Timing

Paul Price of the *Buffalo News* says that one of the biggest problems with press releases is that they arrive too late to be used. "We're

a daily paper. We have to have news by the day after it happens or we can't use it. If a candidate gives a speech on a Thursday evening, the press release should be delivered to our office on Friday morning." Price advises candidates to "send releases to us several days ahead of an event. Then follow up with a second release afterward."

Deadlines are important. Take the trouble to find out when the deadlines are for the newspapers you are supplying with news. Then make sure your releases get there in time. Maintaining a computer database of editors and newspaper deadlines can expedite the process.

Be careful not to be too efficient, though. Your news shouldn't arrive so early that it must be saved for more than a few days.

And don't let over-efficiency trap you into making mistakes. J. Edward Cuddy, who unsuccessfully opposed Congressman Henry P. Smith III of New York in 1970, remembers one serious mistake made by his press staff.

"We had a press committee that handled the releases. They had a system that seemed to be working pretty well. The committee chairman took my calendar and assigned people to send releases out right after each speech. We were getting great coverage for a while," he says.

"But one night I was scheduled to speak before a local veterans' group. There was a

- Proofread press releases before final typing. And make sure they include the ten essential ingredients. They should always be typed, double- or triple-spaced, on one side of the paper only.
- Leave lots of space, at least a third of a page, between the heading information and the copy. Use wide margins. The extra room allows editors to write headlines, make changes, and include instructions for the typesetters.
- Don't put headlines on releases intended for daily papers. For weekly papers, you can include short, lively headlines typed in capitals just above the first line of copy. But even here it's not necessary to include a headline. Leave it out if you're unsure.
- At the top of the page type the release date and the name and phone number of the person submitting it. For maximum flexibility use open-dated releases and label them "For Immediate Release" or "Use at Will." If the information is valid only after a certain date, say "For Release on or after _____ ."
- If the news is exclusive until a particular date, say "Exclusive until _____ ." Releases that must be used on a particular day should say "For Release on _____ ." Try to avoid limitations for use. You'll get better results with flexible timing.
- Indicate the end of your release by typing "30" after the last line. At the bottom of each page of a longer release type "more." Label subsequent pages with the candidate's name and a page number.

mix-up with the schedule and I never made it to the meeting. Unfortunately, the releases went out anyway and were used by two papers the next day. The veteran's group was justifiably angry and complained to the papers and to me. We apologized and explained, but I know that mistake cost us voters."

For news where you have some flexibility in timing, such as announcements of candidacy or statements of position, plan to time releases to enhance your overall strategy and to take advantage of slow news periods, such as weekends.

Style

Newspaper style is the manner in which information is uniformly handled to give the paper, which is put together by many different people, a sense of unity and continuity. Newspapers try to be consistent in the way they handle such details as abbreviations, titles, and standard spellings.

Style also encompasses the larger issues of what type of news is covered and what format is used for routine announcements such as weddings, meetings, and calendar listings.

Because most newspapers aim for unbiased coverage, their styles usually reflect a careful neutrality. Your releases should too.

"There's one really effective way to develop a style that meshes with the papers you're using," says Alice E. Galzier, a publicity specialist who has worked for charitable organizations and social service agencies, as well as political campaigns.

"Make copies of all your releases. When they appear in the paper, cut them out and compare the clippings with the original releases word-for-word. Study the changes and make note of them. File the clippings and the releases in a press book. As you gain experience, you'll see fewer and fewer editorial changes. You'll learn from your mistakes."

Preparation

It goes without saying that your releases should be as professionally and competently prepared as you can make them. Double-check each release to make sure it includes all of the ten essential ingredients and prepare it according to the guidelines that accompany this article. The preparation of your press releases reflects on your candidate. Remember, voters often judge a candidate's abilities to perform in office efficiently by how well his or her campaign is run. There are votes in well-organized effort.

Sallie G. Randolph

Speechwriting: An Acquired Art

Craig R. Smith

Ronald Reagan's political success has been rooted not just in what he had to say but in how well he said it. The same could be said for Franklin Roosevelt and John Kennedy in their eras. As any longtime observer of politics can confirm, there are relatively few political communicators of the caliber of Reagan, Roosevelt, and Kennedy; in fact, many (if not most) politicians are barely adequate as public speakers. Sooner rather than later, major public officials come to depend heavily on their speechwriters to craft appeals that are at once substantively convincing and stylistically attractive. Few aides possess the skills to do this well, but one who does, former Ford presidential speechwriter Craig Smith, explains how political speeches can be constructed for maximum impact and effect. His frank appraisal of speechwriting techniques nicely blends belief in the power of ideas with recognition that timing, symbols, and appearances are elements as powerful as substance in politics.

Jean Paul Sartre once said, "We make ourselves what we are." Nothing is more influential in this creative process than communication, and particularly persuasion. The problem is that because we talk so much, and because we learn so much so early, we often take the art of public speaking for granted. Politicians are no different. Most of them fail to understand that they are known primarily through their speeches, through what they say and how they say it. Many I have worked for use speechwriters to frame issues or to phrase stylistic lines, but few use all of the writer's talents. They assume they can handle most situations themselves.

It is not until the politician is embarrassed by a bad newspaper column or silent crowd that he turns to a speechwriter for help. At this juncture, a second mistake is usually made. Instead of hiring a professional speechwriter, the candidate turns to a journalist or a novelist. Journalists usually write for the eye; fiction writers not only write for the eye but tend to have styles that are immutable.

An effective speechwriter writes for the ear; he is a rhetorician. He understands that a speech is a moment of confrontation between an audience and a speaker. That the audience is not universal, but specific; that the message is not for the ages, but for a certain moment; that the speech itself is neither prose nor poetry, but a persuasive attempt to change attitudes; that speeches are invisible for an audience—they can't go back up a page and recheck what they saw before. Thus, speeches are necessarily more organized and more repetitive than printed prose. In fact, a speech that *reads* well probably is not an effective

Craig R. Smith served as a full-time speechwriter for President Gerald Ford.

speech, just as a passage that *sounds* impressive is not likely to be good prose.

All this means that speeches, while they provide useful media copy when properly rewritten, are as different from written documents as elephants are from donkeys. An effective speechwriter will have been steeped in rhetorical theory and understands that the audience must be analyzed, the speaker's credibility enhanced, the emotional tone of the moment reshaped, the issues well researched and properly framed, the style made fascinating for the ear, and the delivery attuned to the moment.

Analyzing the audience

While a general theme or a specific message may be in the mind of the speechwriter when he begins his draft, not a single word should be typed until the audience for the speech has been analyzed. All of the strategies of speechwriting arise out of the audience because the speaker's primary objective is to persuade the audience. But how does one analyze an audience?

As a practicing speechwriter, I know how frustrating this task can be. On the campaign trail, or even in the White House, I have received speechwriting assignments that contain no description whatsoever of the audience. Even in the best campaigns, the speechwriter may be given only the advance man's assessment of the group to be addressed. This is a terrible error unless the speech is not really intended for the specific audience to be addressed, in which case the writer still needs an analysis of the possible *intended* audiences.

Audience analysis can be accomplished in several ways. First, the advance people should make it part of their duties to ask as many questions about the composition of the audience as possible. Can the audience be divided into age groups, sexual groups, or occupational groups? What religious affiliation predominates? How many people will be present? What issues are they concerned with? What values do they hold? What will the physical conditions for the speech be?

These latter two questions are difficult to answer on a short-term basis. Often a local audience will be a microcosm of the national audience and in such cases Gallup, Harris, and other polls can be used for guidance. Try to use the most relevant poll data to determine "hot" issues in the area or within the age group or interest group addressed.

Perhaps the most effective use of poll data was accomplished by the Nixon speechwriters in 1968. The composition of parts of his 1968 nomination acceptance speech to the Republican Convention reveals how poll data can be used to carve out a majority of supporters from a diverse audience.

Nixon knew that he faced a double audience: the voters at home watching him on television and the delegates on the floor of the convention hall watching him in person. Furthermore, poll data revealed a deep division in the national audience over the course the United States should follow in the Vietnam war. Forty-three percent of the home audience characterized themselves as "hawks," while forty-two percent saw themselves as "doves." There was more unity among delegates on this issue.

But what complicated Nixon's task was the fact that Vietnam was the most important question for both audiences. Thus, he could not ignore the issue. Nor could he ignore crime and the economy, which his polling data had revealed were the second and third most important issues for the voters and delegates.

Nixon solved this dilemma in several ways. First, he structured the speech so that the delegate audience was placated early on. The speech addressed intraparty issues such as unity and victory, thereby forming some consensus among delegates by using issues they were concerned about. But when Nixon turned to his national audience he did not forget the delegates.

Craig R. Smith

He began by talking about the *problem* of Vietnam, thereby satisfying the need to hear something about it. But because his national audience was divided on the issue, Nixon skirted proposing a specific solution. Instead, he argued that he had a plan to solve the problem but could not mention it lest he disturb the delicate negotiations underway in Paris. *LESSON:* To be effective when facing an issue that divides an audience, talk about the problem and avoid being specific about solutions.

Next, Nixon turned to crime and the economy. He knew that both audiences were united with regard to the solutions they preferred. At least seventy percent of each audience wanted stronger law enforcement, a change in the Supreme Court, less spending, and less big government. Thus, Nixon not only discussed the problems, but gave very specific solutions to them. *LESSON:* Where there is consensus, seize on it specifically.

Nixon was able to achieve considerable consensus because his pollsters not only provided him with a list of problems the nation and the delegates wanted to hear about, but they *rank ordered the problems and then polled the audience on what they thought the solutions to those problems should be.* Nixon arranged his speech so as to placate interest groups and yet appeared to be speaking specifically at the same time. And this he did as he wandered around Montauk Point writing on yellow legal pads, with the help of modern polling.

Finally, a thorough analysis will not only include demographics and issue-positions, but will *formulate values.* Values are deeply held beliefs that serve as guides to people in the decision-making process. To get at them is a very difficult task, but several methods have proven effective.

First, "focus groups" composed of a cross section of the audience can be brought together and observed. If properly questioned, they will normally reveal the values held by the group as a whole. Second, some groups, particularly those concerned with single issues, will have

values that are readily apparent. For example, many anti-abortionists are deeply religious. Third, past voting patterns can be analyzed to reveal trends over time. Blue collar workers, for example, hold a cluster of values concerning the work ethic. Their voting record on such issues as busing and affirmative action exposes this cluster of values.

Since values are deeply held, they often present the speechwriter with concepts of constant and universal appeal. Opinions can change rapidly, but values such as courage, commitment to children, and patriotism are steady. Often, speakers must address these values instead of the more volatile issues.

Formulating the issues

Most speeches seek to make a point, to convey a message, to change attitudes. At the outset, the speechwriter needs to know what the speaker is trying to accomplish. If the speaker wishes to change the minds of his colleagues on certain issues on the floor of the Senate, his speech will have a different cast than the speaker seeking to use the issues to get his audience to vote for him for public office. In the former case, the formulation of the issues with supporting arguments and evidence becomes an end in itself. But in the latter case, the issues are used to open the listener to persuasion which then seeks to identify the speaker with the listener.

How does one frame an issue for presentation in the speech? Assuming the speaker's purpose is to move his audience closer to his own position, and assuming that audience has been analyzed, the speechwriter must begin with extensive research. He must know what arguments can be launched against the position to be taken so that he can preempt them. He must know what the best evidence available is for his argument. And he must know what pieces of that evidence the particular audience will need to make their decision as well as which parts of it they will accept as persuasive.

The following questions can help the speechwriter check to see that his *evidence* is sufficient:

- How many *examples* are needed to establish the point with this audience? Should these examples be objective or picturesque?
- What *sources* of evidence are particularly attractive and credible with this audience? What authorities should be avoided?
- Can this audience understand *statistical* evidence? How much explanation of the data is needed?

Evidence needs to be built to a conclusion. Such a construction is an argument. The following questions should be asked about the form of the *argument* to be used to present an issue:

- **Should the argument be inductive or deductive?** That is to say, should you begin with your conclusion and support it, or should you lead your audience to your conclusion through evidence and argument? The answer to this question depends on the attitude of the audience toward the particular issue.

If they are hostile to the speaker's position, it is wise to withhold the conclusion until a solid set of facts and premises have been laid down. If you begin with the conclusion in this case, the audience will immediately reject it and question the evidence you use to present it.

If the audience is in agreement with the issue in question, begin with the conclusion and reinforce it. This will lead to greater identification between speaker and audience and will strengthen positions already held.

- **How much of the argument should be stated?** A good speechwriter knows what is called the "enthymematic process." This phenomenon occurs every time the audience supplies a premise that the speaker leaves out. It happens all the time. For example, if a speaker says, "Jones is a liberal and I don't think we should vote for liberals," the audience will fill in the missing premise; that is, "We should not vote for Jones." This saves time and prevents the speech from becoming boring when the speaker keeps stating the obvious.

But the enthymematic process can be used more subtly. In his 1968 acceptance speech, Richard Nixon promised "peace with honor." The vagueness of the phrase allowed moderates and conservatives who supported Nixon to fill in their own meaning for his phrase. Thus, Nixon was able to remain the choice of diverse groups through deft phrasing that played to the enthymematic process.

Enhancing credibility

Aristotle once argued that a speaker's credibility was perhaps his most potent persuasive tool. Certainly, in an era of image often given to the cult of personality, credibility becomes an overwhelmingly persuasive factor. There are two components of credibility that will not be discussed here. One is that magical quality called *charisma*: either a speaker has it or he does not. And in all cases it must be dealt with on an individual basis. Second is *prior reputation*. In every case, before a speaker opens his mouth, some sense of the man has preceded him, whether it is because of the cut of his clothes or because he has been in the news.

What is more important here are those factors over which the speechwriter has control. The first is *expertise*.

A speaker must know, or at least appear to know, what he is talking about. Therefore, how a speaker handles the issues can have a significant impact on the audience's perception of the speaker's expertise. The use of statistics, specific solutions, and privileged knowledge all add to the sense of expertise and thus contribute to credibility. It is no accident that Walter Cronkite was the most trusted man in America; he expertly handled the news for many years.

The second factor is *goodwill*. A speechwriter needs to make sure that the speech conveys to an audience the fact that the speaker has *their* best interests *at heart*. This is a difficult task in the political world, where most speakers are perceived to be merely advancing their own careers. The use of issues of interest to the audience, and references to local problems and members of the audience, all help to convey goodwill.

The third factor is *character*. When and how has the speaker demonstrated character? While George Bush's experiences in World War II may not qualify him for the presidency, they do reveal that the man has courage and can make tough decisions, all of which enhance his character and thereby the audience's sense of his credibility.

The fourth factor is *congruency*. The speechwriter needs to be sure that the speech is internally consistent. That requires a close examination of the evidence and argument used in the speech. A presidential candidate once said, "Twenty percent of the poor go to bed hungry every night. That means that one-fifth of the people in this country need welfare aid." If it wasn't obvious, his speechwriter should have informed him that twenty percent of the poor is not the same as one-fifth of the entire population

The speechwriter also needs to be sure the speech is externally consistent; that is, does it jibe with the facts the audience already knows? A speaker telling a group that unemployment is low across the country in an area where unemployment is high will not have much credibility!

The final factor of importance is *spontaneity* of delivery. In 1969 Senator Edward Kennedy addressed the nation regarding the tragedy at Chappaquiddick. He read from a prepared manuscript, losing his place several times. This lack of spontaneity reinforced in the minds of his audience a sense that something was being covered up. Richard Nixon faced the same problem in dealing with Watergate. When he read his speeches he was automatically unspontaneous and lost credibility. But when he held press conferences, where no script was possible, his answers seemed more believable to the public. The format of the speech thus becomes a crucial factor in enhancing the speaker's credibility.

Emotional tone

Another elusive matter is that of appealing to the emotions of the audience. Often, an emotional appeal is essential if persuasion is to be sealed. But if the speaker goes too far, the results can be catastrophic since persuasion not backed by argument and evidence evaporates very quickly. There is a sure-fire three-step approach for speechwriters wishing to appeal to the emotions.

- First, determine what the current emotional tone of the audience is. Are they *angry* over inflation? Are they *frustrated* by the federal government? Are they *apathetic* about politics?
- Second, determine what mood is most compatible with your message. Do you want the voters *mad* at Washington? Are you writing to *calm* the voters down? Do you want the audience to be *sympathetic* toward refugees?
- Third, and here's the rub, what words, images, and arguments will move the audience from its present state of mind to the one compatible with your message? Often you need only enhance an already existing mood. On other occasions you need to move the audience to another state of mind. In such cases, one image can be worth dozens of examples or facts. A well-crafted picture of starving refugees is far more likely to cause sympathy for their plight than a list of statistics about how many there are.

Always remember that emotions are volatile and interact with each other. Almost any speech will touch on a myriad of emotions ranging from fear to guilt. The effective speechwriter will keep a tight rein on all of these strategies.

Organization

Once the above strategies have been digested, the speechwriter is ready to organize these appeals into a coherent speech. Organization enhances a speaker's credibility and usually determines how much of the speech is retained by the audience. Organization is a crucial part of speechwriting and one of the few elements over which the speechwriter can have some control.

The introduction of the speech should be written last, after the other sections are complete. A good introduction has at least four parts. First, the *opening* should focus attention. Analogies, stories, and historical parallels can all be effective in getting attention. The opening remarks set a tone and often help the audience determine what frame of mind they are expected to be in. Frivolous remarks may result in the audience losing interest in the entire speech. Occasionally a truly shocking or controversial remark is in order if it serves to get a rambunctious crowd to listen to what follows.

The opening should flow naturally into the next part of the introduction: the *statement of the topic*. Often this is done in general terms. In the case of a hostile audience, one should not disclose the conclusion the speaker is going to reach.

Third, the topic should be *related to the particular audience present*. Normally, this is done by telling the audience why the topic is important to them, to the area in which they live, or to the business in which they work.

Finally, a good introduction ends with a *preview of the organization* to follow. This gives the audience something to hang their expectations on, while at the same time imparting a sense of control to the speaker.

The body of the speech can be organized around a number of patterns. The important thing is organization. Tests have shown that organization leads to greater retention of message, higher esteem for the speaker, and better reviews from the media.

Speechwriters with bright and cooperative clients can devise intricate and persuasive structures for their speeches. Less bright and less cooperative clients require simpler structures as do less formal speaking situations. Here are some useful models:

- **Causes and effects**. A discussion of a major problem can often be divided into its causes and effects. If the speaker wishes to take a stand on an issue, he can conclude with a solution based on his "balanced" analysis of the topic. I recommend discussion of no more than three causes and three effects, treating each as a separate unit so that they stick in the mind of the listener.

- **Advantages and disadvantages**. Often known as "pro and con," this method of division allows for balance and the appearance of an unbiased approach to the topic. The speaker has the option of reaching a conclusion or leaving it to the audience based on the information he has supplied them.

- **Problems and solutions**. Speakers wishing to take a stand and wishing to cover several different topics can use this method of structuring the speech. Again, transitional language should be used to keep the structure clear in the mind of the audience. For example, "Now that we have examined these problems, I would like to examine some proposed solutions."

Conclusions are very important. Often called perorations because they are speeches unto themselves, conclusions require great care. I suggest the following steps:

- First, summarize the speech. The longer the speech and the more intricate its structure, the longer the summary must be.

- Second, if you wish to deliver a conclusion, this is the place for it. All of the arguments and evidence have been delivered; the emotions have been stirred; and the audience sits ready to hear your judgment as a credible speaker.

- Third, the emotional tone of the speech should be reinforced. Roman orators sometimes referred to this moment as the anticlimax when once again the orator lifts the spirits of his audience to an emotional pitch. I suggest at this point that the speaker refer back to the opening of the speech. This tactic gives the speech a sense of unity and also signals the audience that the conclusion is near. It is a handy way to exit, not always the easiest thing to accomplish in a major speech!

Style in language

Most writers understand that style is nothing more than word choice. Good writers understand that choice is everything. Buffon, the French academician, once said that style is the man himself. Buffon may have hit on a democratic principle of style. Each of us has our own style that we are most effective using. The question is how do you find your true style, and then how do you enhance it?

Harry Truman found his style in the rough and tumble of the 1948 presidential campaign. Contrary to the advice of most of his writers, he began to speak extemporaneously, and to use language that many thought was unbecoming and, thus, unpresidential. The discovery of his own style provided Truman in part with one of the biggest upsets in political history. John Kennedy seemed born with his sense of style and brought it to fruition in his inaugural address.

But what can the speechwriter do to locate and enhance his client's style?

• First, try to isolate those moments when your client is at his best. Record them; listen to the phrasing, the word choice, and the pace. Using that material as a kind of stylistic essence, try to improve it by adding more sophisticated structures, more colorful language, and a few stylistic devices.

• Second, try to remember that style should reinforce message, not smother it. Some speakers use so many devices that the message is lost and the speaker sounds pretentious. Candidate Ronald Reagan was particularly effective at using clusters of images to reinforce the ideas of his speech. The images never get in the way of ideas; they provide instead an almost subliminal backdrop for them.

Often a touch of repetition can add elegance even when the phrase repeated is one the speaker came to naturally.

"If you want to buy a house, it will cost a great deal more than it did just a few short years ago.

"If you want to start a business, the overhead will be prohibitive.

"If you want to save, the inflation rate will wipe out your gain."

Here a very simple phrase, *"If you want . . . ,"* is repeated to give the message emphasis. As an aside, I would add that these devices become monotonous only after the third use.

• Third, a section laden with issues or arguments is likely to sustain itself, so stylistic devices should be kept to a minimum here. But emotional or transitional sections, particularly introductions and conclusions, normally have less substance and require more style.

President Ford's nomination acceptance speech at the 1976 Republican Convention is a case in point. The speech is full of evidence and specific positions, but the transitions are highly stylized to relieve the factual onslaught.

• Fourth, speechwriters should try to develop an understanding of as many different stylistic strategies as possible. Since style is highly individualized, it is well-served by very diverse strategies. The Romans developed over 450 different tropes and figures of language. Shakespeare used these tropes and figures often in his plays, and they, few would argue, contain some of the best speeches ever written.

The most common stylistic devices include *metaphor, analogy, allegory, irony, hyperbole, alliteration,* and *balance.* A good speechwriter will have mastered these and other devices. He knows that an oxymoron such as, "We must never negotiate in fear, but we must never fear to negotiate," will be retained by the listener because it holds attention with a poetic touch.

Often the best stylistic devices are composed of the simplest words: "The only thing we have to fear is fear itself. . . . The business of America is business. . . . of the people, by the people, for the people. . . . Speak softly and carry a big stick." Franklin Roosevelt took care to see that each word in his speeches was apt as well as on the list of the most common words in current societal usage.

• Fifth, the expert speechwriter realizes that style, like the other components of the art, cannot be isolated from the entire speech-writing effort. The words a man chooses say something about his personality. They must be geared to the comprehension level of the audience. They must be compatible with the mood conveyed.

Too often writers try to remake their clients into literary giants. While "the grand style" may be effective with a few, for example a Kennedy or a MacArthur, it usually opens the ordinary speaker to ridicule while making him very uncomfortable. Effective style is so rare in a society constantly degraded by the crassness of commercial television that a little style will go a long way.

• Finally, the effective speechwriter knows that the art of writing lies in rewriting. Most good speeches go through at least five drafts, with the client participating in much of the redrafting. F.D.R.'s major speeches usually were drafted eight to twelve times. He was intimately involved in the process. Perhaps that is why he knew his material so well, and his speeches bore his own indelible stamp despite the fact that he had a large staff of writers.

Communicating is the most important thing a politician does. If he has advisors for other major functions, he should certainly have one for his speeches. And the person he selects should be fully versed and up-to-date in the field. An effective speechwriter needs to know his craft, including adjusting the politician's rhetoric to factors of personality, audience, emotion, style, organization, logic, delivery, and motive.

A major speechwriting staff will include an audience analysis unit and a research unit. A ready library of quotations, witticisms, and reference material will be on hand. But most important of all is the hiring of a writer who is thoroughly steeped in rhetorical theory, the art of finding in any given case the available means of persuasion.

Craig R. Smith

Door-to-Door Campaigning:
How to Get the Most out of Your Pedometer

Lorene Hanley Duquin

Former U.S. House Speaker Thomas P. "Tip" O'Neill lost his first race for local office in Massachusetts by a tiny margin. He was puzzled by the defeat because he thought he had counted his expected votes carefully before polling day. To his great surprise, O'Neill was later told that one of his neighbors, a close family friend, had not voted for him. When the future Speaker confronted the man, he explained simply, "Tip, you never bothered to ask me for my support."

Even in this age of television and direct mail appeals, citizens like to be asked personally for their votes. In statewide or national campaigns, only a tiny percentage of the electorate can usually meet the candidate on the campaign trail, but a local race can be personalized to a much greater extent. Lorene Hanley Duquin describes the age-old techniques of door-to-door campaigning in this article, and her homespun advice for the candidate-on-foot is both practical and sometimes amusing.

Angry constituents, barking dogs, tired feet, worn-out shoes, and blisters. Door-to-door campaigning can be hazardous to a candidate's emotional and physical well-being. But in many local races, it can also mean the difference between winning and losing.

Why? Because even in these days of sophisticated campaign techniques, voters are still impressed and complimented when a local candidate takes the time to deliver his or her message in person. That personal visit allows the voter to see and hear the candidate, to ask questions, and then to tell all his or her friends and neighbors about it. One visit can create a positive ripple effect throughout the district.

But too many political newcomers and many incumbents don't use door-to-door effectively. Many start walking without a plan and waste valuable time trying to reach *every* voter when they should be concentrating on finding the *right* voters.

Others give up before they even begin because the thought of walking up to even several hundred homes is appalling—and it may mean several thousand.

And then there are always a few who assume door-to-door is a magic formula for success

Lorene Hanley Duquin is a political writer and campaign advisor in western New York State.

when they would be much better off using other campaign tactics.

Effective door-to-door campaigns are carefully planned and systematically executed. They are specifically designed to best utilize a candidate's time in his or her district. Then the door-to-door contact is reinforced by other campaign tactics. While it may appear to be very informal, smart candidates know that their successful door-to-door program is just one small part of their overall campaign strategy.

The importance of strategy

"No matter what political level you're on, it's important to realize that in a campaign, time, money, materials, and workers are limited resources," says Jeff Spencer, now a Buffalo attorney. "The problem every candidate must face is how to maximize those resources so they have the greatest impact on the electorate."

Spencer was a Syracuse University graduate student in 1973 when he developed a successful door-to-door program for New York State Assemblyman Robin Schimminger. Although Spencer is no longer involved in professional politics, his theories on strategy and door-to-door as a campaign tactic can be applied to any political race because they are based on military principles.

"I've always been interested in military history," Spencer says. "When I was active in political consulting, I would take military strategy, decision theory, and organizational theory and apply them to political campaigns.

"For example, in the military, if you're in a defensive position, you'll need fewer men than if you're in an offensive position. It takes a whole company or four platoons on the offensive to overcome one platoon on the defensive. Now if you apply that to a political campaign, and you're the incumbent with a strong base, you can see that you don't need as many resources to hold your territory and win the election. But if you're the challenger, the greatest amount of your campaign resources must be spent attacking your opponent's territory and capturing enough of it to win. But while you're attacking, you still have to keep a minimum amount of resources in a defensive position to protect your own base and whatever new territory you've captured."

In many cases, door-to-door campaigning can be an effective means of attacking an opponent's base. But a good overall campaign strategy makes the best possible use of all campaign resources. So in addition to door-to-door, it's essential to have a defensive strategy that will reinforce and protect your base.

The plusses and pitfalls of door-to-door

Whether you should use door-to-door or not will depend on the size and character of your district, your personality, and the amount of time left in the election.

For example, in a race for school board in a large district where there is always a low voter turnout, door-to-door would be a less efficient way to use a candidate's time.

It would be better to locate the people who would be most likely to vote in the school-board race: teachers, parents of school-age children, members of taxpayer organizations, senior citizens. Since the chances of zeroing in on these people in a door-to-door campaign are slim, the candidate would be better off planning hand-shaking campaigns at PTA meetings, senior citizen centers, and other community events that attract these probable voters.

Similarly, in a higher level race, a candidate's time is often better spent meeting large numbers of people. For example, when Rep. John LaFalce of New York first ran for Congress in 1974, he already had good name and face recognition because of his previous elections to county and state legislative seats. Since the congressional district was large, LaFalce's time was better spent shaking hands at plazas, businesses, industries, and community centers in the area. People already knew him, so having the opportunity to shake his hand was

Lorene Hanley Duquin

impressive because he had political celebrity status. A door-to-door campaign would have limited the number of people LaFalce could have reached.

Chuck Swanick, on the other hand, was a political newcomer when he first ran for an upstate New York county legislative seat in 1979. Unlike LaFalce, no one knew Swanick. Since there was a good chance that a voter who met Swanick at a plaza would consider it more of an annoyance than a privilege, his campaign strategy emphasized door-to-door where voters would be impressed by an energetic young man who was taking the time to walk to their homes.

Determining whether door-to-door is right for you

Before you decide whether door-to-door should be part of your political strategy, ask some questions and do some investigating. Here are a few suggestions:

- Drive around the district. Examine the types of homes, the neighborhoods, the number of apartment complexes. Going door-to-door is difficult in rural areas and impossible in some apartment buildings, co-ops, and condominiums where soliciting is prohibited and tight security prevents anyone but residents from entering.
- Know your opponent. If he or she has a history of using door-to-door successfully, you may have to follow suit.
- Talk to people who have run for office before. Ask them why they did or did not use door-to-door and whether they think it would be effective.
- Ask your political party leaders for advice. Is door-to-door expected in your community? If not, would it give your campaign an edge?
- Take a look at the physical size of the district. Is door-to-door realistic? Or could your time be better spent in other ways?
- Study the voter enrollment in your district. Do you have the political advantage or are you the underdog? Would you use door-to-

door as an offensive tactic to turn votes or as a defensive tactic to hold your base?

Setting up your plan

Once you've decided to use door-to-door, formulate a plan. Start by determining how much time you can spend on canvassing each day and how many days of the week you can walk. Some candidates might be able to walk every day, while others might have only weekends available.

A good quality door-to-door contact that will make an impression on a voter usually lasts between three and five minutes. At that rate, you could make about fifteen contacts an hour. Multiply fifteen by the number of hours you plan to work each day to find the average number of homes you can reach daily. Then multiply that by the number of days that you'll be walking between now and Election Day.

For example, let's suppose you planned to spend two hours a day on door-to-door campaigning. Multiply that by fifteen contacts an hour and you've got an average of thirty homes you can reach each day. If you planned to walk every day and there are three months or ninety days left until the election, you'll be able to reach 2,700 homes at best.

But remember, that means *walking every day for two hours no matter what the weather conditions are and no matter how you're feeling any particular day.* And it doesn't take into consideration the fact that at many of the houses no one will be home.

Doing this little calculation does have one advantage, though. It will give you a basis for developing a door-to-door plan.

For instance, let's suppose there are fewer than 2,000 homes in your district. You now know that you have a pretty good chance of reaching every home if you spend two hours a day for the next three months. But if your district is larger than that, you'll either have to increase the amount of time you can spend on door-to-door or find some other way of getting the most out of the time you can afford to spend.

Targeting

Finding a more efficient way to reach the voters is called targeting. Instead of walking to every home, you walk only to the homes of those voters who you decide must be contacted in order to win. Targeting is usually based on three theories:

1. There are many homes in the district where residents are not registered to vote. Since they can't vote in the election, it's a waste of the candidate's time to stop at their doors. But if you want these homes contacted *some way*, you'd be better off sending a volunteer with registration forms who might be able to convince these people to register. If they do and they know the forms *came* from you, they'll probably *vote* for you. If they don't, you haven't lost any of your valuable time and you have nothing to worry about because they won't be able to vote for your opponent either.

2. In every district there are some homes where only one registered voter lives, homes where two voters live, and homes where three or more voters live. A smart candidate who doesn't have much time will focus his or her efforts on those homes where the most voters can be reached.

3. In every district there are people who do not vote along strict party lines. If you can identify them and convince them to vote for you, it may provide the extra votes you need to win.

Putting the theory to work

Dennis Ward, an Amherst, New York, attorney, used these theories when he developed what he calls a "Swing District Targeting Program" for his brother Dan, who was elected to a county legislative seat in 1975.

"Our goal was to reach 80 percent of the voters," Ward says. "In order to do that we had to start in March and work right through the November election. We also realized that it was more important to contact some voters than others. So we took a comparison of five previous elections to see how the Democrats and Republicans in each district voted. Since my brother was running on the Democratic line, we looked for districts where the Republicans had a history of swinging over to the Democratic lines. Then we rated each district.

"The districts where the Democrats and Republicans tended not to deviate from party line were classed as low priority. We figured the Democrats would vote for us anyway and the Republicans probably wouldn't. The swing districts had a high priority."

In Ward's high-priority districts, the candidate walked to the home of every registered voter. He carried voter affiliation sheets so he knew where the registered voters lived, what political party they were enrolled in, and how many registered voters lived in the home. Each person the candidate spoke to received a telephone directory of important government services. The directory was designed so the candidate's name appeared in bold type. After he left each home, the candidate put a plus mark next to the name of the person he had spoken with. Each week, a campaign worker would send a hand-written thank-you note to the people who had plusses next to their names. The thank-you note was designed to reinforce the visit in the mind of the voter.

"Since we started so early, we had to adjust our strategy because the voters we reached in March are not as attuned to the election as the voters in September or October. But we figured that the candidate makes the best possible contact and even if the early ones were not as effective, since we had touched the voters, they would remember it nonetheless. We always reinforced those early contacts later in the campaign with phone calls and other campaign tactics that built up our name recognition and momentum in the district."

Sometimes a candidate *appears* to be going door-to-door when in fact he or she is only going to very special doors. Len Lenihan waged that kind of campaign for a seat on the county legislature in Erie County, New York, when reapportionment left him in a district that had a 5,000 vote advantage for the other party.

Lenihan's door-to-door campaign was so finely targeted that there were often streets where he would actually visit only a few homes on the entire block. So instead of walking through the neighborhoods of his district, Lenihan had a campaign volunteer drive him to his targeted homes. This idea of using a driver would also be advantageous in rural areas or in suburban communities where homes are spread far apart. And if there should be an unfriendly dog, you can always jump back into the car!

"Once you understand that time won't permit you to walk to everyone's home, you have to sit down and decide exactly where you *want* to go and where you *have* to go," Lenihan said. "At first, I was opposed to using a driver because I wanted to be seen walking down the streets informally. I didn't want it to look like I was picking and choosing the houses I went to. But in terms of productivity and effectiveness, a driver is the best way—especially in the fall when it starts to get dark early and you want to hit as many targeted homes as possible."

Lenihan also used thank-you notes to reinforce his visits at the door. His notes were preprinted but he always took the time to jot down a personal message on the note.

"To me, the most effective thing about the note is that personalized message," he says. "I might write *Thanks for the iced tea* or *Your dog was cute.* In some cases there wasn't anything particularly different about the visit so I'd just write, *Mrs. Smith—I enjoyed talking to you.*"

Perfecting your door-to-door technique

"I always fall back on my experiences as a part-time mailman when I was in college," says New York Assemblyman Schimminger, who has used door-to-door campaigning in every political race he's entered. "The first cardinal rule of door-to-door is: *Train your eye to spot the ominous chain or rope.* It's a sure sign that the home is also inhabited by a dog.

"Cardinal rule number two is: *No vote is ever worth a fight with an angry dog.* It's always better to skip the house than to run the risk of being bitten."

Finally, here are several other door-to-door tips from successful candidates:

- Introduce yourself and briefly tell the voter what office you're running for and why. For example, you might say, "I'm running for Town Supervisor because I think the office needs more attention than a part-time administrator can give it. I plan to work full-time at the job."
- Always apologize if it's apparent that you've interrupted a resident's nap, meal, or other activity.
- Don't ever get into an argument with a resident at the door. If the person doesn't agree with you, leave.
- Always give a piece of campaign literature or a campaign novelty to the voter. Sports schedules, phone directories, and library schedules have an added advantage because the voter tends to keep them longer than he or she would a brochure listing your qualifications.
- Never canvass after dark. People don't like opening their doors to strangers after sunset.
- Avoid canvassing during important televised football games.
- Don't dress too formally. But don't dress too casually either. Never appear eccentric or sloppy.
- Don't take notes about your visit while the resident can see you.
- Keep your message short. Remember: three to five minutes at the door is best.
- Don't take it to heart if someone slams the door in your face. It's unreasonable to expect that everyone will vote for you. Just shrug it off and keep on walking.

Paid Canvassing:
Getting Politics Back into the Streets

Pat McCoy • Ned McCulloch • Peter Wood

The candidate is not the only one who can profitably campaign door-to-door. His or her volunteers—and sometimes paid workers—can canvass key neighborhoods on the candidate's behalf. In fact, in statewide contests where the electorate can number in the millions, a coordinated program of paid and volunteer canvassing by party and campaign activists is the only feasible way to reach a substantial number of voters in person.

The authors of the following article propose that the best method of high-quality personalized campaigning is a professionally directed paid canvassing program. Under this scheme, canvassers pay their own salaries (at least ideally) by soliciting money door-to-door for the candidate's cause at the same time that they deliver literature and assess the residents' voting preferences. This technique is borrowed from interest groups (such as the environmentalists) that have raised considerable money for many years using door-to-door canvassing.

If you have a cause or a candidate to promote and need to broaden your support, you may want to consider a paid canvass. Canvassing has come a long way from those days when a few loyal volunteers would walk their block to drop campaign literature or collect small campaign contributions. Several large professional canvass operations have sprung up across the country in recent years, usually as outgrowths of ideological organizations. They offer an obvious payoff: face-to-face contact with tens of thousands of people who are polled for support and prompted to contribute money, time, and votes.

Mr. Wood and Mr. McCoy have served as national directors of the Acorn Canvass. Mr. McCulloch is the Washington director of Acorn Associates, grassroots campaign consultants.

Why has the paid canvass generated so much excitement among politicians? The answer lies in the intensity of resources required by this activity. Door-to-door canvassing is the most powerful voting contact technique, but any significant effort consumes endless staff and worker man-hours. Therefore, over the past decade, campaign managers have increasingly substituted direct mail, media, and phone canvassing for the traditional volunteer-staffed door-to-door canvass. During that same time, however, interest groups have successfully used canvassing to carry their message to millions of voters, while gathering petition signatures and raising funds for their legal and lobbying activities.

The key difference: Interest group canvassers solicit donations at the door of a supporter and use them to provide wages for the canvasser and income for the sponsoring organization. Think of the professional canvasser as a door-to-door salesman. If a crack door-to-door salesman can earn a living selling a product door-to-door, a canvasser should be able to earn a living selling *a cause* door-to-door. With their wages at stake, professional canvassers have an incentive to persistently deliver the message in a convincing manner to as many households as possible.

The bottom line: Canvassing *can* still be a means of reaching thousands of voters with the message of your choice; the problems entailed in running a canvass *can* be overcome by soliciting donations at supporters' doorways and using those revenues to pay canvassers and hire experienced, professional management.

Goals for the canvass

Even a modest professional canvass operation can deliver a message to thousands of households each week within thirty days of starting up. Many professional canvasses now have twenty or more full-time workers in each state talking to 5,000 households and leaving literature at 8,000 households *every week*. That translates into 4,000 to 6,000 people who will sign petitions for a referendum (or a place on a primary ballot), talk to a personal representative of the campaign, and give information that identifies them for subsequent outreach efforts.

Furthermore, the staff is mobile, so it can go where needed at critical stages of the campaign. When targeted by a precinct selection process, and further narrowed by sending canvassers out with registration lists to guide their door-knocking, the impact of the canvass becomes intense: It gets the message to the voter with more power and pinpoint precision than any other voter contact technique. By election day, an operation with twenty staffers working for six months will have delivered a knockout blow of 200,000 to 300,000 powerful contacts.

Although many groups run paid canvasses simply for the voter contact benefits, under the best of circumstances a canvass can be an important fundraising tool. For example, while three percent is a typical response on a direct mail solicitation, good canvassers will get financial contributions from fifteen to thirty-three percent of their cold contacts. The amount of money raised depends on five widely ranging variables:

1. the quality of supervision
2. the canvasser's level of experience and motivation
3. the sponsoring organization's or candidate's appeal to the public
4. the "rap" used at the door
5. the territory being canvassed.

As an example of the "best of circumstances," a professional fundraiser is typically expected to bring at least $80 back per night, with $100 being about the average. In addition, phone and direct mail resolicitations of the canvass contact list have a very high rate of return. The simple logic of canvassing is apparent here: An informed, friendly, and sincere canvasser can be much more persuasive than a form letter or a voice on the other end of the line.

Unfortunately, campaigns cannot expect results in this high range. On each of the five factors influencing fundraising, interest groups have an advantage over most electoral canvasses. Foremost is the level of experience held by the professional canvassing organization. Interest group canvassers are working for a *permanent enterprise* that has operated *year-round*, often for a decade or more. Over time, the canvass develops a stable and expert supervisor staff, and field personnel grow in experience. People in the community have become familiar with the presence of a canvasser at their door. Directors have fine-tuned the rap and the canvass routes. The fundraising return is a result of a persistent investment in experience.

A campaign has a totally different timeline— at best a canvass will start eighteen months before the general election. In addition, electoral canvasses want to log enormous numbers of contacts (as part of their voter contact goal) so they need to field large canvass crews. The combination of little time and large contact requirements pushes canvass expansion to the limit. Campaign managers are always going to pressure the canvass director to spin off additional offices with inadequately trained staff. In all probability, the crews will not be fully trained until election day—and then the canvass operation is out of business. Inexperience has the same effect on all areas of the campaign: People in the community will not be accustomed to a canvasser's request for political donations, the rap will be ragged, and the routes chaotic.

Bringing in the pros

Many of the problems posed by the institution of a door-to-door effort can be solved by hiring an established professional canvass or canvassing consultant. Campaigns rarely try to conduct their own polling or create their own media; it is equally ill-advised for them to try to run their own professional canvass. Canvassing has now been a big business for ten years, and there are many pros running canvasses for consumer, citizen action, environmental, and feminist organizations. Several of these groups will conduct outside consulting with campaigns interested in setting up a paid canvass. Once the campaign manager has hired consultants, or an existing professional canvass, the campaign staff has access to years of canvassing experience. Then it becomes the consultant's responsibility to hire, train, and motivate professional canvassers; to deploy the canvass crews effectively day after day, week after week; and to develop raps and petitions that work at the doors.

In drawing on this wealth of experience, some campaigns have adopted a turn-key approach: they pay an existing canvass (usually one already operating in their area) to carry their message to the voters. When possible, this approach has the advantage of requiring the least supervision from the campaign staff. Yet, inevitably, conflicts arise over the primary purpose of the canvass—money or message. The group currently sponsoring the canvass operates it almost exclusively as a fundraising tool. Any perturbations that lower the fundraising yield are not going to be well received. In comparison, the campaign is going to be much more interested in making quality voter contact. A canvass that raises no money—even a canvass that loses *reasonable* amounts of money—is still a superior voter contact tool.

Targeting is an excellent example of this divergence of goals: A professional canvass takes in more money by restricting its doorknocking to upper middle-income neighborhoods. But most Democratic and Republican campaigns would like to restrict doorknocking to households with registered voters (and in a primary, registered party voters) in low-income neighborhoods. Arrangements can be worked out for the campaigns to subsidize takes "below quota," but they should not expect professional canvasses to be very flexible on targeting canvass routes (or a host of other items: the rap, salaries, working hours).

Therefore, campaigns often choose to build their own canvass. If the campaign can supply the canvass consultant with two or three capable staff persons as core trainees, they should be able to field a canvass with ten canvassers per night four to six weeks after startup. Additional core trainees can help the canvass generate large numbers of contacts immediately, and—as additional canvassers are hired—may become supervisors in the expanded canvass staff. In the end, the decision is one of money and time: A campaign with time but no money should try to build its own canvass. Consulting fees will be lower and flexibility greater.

Setting up a canvass

The bare-bones minimum staff to begin a canvass consists of two people: a canvass director and field manager. Professional

Pat McCoy • Ned McCulloch • Peter Wood

consultants will probably have to fill these roles during the start-up period, even with the presence of the core trainees. The canvass director's primary responsibility is to perform all of the office work associated with the canvass—from interviewing potential canvassers to keeping the books. Other duties of the director include supervising the field manager, setting up canvass routes, maintaining accountability, and acting as liaison between the canvass and campaign staffs. The field manager assigns the territory, drops off and picks up the canvassers, trains them, and helps enforce standards.

Procedurally, the first step in establishing an electoral canvass is to identify two or three campaign staff persons interested in working on the project. One of these people will become the canvass director, the others field managers. Once identified, this staff should be detached from campaign responsibilities and sent to train with a professional canvass. After several weeks of such exposure, these campaign staffers will return to the campaign and form the core of the canvass crew. At this point, the consultant travels to the campaign site to supervise the startup of the canvass; additional personnel are hired and trained, systems are developed, and the canvassing hits the streets. After two or three weeks, operations should have smoothed sufficiently for the "core canvassers" (who by now have four to six weeks of training and experience) to take over the roles of canvass director and field manager. Yet even after the consultants stop full-time supervision, they should continue to come back on a regular basis until the operation is running smoothly.

The advantages of professional management

It is reasonable to expect a staff of ten to fifteen canvassers within a month, if you have a good labor market *and* an adequate supervisory staff. A popular candidate or cause will ease recruiting problems by pulling in additional inquiries from people who are already employed but want more meaningful work.

Other responses will be generated by recruitment on local college campuses and in areas where supporters are concentrated. If an ad in the local paper gets fifty or more inquiries, staffing the canvass with door-knockers will not be a problem.

Normally, canvass expansion is limited by the shortage of experienced supervisory staff. Opening new offices is an example. Expanding canvass offices across the state has the obvious advantage of increasing the volume of voters who can be reached by the canvass. More important, they add recruitment bases to feed the voracious appetite for canvassers. But each new office requires an additional canvass director and field manager.

A consultant can be a source of trained personnel, but should only provide it during the start-up period (and possibly for the get-out-the-vote effort). A good canvass brings a lot of workers into the campaign. These people pay for themselves while in training, affording the campaign staff an opportunity to assess the skills and commitment of their new recruits. Many talented personnel uncovered by canvass recruiters have later taken on greater duties within the canvass or campaign. Staff development is the key to molding a canvass into a professional operation that can perform consistently year-round, year after year.

The candidate's role

The candidate's interaction with the canvass staff is an important ingredient in motivating the troops to stay with a job that has some very frustrating and discouraging moments. It is important for the candidate to maintain a regular presence and show genuine interest in what kind of feedback the canvassers are getting from voters.

A large part of each canvasser's motivation in taking the job (and sticking with it through the most trying moments in the field) is his commitment to the candidate. A briefing or meeting with the candidate once every two to three weeks to get updates on the campaign or trade stories can suffice—just so the staff feels that they are an important part of the campaign. They are, in fact, the most personal embodiment of the candidate to thousands of people; make sure that they are well-informed and that their message is positive.

A big bang for the buck

Should a self-supporting canvass operation be an integral part of *your* campaign? In terms of economics, the answer is usually an emphatic *yes*.

Compare what you get out of a canvass to other voter contact techniques. For example, mailing a brochure to 4,000 households requires high packaging costs and postage. A canvass can get the brochure out to all 4,000 homes without these costs *and* adds hand delivery to 2,500 voters in the process.

A phone bank can ask questions of voters, yet the phone calls usually have to be used in combination with a mailing coded to each voter's response. This combination usually carries a cost per contact of *at least* a dollar. A canvass is the only voter contact technique that can reach into households (with and without phones), deliver the candidate's theme in an eye-to-eye contact with the voter, leave a piece of literature in the voter's hand for later perusal, and do it all at a low cost.

No serious campaign should be without one.

Special Event Fundraisers

Karen Feld

Just a few decades ago, it was not uncommon for a candidate to raise most or all of his or her campaign treasury at a single cocktail party or dinner. With most statewide races costing millions today—and even a competitive U.S. House campaign requiring well over a quarter of a million dollars per candidate—fundraising has become a full-time, continuous operation (maybe preoccupation) for most candidates. Direct mail (described in a later reading) has received the most attention as a fundraising device, but it cannot be used successfully by all campaigns. Nor will it ever completely replace special events—dinners, cocktail parties, concerts, and the like—in the financial plans of campaigns. Much as the wise investor diversifies his or her portfolio, so must the candidate simultaneously prime many money pumps. The small (under $100) contributor, big donors (over $1,000), and political action committees all require different fundraising strategies.

Karen Feld explains the techniques of special event fundraisers in the following article. Written for an audience of candidates, the piece stresses the importance of detail in planning and executing a lucrative campaign event. Once again, the reader is left with an appreciation for the onerous work necessary to start and run the campaign engine. The technological marvels of modern politics are wondrous in some ways, but nothing substitutes for the nitty-gritty tasks carried out by volunteers, party activists, and paid professionals.

In planning a special event, it is imperative not to get so wrapped up in the excitement that you lose sight of the objective of any political fundraising technique: to raise the greatest amount of money for the least amount of expense and work. But never sacrifice details. A successful event is one that is well planned and executed, whether it's a local bake sale, car wash or marathon run, or a glamorous, celebrity-packed $1,000-a-plate dinner.

In the beginning of the campaign, it is advisable to list the groups you need to target and the amount of money you expect from each. Then map out a basic schedule of the kinds of events you anticipate organizing. If you have any questions about the event being in compliance with federal or local campaign regulations, request an advisory opinion before you begin. This can save countless headaches down the line.

Incumbents may want to kick off the campaign with a big dinner to scare the opposition. A challenger might plan a big event to demonstrate a broad base of support. It's an individual decision. "Start off with what's easiest," says Washington-based independent

Karen Feld is a freelance political writer based in Washington, D.C. She has organized many special fundraising events for congressional candidates of both parties.

political consultant and fundraiser Betsy Crone. This applies at any electoral level and in any region of the country.

The eight-week countdown

A two-month lead time is ideal for planning most events, although many successful extravaganzas have been planned in one month or less. Large $500 and $1,000-a-ticket dinners require more time. Often the hotel ballroom alone must be reserved a year or more in advance.

The following timetable was developed by Brad O'Leary, Republican fundraiser and former executive director of the Texas Republican party. Used by the Republican National Committee and the National Republican Congressional Committee, it is the best of all the plans secured from many major fundraisers. This sixty-day countdown should be followed where applicable for each of the events discussed later.

8 WEEKS AHEAD OF EVENT:
- Select date and format of event.
- Appoint dinner chairman (not your campaign finance chairman). Recruit sponsors.
- Confirm principal speakers' appearances (these should be arranged as soon as a date is set or the date should be made according to his or her availability in the case of a major celebrity).
- Select hotel accommodations for overnight VIPs.
- Confirm dinner location and obtain floor plan.
- Select tables for co-chairmen, tables for individual ticket holders, and press tables (side tables three to five rows back).
- Confirm VIP reception location.
- Prepare card file with addresses and phone numbers for invitation list.
- Design and print invitation.

7 WEEKS AHEAD OF EVENT:
- Appoint treasurer.
- Appoint table sales chairman (if local people are cooperative).

- Appoint individual ticket sales chairman.
- Hold first weekly meeting, possibly a breakfast for the dinner committee. Use this time to motivate your workers. Have the meeting at the same time each week if possible.
- Print tickets. Use a union printer in major urban areas, i.e., get the "union bug" at least on the carrier envelope.
- Appoint dinner committee.
- Purchase first class mailing permit and obtain post office box for return mail.

6 WEEKS AHEAD OF EVENT:
- Issue press release announcing dinner or event.
- Divide table prospect file among dinner committee.
- Mail invitations.
- Recruit volunteers for phone bank to begin three weeks prior to event.
- Set up dinner office.

5 WEEKS AHEAD OF EVENT:
- Issue press release announcing speaker or other VIPs.
- Begin follow-up calls to invitees.
- Select individual to give invocation, if necessary.
- Determine decorations.

4 WEEKS AHEAD OF EVENT:
- Distribute memo listing table and individual ticket purchasers.
- Issue press release announcing dinner co-chairman, items to be auctioned, or anything of special interest.
- Plan menu for VIP reception, if any.

3 WEEKS AHEAD OF EVENT:
- Distribute list of table and individual ticket buyers along with a list of those invited who have not yet responded favorably.
- Press release if applicable.
- Mail head table invitations if there is a head table.
- Hold luncheon or cocktail party for co-chairmen.
- Set up phone banks.

2 WEEKS AHEAD OF EVENT:
- Draft and print program.
- Confirm master of ceremonies and speaker itinerary.
- Final ticket push.

1 WEEK AHEAD OF EVENT:
- Press release with final information on speaker, dinner, and ticket sales.
- Total ticket sales.
- Contact co-chairmen to make sure they are using their tickets.
- Draw up seating charts.
- Give estimate of number of guests to caterer two days before.
- Follow up and confirm all details of room, entertainment, food, beverage, flowers, security, photographer, microphone, podium, and arrangements for arrival of candidate and VIP guests, meeting plans, hotel, ground transportation.
- Have a "walk-through" the day prior to event.
- Brief the candidate on the kind of audience and provide him with names of key people.

WEEK AFTER EVENT:
- Follow up thank-you notes to workers and contributors.
- Bookkeeping—bank net proceeds and dissolve all dinner accounts.
- Collect outstanding pledges.

Fundraising plans, budgets, ticket prices

The first part of any successful plan for a fundraising event is a realistic budget, an estimate of expenses, and the projected amount of income. "A balanced campaign will raise one-third of its money from direct mail, one-third from dinners and special events, and one-third from county finance committees," says Republican fundraiser O'Leary.

The lavishness of the event should determine ticket prices. For example, it is simply not cost effective (and therefore a waste of time) to have a seated dinner at a hotel in a major city for less than $100-a-person. Whenever possible, arrange for items to be donated. "Avoid expensive gourmet, catered food and open cocktail bars," suggests Betsy Crone, fundraiser for the National Women's Political Caucus and other liberal candidates and causes. "Never use expensive bottled wine even at the fanciest event—use good house wine in a carafe," says Mary Drape, Director of the Republican Senate Majority Fund, Senator Howard Baker's political action committee (PAC).

The less your costs and the more you charge, the greater your net is. Brad O'Leary uses the following table to show what you will achieve with different ticket price structures (dinner goal of $100,000 assumed).

Ticket prices vary with the type of event, the seniority and power of the candidate, and the city in which the event is held. Washington, D.C., prices rarely fall below $250. A ticket that was $250 just two years ago is now $500. An incumbent senator or committee chairman can usually charge $1,000-a-head.

"Any event will be costly, time-consuming, and is part of the building process," says Crone. "The person who is a $25 donor in January, gives you $50 later, and then becomes a volunteer," she adds. If the event is for the

Ticket Price	Number	Cost	Gross	Net
$ 25	4,000	50%	100,000	50,000
$ 50	2,000	30%	100,000	70,000
$100	1,000	10%	100,000	80,000
$250	400	18%	100,000	82,000
$500	200	14%	100,000	86,000

challenger or a relatively unknown incumbent, don't start off with a $500 dinner. Start small and build, she advises.

"Campaign fundraising events should be targeted for different size donors—large, medium, and small." They should appeal across the board—to the $15, $25, $50, and $75 donors, as well as the $100, $500, and $1,000. "In any case, you don't want costs of the event to exceed one-third of the total projected income," comments Crone. "If you are going to go through the pain and agony of a fundraising event, the purpose is exclusively to make money."

Choosing a time and venue—scheduling the event

Frequently the time of the event (which often determines the type of event) must be selected on the basis of the candidate's political or travel schedule. For example, if a candidate is staying overnight in a particular city and has the morning free, a breakfast is an ideal event. Practical considerations should always prevail.

Other considerations include the lifestyle of the people in the particular city. In Miami, breakfasts work well because the people are up and out early, says Mary Drape, who also advises, "Never do a breakfast in Chicago because even wealthy people use mass transit and many have to commute an hour." In Texas, luncheons are popular because custom dictates long lunches. In Southern California, 4:30 P.M. is an ideal time for a cocktail reception because people leave work early, whereas in New York or Washington, you would organize the same reception for 6:00 or 6:30 P.M.

Representative Newt Gingrich (R-Georgia) has found business receptions in his congressional district worthwhile. He invites business people at $25 each to stop by his office in Atlanta for wine and cheese on their way home between 4:00 and 6:00 P.M. Most important, be sure the time and place is convenient. "You don't want people to have to go across town at rush hour," says Crone. Be flexible and practical. "If Joe Smith has done successful breakfasts in a particular city, then do a breakfast," advises Drape.

Fundraising events should be fun, so be imaginative in selecting the venue and the type of event. Make the event something special, something people in that community couldn't do on their own. Bring in a famous celebrity or have a theater party on the opening night of a sold-out performance, or a movie party before a blockbuster film opens to the public. Do something people will talk about and enjoy. For example, try *not* to offer the overly familiar atmosphere of the Capitol Hill Club or Democratic Club in Washington, although the expenses will probably be less at those locations.

In selecting a room at a hotel or hall, be sure that it will accommodate the expected number of people and that it is neither too big nor too small. In general, a small room packed so tightly that no one can move is just as bad as a cavernous room for only thirty people.

Whenever possible, hold the event in a room with windows rather than a basement restaurant or banquet hall. Brad O'Leary suggests a room with a low ceiling, windows, and a view if possible: "Create an atmosphere for people to give."

The closer the guests are to the candidate or VIP guests talking, the better. Private homes limit the number of guests, but the price is right, and they often provide an intimate atmosphere. Find a home that people will want to see and may not be invited to otherwise. It may be the home of a celebrity or someone who has an outstanding Chinese art collection. Such an approach is as much a requirement in Peoria as in Washington, D.C.

Local candidates, looking for Washington-based PAC support, must schedule their fundraising events early in the campaign cycle. There is tremendous competition for the available political action committee (PAC) money. Sixty percent of the national PACs are located in Washington. Most lobbyists get 400 or more invitations a year to congressional fundraisers. Successful Washington fundraisers early in the campaign cycle can serve to scare off potential opposition. They can provide early seed money for the campaign and funds that cannot be raised in the district. To avoid scheduling conflicts, the Democatic and Republican National Committees, as well as their congressional counterparts, mail out lists of Washington fundraisers many weeks ahead of the events. Ted Miller, manager of the Republican Capitol Hill Club, suggests strongly that fundraisers be booked months in advance. "We average five a week," says Miller. The same is true of the Democratic Club.

None of these suggestions guarantee success, but if the details are right, the potential for success is greater.

Staffing—who does what?

You may want to hire a professional fundraiser to handle the details of your event. They work either on a flat fee basis, such as Nancy Cole of Fundraisers Unlimited (who charges $2,000 plus expenses to handle the entire event), or on a percentage basis, generally fifteen percent off the top of every contribution. Fees are usually determined by the amount of time needed to organize and carry out the event, from beginning through the follow-up. "Normally, I charge a management fee based on time—about $90 an hour," says Brad O'Leary. "It takes more hours to raise the same amount of money for a nonincumbent (than an incumbent), and it also takes more hours in smaller cities," he adds. Therefore, the cost budgeted for such services should be higher under these circumstances.

Enlist the help of a pro to ensure things run smoothly if you are doing a nontraditional event, such as a concert or auction. This is definitely worth the extra dollars. In the case of Sunshine, an advertising and promotion group that promoted the Fleetwood Mac concert on behalf of the (Birch) Bayh for Senate committee in Indianapolis in 1980, the fee was 12.5 percent of the net. "They did everything, handled all the logistics. That's the preferred way to go," says Darry Sragow, who coordinated the concert for the Bayh committee.

In addition to the campaign staff, a host committee should be formed to assume all responsibility for the fundraiser. These people are reliable volunteers and supporters who do everything from addressing invitations and writing thank-you notes, to making follow-up phone calls. They must be carefully supervised and motivated. "Be specific in what you ask people to do," advises Crone. "Ask twice as many people as you need to work. Give clear instructions and a deadline," she adds. "For example, instruct volunteers to call these five people by Wednesday to be sponsors." In general, volunteers usually play a critical part in any fundraiser and the campaign committee may wish to undertake special volunteer recruitment efforts just for the fundraiser.

Invitations

"A wedding-type invitation is boring. Have a fun invitation," says Crone. "The invitation is a statement about the kind of party it's going to be." Crone advises concentrating effort and money on the invitation rather than on the details of the event, because "even the greatest caterer can't serve great food for a crowd."

The invitation is the sales pitch. Its appearance and content are perhaps the key elements in your fundraising appeal. The style of the invitation varies with the type of event and with the personal preference of the individual in charge. Regardless, it must be an attention grabber and should be mailed four to six weeks ahead of the event.

The kind of invitation Crone likes to see is one such as that used to invite potential contributors to a "New York Block Party" in Washington in 1980 for Karen Burstein, a Democratic candidate for Congress in a New York congressional district. The invitation pictured a 1920 New York street scene complete with old-fashioned vendors. The invitation also listed the sponsors—four members of the New York congressional delegation. It let the invitees know they could expect street musicians, New York egg creams, and ethnic foods. The invitation listed Burstein's qualifications, gave a brief biography, and listed additional sponsors on the back—all of whom had *paid* to have their names listed, all names recognizable to Washingtonians (in this case, people active in both the Carter and Kennedy presidential campaigns). It also included some names Washingtonians would recognize from New York (people active in labor unions, implying endorsement by these organizations). The invitation told something of the issues Burstein cared about by including names from the National Abortion Rights Action League. All these things can be implied on the invitation without being explicitly stated and are especially important for a nonincumbent having a fundraiser in Washington.

"Have the invitation designed by an artist, not a printer," advises Crone, who allows at least one week for the design and approval process. The invitation should include the time, place, kind of event (cocktail, buffet, etc.), ticket price, and a *brief* sales pitch—two or three sentences that say something about the candidate or issue—and a contact person and phone number. It should also offer invitees the option of being a sponsor (and thus paying more), or of contributing even if they are unable to attend the event. Also included should be instructions on how to make out the payment check and other information the campaign committee must have for legal compliance (name, address, phone, occupation). A reply card and return envelope are essential. The invitation carrier envelope should have a handwritten address and be mailed first class with a real stamp.

Rich Jalovec, a Democratic challenger for a congressional seat in an Illinois district, ran what he calls a "trendy" campaign. His invitations for a preelection country western

night held in his district took the form of a wanted poster. They said "Wanted for Congress: Rich Jalovec" and pictured the candidate in a cowboy hat. The party was a western barbecue and included riding a mechanical bull, as in the movie *Urban Cowboy*. Country western bands entertained. The invitations also noted the "Reward: Best Representation." About 1,000 people attended at $10 each, mostly profit since the mechanical bull and roasting steers were donated.

Personal letters are more effective than plain invitations to events in Washington when the goal is PAC money. Political consultant Hank Parkinson uses a form letter that he mails to a carefully culled PAC list. The first three paragraphs are the same on all letters. Parkinson includes quotes from the candidate, tells how comfortable his recent wins have been, and then notes that this year is going to be different. It will be a tough contest so the candidate needs money. The fourth paragraph is the variable one. In this paragraph, Parkinson gets specific. For example, if the letter is going to the president of a labor union, this paragraph describes the candidate's support for the union. The variable paragraph notes past union contributions and asks for a contribution again. The letter, prepared on a word processor, is signed by a well-known local lobbyist or attorney. It includes a postscript: "One of the candidate's campaign workers will call you in a day or two."

Parkinson used this approach in 1980 for a $350-a-plate fundraising dinner he organized for Representative Berkley Bedell (D-Iowa) at The Broker restaurant on Capitol Hill. The letter went to 200 carefully selected PACs. In each letter the first three paragraphs were the same. However, there were fourteen different versions of the fourth paragraph. Parkinson has done this type of package for other candidates and uses up to thirty-one variable paragraphs based on giving categories isolated by the computer. "The secret is phone follow-up with trained callers working from a good script," says Parkinson, who averages a sixteen percent response rate with an average contri-

Karen Feld

bution of $606. He pays his callers $7.50 an hour. Parkinson is able to prepare and mail this type of invitation for $15–$29 per letter. The cost depends upon the number of variable paragaphs and the number of long distance calls out of D.C. For Bedell, he raised $11,500 in the first two weeks. He estimates a four to one return ratio, raising four dollars for each dollar spent.

Parkinson says the advantage of this type of invitation and Washington fundraiser is that it takes no campaign staff time and allows excellent management controls because it can be stopped at any time it ceases to be cost effective. "It's the most productive program for fundraising I know of."

Mailing lists

The key to successful fundraising is a good list. "A good list should get an eight to one or ten to one response," says Mary Drape. Lobbyists can help by donating mailing lists to campaigns. When planning Washington fundraisers, ". . . branch out to ten different industries," suggests Drape.

Target invitations for Washington events to lobbyists and PACs who will find it difficult to turn you down. Make them feel important. For example, Alaska Senator Mike Gravel preceded his 1980 fundraising invitations with a series of letters on official stationery to energy PACs. The letter reminded them of his opposition to the windfall profits tax. Generally, it is a good idea to supplement such a targeted PAC list, which will vary depending upon the candidate's committee assignments and areas of interest, with names of the candidate's friends and official contacts, such as leaders of groups who have invited the candidate to speak and constituents and others who have come to visit him on specific issues.

Follow-up

Phone follow-up on the invitation list should start within a week to ten days of their arrival. If time or staffing doesn't permit follow-up on the entire list, at least follow up on a targeted smaller list.

Bruce McBrearty, president of Campaign Marketing Group and an independent consultant to Republican House and Senate candidates, advises sending a follow-up letter ten days after invitations are mailed and then following up with phone calls two to seven days prior to the event.

"A call is more personal than a letter. The only thing better is a personal visit," says McBrearty, who once directed the annual $1,000-a-plate Senate-House dinner for the Republican National Campaign Committee. He recommends calls for events priced at $50-a-head or above. "Even at $25, you make more money than it costs you." Although he uses trained telephone communicators, "even a bad follow-up is better than none at all," says McBrearty.

Follow-up after an event is the least popular task when it comes to fundraising, but one of the most important. "No event chairman likes to go back and armtwist his or her friends to get money when the check hasn't arrived," says Mary Drape. "But I can call and say, 'I'm from Senator X's office. The senator really enjoyed meeting you at the event. Money is tight now, so the faster we get the checks in, the more help it will be.'" She strongly suggests that the campaign staff take that load off the chairman of an event. "We provide the chairman with lists of our known supporters in the area; they get them there. Then I do the thank-you's and financial follow-up. I keep control," says Drape. Personal thank-you notes should be mailed in a timely fashion. Table buyers and other large contributors should be thanked personally by the candidate.

Summary

Special events have proven to be a successful fundraising option in recent years. Any profitable event must be well-planned with sufficient lead time. All details should be handled professionally and with careful follow-up. Regardless of the size of the event, and whether it is to raise funds for a local candidate or a national race, keep in mind the main objective: to raise the largest amount of money for the least amount of expense and effort. Plan and adhere to a realistic budget.

In selecting ticket prices, make an objective assessment of the influence of your candidate and his willingness to use that influence. Determine your target—PACs or individual contributors.

As in other fundraising techniques, a good list is the key to success. The invitation is the sales pitch to that list. Make sure it's attractive.

The same basic formula can be adapted to a rock concert, a sporting event, or a yard sale. All require imagination without disregarding practicality. If you follow these guidelines and give people something to talk about other than the familiar, your special event is destined to be a successful fundraiser for the candidate.

Part Three

Advanced Campaign Technologies

Campaign Commercials and the Media Blitz

John Witherspoon

The most visible aspect of modern campaigns is the media advertising. Paid political spots are almost universally considered an essential element of a winning candidate's strategy. This is true even though most political observers are hard-pressed to name more than a half-dozen campaigns where media clearly made the difference between victory and defeat. It is all a matter of guesswork, in any case; voting research data can only rarely conclusively point to one aspect of a campaign—whether paid media or something else—as the decisive event in an election. The simple act of voting is, in fact, exceptionally complex.

Whatever the truth of the matter, candidates and their staffs, families, and volunteers believe paid media to be important, so no serious contender for high office can afford to be without it. As a result, political media consultants, such as the author of this article, have become indispensable campaign agents and strategists. John Witherspoon offers some colorful examples of many kinds of political advertisements— from "talking heads" to "comparison spots"—and he discusses the purposes served by the television commercials at each point of the campaign schedule.

The *"science"* of political advertising as practiced in the computer age is primarily concerned with counting, defining, and quantifying media buys and audiences in order to carry messages to the voting public in the most cost-effective ways possible. But without the *"art"* of political advertising, this technology is wasted. As Roy Spence, one of Walter Mondale's 1984 media consultants, said, "Effective communication in political advertising is called winning. If your opponent gets more votes than you, you haven't effectively communicated!" The subject of this article is the art of winning: creating and producing a

message that will capture the attention, imagination, and *votes* of its audience.

Commercial and political advertising: how different?

First of all, several federal agencies regulate the content of commercial advertising, but they have no say in political advertising. The networks turn down many product commercials submitted to them for violation of one code or another, but First Amendment rights prevent application of these same codes to political advertising.

Second, as one ad man paraphrased Abe Lincoln, "In the free market, you can fool some of the people some of the time, but in a political campaign, you only need to fool half of the

John Witherspoon is Vice President of Marketing/ Creative Services at Hayes Productions, Inc. of San Antonio, Texas.

people once." This is by no means meant to be a condemnation of political advertising—nor of commercial advertising. Our belief is they are essentially the same: an effort to persuade the voluntary exercise of freedom of choice—one in the marketplace and the other at the polls. And like commercial advertising, political advertising that *works* will put across an honest representation of the candidate. The candidate is the message.

One big difference, of course, is timing. If all is not ready for a grand opening of a store, you can, as a last resort, postpone it. Grand openings are never postponed in politics. A commercial advertising campaign can take several years to increase a market share by, say, eleven percent. A political campaign has a matter of weeks to convince more than fifty percent of the voters to pick the candidate.

Beyond research: strategic considerations

Everyone recognizes the importance of research. As Lionel Sosa, a well-known marketing consultant, put it: "If you fly by your guts, you're nuts!" The polls, daily trackings, focus groups, and the many other techniques of gathering, compiling, and sorting numbers are the very stuff of which a persuasive communication effort—political or otherwise—is made. Software companies, nonexistent a few years ago, now provide campaigns on all levels with sophisticated technologies for fundraising, budgeting, polling, targeting, opposition research, and media buys.

Everyone has access to the science. And that is precisely the point. From this science, to which you and your opponent both have access, someone must extrapolate a creative strategy. Someone must decide what, when, and how much.

Early name recognition

Political advertising production for television will fall basically into one of three categories:

1. Name/Face Identification

2. Positioning/Issue Spots
3. 11th Hour Blitz

One of the early innovations that we translated from the commercial production world to politics was the animated campaign logo. By using your campaign print graphics—your logo—on television, you reinforce recognition of your candidate's name as seen in newspaper ads, signs, bumper stickers, and so on.

When time and budget permit, consider animating the logo. Research by Dr. George Shipley, an Austin-based pollster and consultant, indicates a thirty percent increase in recognition when the logo is animated. This does not, of course, mean that recall equals votes, any more than recall equals sales. It does mean they know you are in the race. If you can incorporate a face into the logo, so much the better. Incumbents generally already have a high degree of voter awareness. The first priority for a challenger is early name recognition; the sooner the voters know the players, the sooner they can compare.

Animated logos, when produced with digital video units—squeeze zooms, line expansion character generators, etc.—can be completed in a matter of hours at a post-production facility for well under $1,000. Five to seven seconds of logo animation produced on film on an animation camera will require at least two weeks at a cost of $3,500 or more. The difference is more than just technique, however. The film animation produces a better image on the screen, a more "finished" look. The vast majority of network programming and advertising is still shot on film.

Both techniques require talent. A well-designed, well-produced logo is far more than just fluff. It can significantly increase name awareness, which translates to more market penetration per dollar.

Early television advertising can be a "best-defense-is-a-good-offense" situation. Pollsters for Senator Russell Long of Louisiana discovered prior to his 1980 bid for reelection that there was a potential "softening" of the solid position the Long family has held in Louisiana politics. Campaign leaders produced an extraordinary thirty-minute program documenting the career of Huey Long, complete with seven or eight minutes of remarkable footage of the governor in action, and continuing with the job that his son Russell was carrying on in Washington. Six months prior to the election, the show was aired with a substantial media budget. The result? Not one opposing candidate filed.

Positioning and issues

The bulk of your production dollars will be spent in positioning your candidate in the field and clarifying and comparing his or her position on the issues. After your name identification dollars are spent, you face the big budgetary question. "How do I allocate my media dollars?"

In congressional or statewide campaigns, it is not unlikely that fifty percent or more of your total dollars will be spent on media. Borrowing some guidelines from Madison Avenue, up to twenty percent of this figure may be spent on television production. Half of your total media buy will probably be in the last three weeks of the campaign. This buy will be made well in advance of the air dates based on projected dollars available. Competition for time is fierce in these closing weeks.

An important caution: There are never enough dollars, but a contingency production budget *must* be established for the unexpected in the "11th Hour." More on this later, but first, let's look at the types of spots available—a smorgasbord of commercial options.

The talking head
As the name implies, the camera is aimed at the candidate and he talks. In the case of charismatic (and photogenic) candidates, such

In a variation of the "talking head" spot, Judge Roy Barrera used courtroom props to establish his experience as an incumbent and overcome his youthful appearance.

Judge Roy Barrera

Senator Lloyd Bentsen used simple hanging placards to emphasize the critical issues and dress up his "talking head" spot.

The placard designs were popped on the screen to become part of the logo tag as a last subliminal reminder to the viewers.

John Witherspoon

as Texas Senator Lloyd Bentsen or San Antonio Mayor Henry Cisneros, this is probably the most effective and definitely the least expensive type of spot available. It can also be the dullest for the viewer.

American flags and bookshelves full of leatherbound law books are common props to give "atmosphere" to a "talking head" spot. Texas District Court Judge Roy Barrera appeared in his judicial robes behind the bench to establish his incumbency and overcome a deceptively youthful look. Lloyd Bentsen's credible delivery was reinforced with three simple hanging placards visually strengthening the issues he was discussing. The three cards were then animated into the closing logo tag.

Production costs are minimal for this type of spot. A thirty-second commercial, shot in studio with a few props, can easily be completed in an afternoon at costs beginning at a few hundred dollars—if your candidate is not rushed with an overly busy schedule that interferes with his remembering his lines or reading the teleprompter. Remember, a tired, ragged-looking candidate on the day of taping will look that same way every day the spot is run!

The candidate in action

Not all candidates are trained actors. Although a public servant may speak for himself, he or she may not speak in a particularly viewer-appealing manner. Nothing can be more frustrating to campaign workers than a qualified candidate that just does not "come across" on the air.

Another option is to show the candidate among the voters or, in the case of an incumbent, at work. This is an excellent way to target voters and issues; a candidate among senior citizens cares about Social Security issues, one with a group of students shows an interest in education, and so on.

This is a good point to reiterate the basic truth of political advertising: "The Candidate

Showing your candidate among a group of senior citizens—as this DeConcini spot did—makes a powerful visual statement about his/her feelings on Social Security and social welfare issues.

is the Message." Jim Mattox, current Attorney General of Texas, projects a "fighter for the citizens" kind of personality. To present him any other way would be deceptive and counterproductive. Shots of Mattox with his jaw jutting, making no-nonsense "I'm not going to take it" positions were used in spots that concluded with the campaign line "the tough DO get going!" Lloyd Bentsen is a dignified statesman and family man. Spots of Bentsen showed him fishing with his grandson, with a voice-over about the kind of America the boy would inherit. Bill Hobby is a comparatively quiet, hard-working lieutenant governor. He was shown working after hours through a lighted window in the statehouse and at planning sessions with charts and pie-graphs.

In almost all cases, this type of spot is more expensive than the "talking head." Because they are shot on location, they require a crew, equipment, lighting and sound equipment, and extensive post-production. While very effective, it would be difficult to produce a "candidate in action" spot for under $2,500, and they can cost as much as $7,500 or more. Nonetheless, these are your bread-and-butter vehicles for presenting your candidate and the issues.

Man on the street

Applied to politics, this is a version of the testimonial. It is risky in commercial advertising and, because of the time constraints, much riskier in politics (unless you have a large budget).

The problem is money and credibility. A usable, spontaneous "testimonial" is rare, and there is only an occasional diamond among many lumps of coal. That means dozens of interviews must be conducted to secure one good one, or hundreds of feet of film or tape used to get a ten-second comment.

Slice of life: paid performers

The practice of using actors, actresses, and on-camera announcers may be one area where

No "Mr. Nice Guy," Texas Attorney General Jim Mattox was shown with jutting jaw and firm profile to match his slogan "The tough DO get going."

John Witherspoon

Texas Lt. Governor Bill Hobby took the hard-working public servant approach.

Another ''candidate in action spot'' shows Hobby working and planning in the state Capitol.

commercial and political advertising do not mix. It is difficult enough for the best minds in Hollywood to create realistic, believable dramatic situations; I have rarely seen it done in politics. It is not that the actors or announcers do not perform believably; it is that the viewer will correctly perceive it as a person getting paid to say something nice about the candidate. It is also expensive. Using professional talent, sets, makeup, and wardrobe can easily bring the cost of a thirty-second spot into the $20,000 and over range.

On-camera announcers, if they have a reason for being on camera, can be effective. In a recent primary for a Texas county commissioner's seat, the underdog nonincumbent candidate utilized a paid announcer walking among door-sized panels with news clippings about his opponent mounted on them. It was only at the end of the spot, when the announcer pushed one of the panels into another, that the viewer realized the panels were the back sides of dominoes. The closing cutaway of dominoes knocking each other over created a very powerful visual strengthening of the message. The domino props and the paid announcer were the main expense items. The cost was under $3,000 and the candidate pulled about sixty percent of the vote.

Attack and compare

The result of "attack and compare" production is to create distinctions. We have produced countless variations of a split-screen check list, with Candidate A on the left and Candidate B on the right. In many cases, when the honest facts of voting record, experience, or accomplishments justify it, this comparison can clearly show the voter the alternatives. For the most part, a spot of this type can be produced rather inexpensively: from a few hundred dollars for text on the screen to $1,500 or so for more advanced visuals.

We have produced some interesting variations. One "weathervane" spot, designed to illustrate how unpredictable the opponent was,

In this "attack and compare" spot, the announcer makes his case against the opposition in a large set filled with monoliths. . .

John Witherspoon

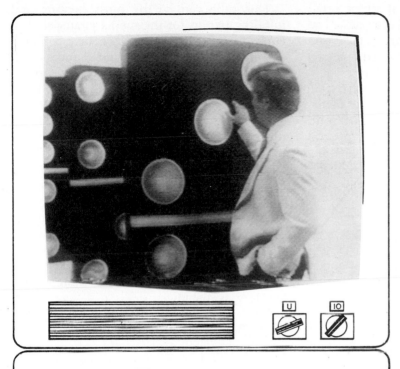

Behold: the monoliths become dominoes when seen from another angle. . .

And the action to illustrate the disastrous effects of voting for the opponent.

actually used a weathervane spinning erratically as the voice-over announcer described the opposition's apparent change of positions. In another spot, a split-screen comparison showed four needles of a lie detector as a background. As various statements were read, the needles on the opposition's side of the graph went wild with deception. The word "liar" was never uttered. And a commercial in a recent Texas race showed unidentified hands plopping a carpetbag on the table and removing momentos of the opposition's past political and business failures.

The 11th hour: the media blitz

It is in the closing weeks, frequently the closing days, that downright nasty things can happen to a campaign.

Some races, of course, have by this time been decided. Most have not. Frequently the daily trackings are showing mixed trends or inconclusive results. The knee-jerk reaction is to unload with everything you have.

This time can be the most exciting and fulfilling period for the media strategist. The atmosphere lends itself to a creative combustion that can sometimes move more than mountains; it can move big blocs of voters.

If there is one constant in this 11th Hour equation, it is to start early buying time to air your media blitz. Your ads won't do you much good if you can't get them on. Your media-buying service should purchase all the air time you can afford many weeks prior to Election Day, because the September to November period is television's busiest season with commercial advertisers and other candidates putting a strain on availabilities. When buying time, buy back from Election Day, buy heavy for the final week or two, and add spots for earlier time slots if more money becomes available.

There may be issues in your campaign that lend themselves to anticipatory, or early, production. That means producing a spot and leaving it on the shelf "just in case." We have

This "weathervane" spot was used to drive home the inconsistency of a candidate's voting record.

John Witherspoon

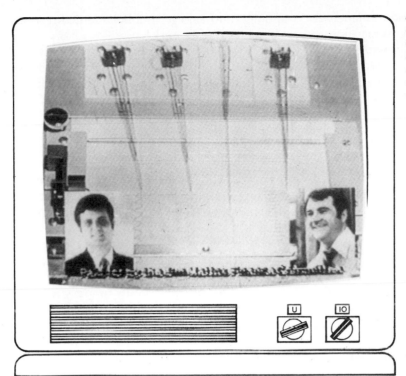

produced dozens of these, most of which were never pulled off the shelf (until after the campaign. Then a campaign staff member hurries over to retrieve the tapes, asking "Are you sure there are no more copies? These are all the masters?"). Professional integrity, and in some cases common decency, prohibit me from discussing any details of these. The visuals usually show large amounts of currency going into pockets or coming out of brown bags.

A more positive reason for producing spots that may never run would be anticipating an event that could go one of two ways and materially alter a race: a labor strike, pending legislation, an important endorsement, foreign events. The candidate may see an advantage in clarifying his position. In such an instance producing one or two spots early on is a prudent use of your most limited resources: time and money.

The point is that time is very precious as you approach Election Day. Even a single

afternoon for a "talking head" spot may be impossible to coordinate. The only advice seems to be to size up your race and, if there are issues such as these, consider anticipatory production and plan ahead. There is the undeniable possibility that you may be spending money on something you may never use, but it's like insurance. You hope you don't have to collect it, but you thank your stars for your perspicacity when you have a loss to claim.

"Quick on the feet" spots

More than likely, your 11th hour blitz will include spots that must get on the air today. Or sooner.

During the 1982 Texas gubernatorial race, Democrat Mark White faced the most lavishly financed campaign in Texas history to reelect incumbent Republican Bill Clements. Early efforts to get a handle on a winning issue seemed to elude White. The strategic decision was made to zero in on a few topics, among them education. The strategy was to maneuver any public debate or media coverage into a discussion of these hand-picked issues.

It worked. The incumbent governor, and some of his appointees, were forced into making some statements that became apparent contradictions to Clement's current positions. These appeared to be the first chinks in the armor of a popular governor.

Each time one of these apparent chinks would appear, White's campaign staff, headed by Roy Spence, would use a TV spot to pry it into a gaping hole. The technique? They simply "scrolled" the contradictory messages up the screen, and let the obvious conclusions be drawn. This begat Republican denials, and they begat more mistakes, and they begat more spots, and so on, and so on to the Democratic victory.

The above is an example of how it should work: media as a function of campaign strategy. When the strategy begins working, amplify it with media. The "production costs" are inconsequential. The timing is everything. The turnaround time on these spots was probably thirty-six hours from start to on-the-air. The cost could not have been more than a few hundred dollars per spot.

The story of the "John Tower Handshake" is quite another matter. It is now famous in Texas politics and may be the best media campaign story of modern times.

The 1978 U.S. senatorial race in Texas was a heated one of considerable differences in style and substance. John Tower, a longtime fixture and powerful Republican presence in the U.S. Senate, faced Bob Krueger, an urbane, scholarly, eloquent contender.

A paper appeared, allegedly circulated by some overzealous Krueger campaign workers, and authored by an influential Baptist leader. The document made some rather uncensored allegations about the senator's personal life in Washington. In fact, the Baptist had been referring to a different senator, but the paper "appeared," and was "non-denied" by the Krueger staff. Tower publicly demanded an apology, and Krueger publicly denied responsibility. End of Round 1.

At a well-publicized debate at the Houston Press Club, both men were face-to-face for the first time since the standoff. Krueger offered his hand to Tower in greeting. Tower refused and turned indignantly back to his dinner plate, Krueger standing above and behind with his hand extended in gentlemanly manner. The photographers caught the whole sequence, and two sequential photos—of the offering, and the refusal—were run side by side in every tabloid in the state and many outside it.

The result was devastating. Less than a month before the election, the senator's narrow lead began to erode. Efforts to reduce the significance of the event to "it's only a handshake" did not stop the slide. Attempts to change the subject and talk about the issues could not penetrate the Handshake Curtain. Insiders reported a certain resignation among the troops, and possibly in Tower himself, that it was over.

At a meeting of mainly Hispanic voters late in the campaign, Senator Tower told the whole story from his perspective, asked the audience if they would not do the same thing, and received—to his amazement—a standing ovation.

Combustion! Here was the solution. His media consultant borrowed a secretary's typewriter, wrote a thirty-second script, and took it back to the senator who delivered it faultlessly in two takes. The spot starts with Tower sitting on his desk saying, "Perhaps you have seen this picture of my refusing to shake hands with my opponent. I was brought up to believe that a handshake is a symbol of friendship and respect . . . " as the now famous pictures appear on screen, "not a meaningless, hypocritical gesture. My opponent has slurred my wife, my daughters, and falsified my record." The spot concludes with the zinger, "My kind of Texan doesn't shake hands with that kind of man! Integrity is one Texas tradition you can count on me to uphold!"

John Witherspoon

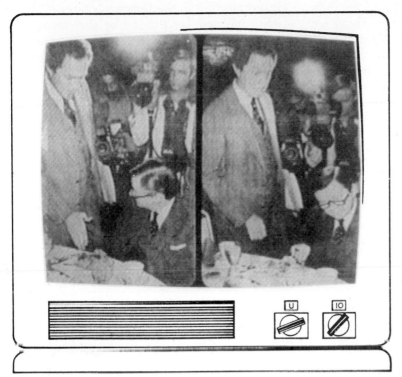

The now famous Tower/Krueger handshake photos. . .

And Senator Tower delivering his side of the story in a late campaign-saving commercial.

Every other spot was pulled and the new one ran in all available time slots. About ten days before the election, the slide was reversed. Tower then started to climb. Daily trackings showed the Tower curve crossed the victory line two days before election in what was the closest election in the senator's career.

No one can say that he or she "won" an election because of his or her television spots. But who, in a major election, would do without them?

Misses and Mistakes:
Sources of Error in Polls

Larry J. Sabato

Good politicians always rely on instinct, but virtually none are left who trust instinct alone. The political pollster and his surveys are omnipresent, measuring moods, sounding out opinions, interpreting trends, reassuring the pols, and revealing the shape of political things to come. Protestations to the contrary notwithstanding, candidates, officeholders, and the general public are fascinated, even mesmerized, by the steady stream of survey statistics that cascade down every conceivable outlet— business, labor, education, political parties and campaigns, and the news media.

In this article, the polls are scrutinized critically, with a look at the polling instruments and some of the potential sources of error in the surveying process. It should be clear at the conclusion of this examination that polls are far less "scientific" and reliable than is commonly believed and that pollsters are not always the vox populi ("the voice of the people") the press claims.

In spite of glowing accounts of pollsters' exploits, some campaigns remain cautious. The caution is fully justified, for the history of political polling is littered with the remains of campaigns that were misled by wayward pollsters brandishing defective polls. A critical view of polling is warranted—and desperately needed. Polling is oversold as a "scientific" profession and as a campaign tonic. Its weaknesses are at least as apparent as its strengths, and there is a frightfully large number of entry points for error in the polling process. Many polls are just plain wrong— poorly done or poorly interpreted. Several sources of potential error stand out, including

prior prejudices and question bias; the construction, analysis, and interpretation of the polling instrument and results, including the sampling and respondent screening processes; and a host of problems with interviewers and respondents.

Prejudice and question bias

California pollster Mervin Field has bluntly posed the "crisis of conscience" question for political pollsters: "Do they provide objective reports, or are they deliberately or inadvertently influenced by the positions of their political clients?" As he suggests, the prejudice may be subconscious and unintentional, but pollsters are not exempt from the quite natural human desire to avoid being the messengers of bad news. Pollsters also sometimes feel pressure to demonstrate change and reveal

This article is drawn in part from Larry J. Sabato, The Rise of Political Consultants: New Ways of Winning Elections *(New York: Basic Books, 1981).*

unsuspected facts of public opinion. (It is a rare client who will gladly pay thousands of dollars to verify everything he or she knew all along.) It is surprisingly easy to skew the results in any direction. Phrasing and ordering of the questions are critical, and a pollster can poll quite "scientifically" to reach a predestined conclusion.

One can find a superb illustration in examining pollsters' work for the opposing sides of labor-law reform legislation in the late 1970s. Both the Chamber of Commerce and the American Retail Federation fought the legislation, designed to reduce obstacles to union organizing, and hired Opinion Research Corporation (ORC) and Patrick Caddell's Cambridge Survey Research, respectively. Union leaders were infuriated that Caddell took business's side since he had a lucrative, standing contract with the Democratic National Committee, partially funded by labor. The liberal Caddell, however, saw no conflict of interest between the two financially rewarding packages. The AFL–CIO countered by securing the polling services of Public Interest Opinion Research. To no one's astonishment, all of the pollsters found substantial survey evidence that the public supported their clients. The polls were not fabricated—although this has been known to happen in and out of politics. Rather, the various findings were a function of how the question was posed. ORC's inteviewers asked whether "federal legislation should be passed that makes it easier than it now is for unions to organize nonunion employees." The triad of potential answers— favoring the easing of strictures, desiring to make it even harder for unions to organize, or advocating no change at all—would be expected to encourage the "middle way," no-change alternative. Pollsters have long noted that respondents, given three choices of amount or degree, will likely select the moderate alternative. Americans' inherent tendency toward compromise and support for the status quo in the absence of compelling need for change was also heightened in this

case by a lack of information about the whole problem. The question had no elaborate prefacing that could have given rudimentary background.

As expected, 22 percent of the respondents favored the proposed legislation, 25 percent wanted a tougher union organizing posture, and 40 percent said the status quo seemed perfectly acceptable. The survey on labor's behalf demonstrated just as convincingly that public opinion was squarely in their corner. About 70 percent of the public favored "a law making it easier for workers in a company to vote on whether or not they wish to join a labor union." The issue for the respondent now turned on the great American qualities of individualism and a citizen's freedom of choice.

These poll results, contradictory on their face, demonstrate the schizophrenic nature of public opinion. As every individual knows from listening to debate, there are usually popular and valid points to be made on both sides of the same issue, and one can find oneself agreeing with principles that lead unavoidably to antithetical conclusions. Careful wording of a question can tap the desired response, as the labor-law example showed. In that case, one suspects that the bias was intentional, but the chastening discovery for pollsters was how frequently bias of some type affects the responses of truly "nonpartisan" surveys. (Since no word is really neutral and every word communicates or symbolizes something, bias in some direction is absolutely unavoidable.) In 1953, two Korean War opinion surveys taken within a month by the same polling firm showed a 37 percent variation in the public's evaluation of the war. Only 27 percent responded favorably to this question: "As things stand now, do you feel the war in Korea has been worth fighting, or not?" But in answer to a subsequent question, which some observers believe tested patriotism more than anything else, 64 percent of the respondents agreed that "the United States was right" to have sent in troops. Long after the

Korean War had ended—shortly after U.S. withdrawal from the Vietnam War, in fact—Louis Harris asked a pair of questions about Korea again. Only 14 percent favored U.S. military involvement "if North Korea attacked South Korea." But a 43 percent plurality favored military action when the question included prefatory background information:

The U.S. has 36,000 troops and airmen in South Korea. If North Korea invaded South Korea, we have a firm commitment to defend South Korea with our own military forces. If South Korea were invaded by Communist North Korea, would you favor or oppose the U.S. using troops, air power and naval power to defend South Korea?

Part of the explanation for the wide variance is obviously the pollster's decision to "educate" the ignorant respondent on the issue. In doing so, though, the pollster is "on dangerous ground," as Mervin Field flatly declared. In seeking to tap a latent disposition, a survey researcher may be creating an opinion where none existed before. On many a prominent public issue, a shocking proportion of the public has no view at all; many people, in fact, may be only dimly aware of its existence.

Construction, analysis, and interpretation

It would be grossly misleading to suggest that polling firms are Chinese take-outs, where what you want is what you get. But the polling instrument and how it is designed are major determinants of a poll's results. Every serious pollster takes the greatest care in the construction of the survey. Pollsters estimate that, depending on the purpose for which they are conducted, between one-third and three-quarters of the questions in their political surveys are standard and used repeatedly. The exact wordings have been devised and tested over time so that there can be a high degree of confidence in their relative objectivity. Identical questions on a series of polls are also useful for comparative purposes (in assessing regional or national trends, for example).

Professional pollsters permit no consultation about the selection of the sample; that task is strictly their own. Even with an expert in charge, however, there is still plenty of room for error. The only acceptable, reliable method of sampling is the "random" or probability one. In this method, each person in the population universe has, theoretically, an equal chance to be selected for the survey, and no element of nonrandom human choice is involved in the selection of respondents. Using census tracts, atlases, and computers, a polling firm first randomly selects a set of sampling points for its in-home interviewees (towns, cities, and so on, where specific respondents will be chosen); finally, the actual homes and even sometimes the individuals within each home are randomly designated. Every major survey research organization now uses random sampling, although this was not always the case. Another form of sampling, the "quota," was assigned part of the blame for the 1948 Truman–Dewey fiasco, when the polls incorrectly forecast an early Dewey victory, and it was widely employed prior to that time. In a quota sample, the choice of the respondents is left up to the interviewer, who is merely assigned quotas of each major population subgroup to interview based on each group's proportion of the population. Quota surveys are nonrandom since the element of human choice is involved, and therefore the theory of probability does not apply.

Clustering interviews within sampling points does not affect randomness; rather, it makes the selection of respondents a two-step random process. But the technique does require that a reasonable number of interview sites be selected and that their geographic locations be diverse. If too many interviews are conducted at a single spot, there is too little heterogeneity to assure a representative sample, and this is where many modern political surveys fall short. The number of interviews conducted at each geographic sampling point ranges from as few as four to as many as a dozen or more. One major public polling group (Gallup) used to assign ten interviews to each of 150 sampling points (producing its total sample size of 1,500), but in the interest of increasing dispersion, just five interviews are now assigned to more than 300 sampling points. Obviously, the costs are greater, but the results are much sounder. It is not uncommon for some political polling firms to maximize their profit margins by clustering fifteen or more interviews at a single place, putting the representative reliability of their surveys at great risk.

Whatever the number of sampling points and the total size of the sample, an automatic probability margin of error exists. The larger the sample, the lower the margin of error. A sample size of about 1,000 carries with it a 3 percent margin of error—that is, the percentages in the survey's responses are representative of the population within three percentage points in either direction. A 5 percent margin of error is found with a 400-person survey.

These statements are made at a "95 percent confidence level." Therefore, in 95 out of 100 surveys of the same population with a comparable sample size, any error in the polls will be within the indicated margin; in the other five surveys, the margin of error would probably be above or below the suggested range. Since hundreds of political polls are conducted each election year, statistical probability discloses that at least a few will likely be off the mark even if conducted flawlessly, with potentially disastrous consequences for the unlucky candidates who have purchased them.

The possibility of disaster is increased by the growing use of "weighting techniques" to "perfect" incomplete samples. In short, pollsters sometimes find it necessary to give extra weight to the answers of respondents belonging to subgroups still underrepresented when all the interviewing is done. These subgroups are by no means purely demographic ones. Gallup increases the weight of respondents who indicate they had been away

from home during several previous evenings, assuming they are much like the people the interviewer could not find in their residences. This guesswork gives more room for error, but its use often cannot be avoided because of the mushrooming proportion of "refuse-to-reply" and "not-at-home" respondents. While once gauged at between 10 and 22 percent of the sample, those who are unavailable or refuse to be polled now total between 40 and 55 percent for in-home interviews and between 25 and 35 percent for telephone samples. About 20 percent of all actual respondents are also "reluctant interviewees" who evade, object, or refuse to answer one or more questions on the poll, so some data are less randomly representative than the overall margin of error would indicate. However justified, weighting is a risky business, as the *Minneapolis Tribune* once discovered. A market research firm based in Phoenix, Arizona, that had contracted to do the newspaper's Minnesota Poll severed ties with the paper after the 1978 midterm elections, charging that the *Tribune's* editors had wrongfully adjusted survey results prior to publication. The original survey findings had correctly predicted a GOP sweep of the major statewide posts, but the newspaper (perhaps getting cold feet about the mildly surprising forecast) weighted the data to reflect what it believed would be a more representative cross section of the state's electorate, with the effect of inflating the projected Democratic vote. Election Day, though, showed the original poll had probably done a better job of surveying likely voters, and the newspaper had egg on its front page.

Flagrant violations of polling procedure occur frequently in yet another area, subgroup analysis. A 400-person poll's summary results, which are drawn from the responses of the entire interviewed sample, may have a 5 percent margin of error, but the subgroup breakdowns by smaller state or national regions or racial and ethnic classifications have much greater margins of error (easily 10 percent or more). A 10 percent error margin means that if the poll showed 50 percent of the black respondents favoring a candidate, the real figure could actually lie anywhere between 40 percent and 60 percent—an enormous margin. Subgroup analysis in small-sample polls is greatly suspect, then, but analyses of the data breakdowns are often made by pollsters as though the margin of error was minimal. A "trend" is established when a candidate gains four percentage points among black respondents from one poll to another, even though the 10 percent error margin clearly obviates any such conclusion. As polling costs increase, the pressure on campaigns to have smaller samples increases, but it does not seem to be accepted that a smaller sample must necessarily entail the price of more detailed analysis.

Loss of precise analysis is an excruciating price to pay, for interpretation is the finest art of the pollster and also is the area where a lack of data can seriously impede a poll's campaign utility. Interpretation can only follow the purposeful and insightful construction of a tightly drawn polling instrument. Only rarely do polls adequately explore the complex mental set of voter attitudes about campaigns, and consequently the findings are superficial. Democratic pollster Peter Hart ruefully gave as one example his 1978 polling in Minnesota for U.S. Senate candidate Donald Fraser. Three months before the Democratic primary, Fraser led his opponent, Robert Short, 67 to 16 percent in a trial heat. Hart was uneasy about the figures, suspecting they did not tell the full story, so he devised a "horse-race" question that dropped the two candidate's names and merely described them using their backgrounds and issue positions. Under these conditions, Fraser had a marginal 49 to 42 percent edge, presaging Short's eventual come-from-behind victory. Screening questions to determine likely voters are also notoriously unreliable and are becoming more so, as voter turnout declines and the Independent bloc in the electorate continues to grow and delays the voting decision until just before the election, or Election Day itself. Although they are just elaborate forms of guesswork, pollsters

have devised complex formulas for screening respondents. Lance Tarrance, for example, classifies respondents on a four-point "propensity-to-vote" scale based on a number of screening questions in the poll and a predictive barometer that uses personal data (such as educational level, age, length of residence, and type of housing). Pollsters are finding it increasingly difficult to deal with the undecided. Should their electoral choices be inferred from the clues they give in answer to other questions, or should they be assigned to candidates on a strict proportional basis? One solution that can be applied to in-home interviewing is the use of the secret ballot. Gallup once reduced the percentage of undecideds from 15 percent to 4 percent with the use of this simple device.

Methodological difficulties notwithstanding, no richer source of polling error exists than the pollster's own frailties. Unless a pollster is extremely careful, he can selectively interpret, seeing what he and his candidate want to see. Not only do pollsters often become too close to their candidates to remain sufficiently objective, but they develop a stake in their own analyses, which can have detrimental consequences for their clients. "If a pollster has done an early survey and made recommendations on how the campaign should go, then as a counselor he's committed to that course of action," Mervin Field explained. "Every poll he takes thereafter is a test of those recommendations. If the policies aren't working, the human thing to do is to say the evidence is not clear-cut." Moreover, pollsters sometimes use the data to inject their personal opinions, or they assume their own views are shared by the general public.

Problems with interviewers and respondents

Even with a perfectly selected sample and a thoughtfully constructed questionnaire, a poll can easily fail. Few observers outside the polling field are aware of the crucial role played in survey research by the interviewers. The interviewers' degree of skill and training is absolutely critical to the quality of a poll's data. The interviewer must be able quickly to establish a rapport (even on the telephone) with a wide range of respondents, who must feel comfortable during the interview if full and revealing replies are to be forthcoming. The interviewer, while appearing at ease, must be on guard at all times to avoid biased phrasing or remarks that might unintentionally sway a respondent. He must be able to stick to the script exactly and to probe delicately, and he must be patient and persistent in the field, not only during interviews, but also in the frustrating task of catching his chosen respondents at home.

Finding good interviewers, training them properly, and assuring appropriate supervision of their activities are constant headaches for every polling firm, and because the measurement of interviewers' preparedness is qualitative rather than quantitative, some firms cut corners in this area without fear of detection. Especially questionable are many of the "partial package" arrangements where a firm provides the questionnaire and sample and the campaign provides the volunteers to conduct the poll. The volunteers are ostensibly trained by the firm, but the instruction is usually rudimentary and the supervision during the interviews wholly inadequate. The unfortunately widespread belief among campaign officials that anyone can conduct a poll, and the willingness of some of the large political polling firms to participate in schemes of this sort, has produced a number of inferior surveys. These cut-rate polls save money, of course, but they are usually cheap in worth as well as cost. Most reputable polling firms have a full-time field director just to do the hiring and training for the high-turnover interviewer posts. Interviewers tend to be students, people between jobs, and middle-aged housewives (who are much preferred because of their tendency to keep the job for longer periods). Strict supervision is required to ensure quality control, and quite commonly plug-in-supervision monitors are used in telephone polling.

It is much more difficult to ascertain the validity of in-home interviewing, and cheating by interviewers is a problem of unknown proportions. While some pollsters claim that less than 3 percent of all professional interviewers falsify questionnaires (i.e., never actually conduct real interviews and fill out the forms themselves), other observers claim that at least a fifth of all interviewers make up some of their returns. There are ways of checking up, of course. Business reply postal cards can be sent to interviewees to verify that an interview occurred and that certain questions were asked, and sometimes, when there are suspicions, respondents can be telephoned directly and quizzed. But most pollsters do not bother to check regularly, lacking the time, the resources, and even the interest to do so.

Fiddling interviewers may be apprehended, but virtually nothing can be done about fibbing respondents. Many people try to please, or at least not offend, polltakers, telling them what they believe they want to hear. Spanish-speaking interviewers in Puerto Rican, Cuban, or Mexican–American neighborhoods might improve frankness, but this is no cure for selective memory. The Survey Research Center at the University of Michigan discovered evidence either of massive ballot fraud or of an amnesia epidemic in 1964 when fully 64 percent of adult voters distinctly remembered having cast their 1960 ballots for John F. Kennedy, who won one of the closest presidential elections in U.S. history. In preelection polls, voters can also lie about their choices, but this dishonesty can be unintentional since, at the time of the questioning, individuals sometimes have not thought through their choices.

Peter Hart also found that people are unwilling to admit forthrightly their prejudices, even to themselves, so the bias must be plumbed obliquely. When Congresswoman Ella Grasso sought the governorship of Connecticut in 1974, voters denied they had much of a worry about electing a woman when pointedly asked about it, but 39 percent confided their belief that a male chief executive would be better when Hart couched the question in terms that made sexism seem more acceptable. (Grasso overcame the prejudices and won overwhelmingly.) People do not readily admit their ignorance, either. A recent survey experiment, asking respondents for their views on the Public Affairs Act of 1975, found fully a third of the interviewees had very definite opinions on the subject. This was especially intriguing because the legislation is nonexistent.

Conclusion and summary

Survey research has made great strides since the primitive and highly inaccurate straw polls of a half century ago, and virtually all politicians, from president to city councillor, have been convinced of polls' campaign utility. As the number of private and public polling firms has skyrocketed, the political pollster has gradually outgrown the role of mere technician, emerging from the cocoon a full-fledged strategist who influences campaign activity in a wide variety of areas. Beyond the campaign, pollsters have assumed the mantel of *vox populi*, becoming in some eyes oracles and philosopher-kings.

Yet for all their impressive qualities and offerings, on closer inspection both pollsters and polls appear surprisingly frail. Polls, after all, are like computers in at least one crucial respect: However awe-inspiring are their powers, they can only do what they are programmed to do. The mistakes of the designer, the interviewer, and the analyst become the poll's failures and, ultimately, the campaign's failures, when combined with the misuses of polling data by the candidate. Like all other new campaign technologies, survey research is more art than science, and the art has notable flaws. At base, public opinion is too fluid for polls to be more than a brief second's snapshot of an object moving in time; viewed in this manner, polls can properly be seen as more historical than predictive. Neither can they quite pierce the interwoven layers of opinions, some brightly colored and others pale, that are held by a public sometimes believing quite contradictory principles simultaneously.

Error-free polls are as rare as perfect specimens in any craft. Pollster and client prejudice not uncommonly shape a poll's results even before the data are collected. Moreover, wholly objective surveys are many times just as biased, however unintentionally. The wording of questions is unavoidably prejudiced, sometimes culturally, always attitudinally. The simple inclusion of a particular question can create, unsuspectingly, a false result by manufacturing an opinion where none actually existed. The construction, analysis, and interpretation of polls is similarly fraught with opportunities for error. The selection of the sample is of fundamental importance, and many factors (such as lack of dispersion) can have harmful side effects. By themselves, the statistical probabilities associated with random sampling guarantee a small degree of error, and the possibilities are multiplied by faulty subgroup analysis, the risky practice of weighting, and the baffling process of screening likely voters. Pollsters can misinterpret surveys quite easily by reading their own views and opinions into the data. Interviewers as well have plenty of chances to skew polling results, and thorough training, proper supervision, and checks to avoid cheating are called for (but not always done adequately). Individuals who are imposed upon to submit to interviews occasionally take subconscious revenge by lying, or selectively remembering, or obscuring their real attitudes (even to themselves), practices that are normally beyond correction but that nevertheless produce faulty polls.

With all this room for error, the average political poll is almost certain to be flawed in at least a couple of respects, and the sooner this is accepted and understood by candidates, press, and public, the healthier and more realistic will be the perceptions of the polling consultant's role in the election campaign and beyond.

12

Voter Registration Tapes:
Mining for New Votes, New Voters, and New Money

Russell W. Getter • James Emerson Titus

One of the basic building blocks for any campaign is the list of voters who are registered and thus eligible to decide the election. A campaign's limited resources should be spent only on attempts to influence this group of citizens; money and volunteer time expended to reach the unregistered—at least after the deadline for registration—are wasted. The authors of this article suggest several productive uses for the voter list: as a door-to-door canvassing device; a source for random-sample polling; a ready-made group for personalized, persuasive mailings; and even for selective fundraising.

The actual names of registered voters are the most prized commodity in American political campaigns. Election Day victory or defeat depends upon the proper prediction by a candidate of the behavior of these select members of the adult populations. Yet conventional wisdom seems to indicate that voter registration lists are of minimal use in campaigning or fundraising. As Richard Viguerie put it: "If you want to do fundraising, you go to fundraising lists. You go to voter lists if you want votes. But why would you use a voter list if you want money? It just

doesn't make sense to do it that way." In other words, registration data are supposedly too costly and too vague to use for targeted fundraising.

As with most political information, registration data are not (in their raw form) orderly and useful for special needs such as raising money, locating unregistered voters, producing turnout on Election Day, conducting telephone opinion polling, and canvassing the precincts. But registrant data *can* be cleaned up and refocused by use of a computer, to the financial and political benefit of campaigns.

Russell W. Getter is Associate Director of the Center for Public Affairs at the University of Kansas. James Emerson Titus has managed several campaigns for Kansas Democratic candidates. The authors would like to thank William Maxwell of Lawrence, Kansas, for his research, which was used as the basis for this article.

Basic data

What do we get when we buy a computer tape of registered voters? We have discovered that statutes vary from state to state allowing, at times, considerable leeway to officials regarding the location, coding, and quality of data.

But with some additions or exceptions in different states, these are the data we are usually buying on each voter:

Person	Place
1. Name	11. Precinct
2. Birthdate	12. Street Name or
3. Gender	Number or Rural
4. Party Affiliation	Route Number
5. Date of	13. Zip Code
Registration	14. Living Unit
6. State	a. House Number
7. County	b. Apt. Number,
8. Township	Letter, or both
9. City	c. Mobile Home Lot
10. Ward	Number

Data use

Let us assume that you have obtained a "cleaned," up-to-date registration tape of a single county. You now have a list of names, but missing are the new voters to be created by a registration drive. For most campaigns, this requires door-to-door knocking in a few highly transient precincts where you hope to pick up names of new potential voters who have moved in during the past year or two.

The data you purchased make it possible to focus registration drive efforts and to use the computerized Unregistered Household Method to blanket precincts systematically with a minimum of lost effort. Further, the application of aggregate precinct voting data, by party, allows you to choose those precincts with the highest potential of new voters for your candidate and party.

Start by sorting the tape of registered voters in the following ascending order:

1. City or township in the county.
2. Wards.
3. Precincts.
4. Street name or rural route.
5. Dwelling number.

6. Apartment number or letter, mobile home lot number or rural route box number, if available.

The objective of this sorting procedure is the organization of all registrants *by household*. This is a key sort for working the streets because it arranges every person (husband, wife, daughters, sons, aunts, uncles, boarders, renters, even grandma and grandpa) under one household heading. The next sort is to arrange households by odd and even numbers so that your workers, like the mail carrier, walk up one side of the street and back down the other. Once you have the registered households spotted, then you can identify the households in which no one is registered. One way to prepare your door-to-door callers is to have someone drive through a precinct beforehand, noting on cards the dwelling numbers *not* contained on the list of households with registered voters.

This unregistered household method of conducting voter registration drives does not address the problem of unregistered persons living in households where former occupants were registered. Also, the method does not identify unregistered persons living in households where at least one occupant is registered. Nevertheless, the unregistered household method is many times more efficient than traditional methods of registering new voters and, at worst, is an excellent complement to the more traditional methods.

The most efficient use of the unregistered household method occurs when aggregate data are also available showing the percentage of voters in a precinct that traditionally vote for one's favored party or candidate. Armed with this information, voter registration efforts can be specifically targeted on those precincts. Targeting voter registration efforts, of course, is desirable where resources are limited and where one thinks that traditional canvassing methods may result in something less than maximum "useful" registration. Useful registration occurs when your candidate or party receives a high percentage of the votes of the newly registered. It is sad but true that many campaign organizations inadvertently register voters for the opposition party or candidate. This can be avoided with the intelligent use of precinct voting returns and the unregistered household method of registering voters.

Canvassing devices

With registrants sorted by household, one may prepare several useful devices for canvassing, depending on who is doing the canvassing work. A perennial favorite is the candidate-centered device that has been found to be so useful for candidates for local offices and state legislative races.

The candidate-canvassing device is a card file of all registrants, sorted in the following order of priority:

1. Candidate's district.
2. Precinct.
3. Street name or rural route.
4. Even-numbered households.
5. Odd-numbered households.
6. Apartment designation, post office box, or mobile home lot.

Again, all registrants will be organized by household, within each set of odd and even household numbers for each street name. The separation of odd and even numbers enables a candidate (or a representative) to work one side of the street at a time.

The computer output can be either cheshire (i.e., plain white computer paper) or gummed labels with up to three registrants per household listed on one label. If there are more than three registrants at a given address, their names will be printed in blocks of three names until all registrants at that address have been listed. Experience suggests that the basic registration information on these labels, in addition to the full names of the registrants, is the ward and precinct, the mailing address, the phone number if it is available, the birthdate or age of each registrant, and the party affiliation.

These labels can then be affixed to 3 × 5 index cards, which can be preprinted with useful questions pertaining to the interests and activities of each registrant. Among the more useful of these questions are previous, present, or potential monetary or time contributions; occupations; interest group or labor union memberships; number of children in the household; whether the residents are owners or renters; etc.

Armed with these cards (which may easily be carried in a coat pocket or purse) a candidate knows the characteristics of household residents before he/she rings the doorbell. Procedurally, the candidate should ascertain the identity of persons in the household and then proceed to note as much additional information about the registrants as possible.

Using this procedure over a period of time, a candidate can soon get to "know" the voters in his/her district in a way that most candidates currently only dream about. Moreover, the newly acquired information may be added to a computer file for personalized mass-mailings if the candidate has the resources with which to take this additional step.

Polling from a computerized data file

It is simply a fact of political life that the usefulness of any information, whether it pertains to voter registration information or not, depends substantially on the degree of access and control one has over the information. Because of the need for timely access and some degree of secrecy and control, candidates appreciate having voter registration data on their own computer systems. The available data storage technology has rapidly improved to the point where it is possible to store several thousand registrar records on a single removable device. For example, a 5 megabyte removable hard disc system will store up to 10,000 registrant records per disc. These data can then be sorted in whatever way one chooses and for several purposes, provided that one has the software with which to manipulate these data. Certainly one of the initial pieces of software that one must develop or purchase is a database program that can not only handle *all* of the voter registration information, but also is capable of receiving any additional information that candidates and their workers might acquire. Telephone numbers and polling results are among the more useful of these additional data.

In recent years, market research firms have developed very sophisticated Computer-Assisted Telephone Interviewing (CATI) systems. These CATI systems either have telephone numbers stored internally or they generate their own numbers with a random digit telephone number generator. In any event, the telephone numbers can be machine-dialed, thus initiating an interview. For political polling, the best method is to enter the telephone numbers into each registrant record prior to the polling phase. For three to six cents each, private firms will match phone numbers with a voter registration tape (Metro-Mail and R. L. Polk, to name only two). These private firms have a match rate of about fifty percent of the names on a voter registration tape, and about seventy-five percent of the households. Equipped with a database complete with phone numbers—albeit imperfect—one may then select registrants randomly for calling.

Once a registrant answers the phone, the interviewer is prompted by a display of textual material and questionnaire items displayed on a video screen in his office. Each possible response category for each question is also displayed, together with a code number for each category. When the registrant-respondent answers a question, the interviewer enters the appropriate response code and then proceeds to the next questionnaire item. The data are stored for each registrant, thus adding to the knowledge-base about each potential voter polled.

Such polling can have many objectives, including an assessment of the relative percentage point advantage (or disadvantage) for the candidate. However, even more useful data may include the likelihood of each registrant to vote and how persuadable each registrant may be to your candidate. This information, coupled with some knowledge of the registrant's positions on issues and the level of intensity regarding them, will enable the campaign to focus its energies on these "undecideds" in beneficial ways.

Personalized mailing to selected registrants

One may generate personalized letters to selected respondents from a computerized listing. In its simplest form, the same letter content is sent to all of the selectees, even though each letter contains the names of one or more persons residing in each household. A more sophisticated version of personalized letters is to tailor the letter's content to the registrant's interests, party, and position on issues—information obtained from registrant records and polls. With computer assistance, one can then select from among a variety of stock paragraphs, matching each paragraph selection with each registrant's predispositions. To reinforce this message, which is matched to a specific kind of registrant, the letter also can be closed with a carefully tailored P.S. message for each type of registrant.

Certainly some persons will object on ethical grounds to tailoring letters to each registrant, usually without considering the implications of such a stand. It is important to note that computer-generated tailored letters *can be* abused, particularly if a candidate appears to be writing contradictory messages on various issues, but this need not be the case if candidates are judicious in composing the stock paragraphs to be stored in the computer. The matching of registrants with specific paragraphs can be as simple as writing about education to a registrant that you already know is concerned about such matters. Similarly, a farmer or rancher probably wants to read what the candidate has to say about agricultural issues, and so on. Since a letter's effectiveness is generally considered to be inversely related to its length—at least beyond three paragraphs—a campaign organization needs the capability to get the correct messages to the appropriate subpopulations. Computer-assisted letters are one way of achieving a high level of effectiveness in this direction.

Multiname household mailing labels

The questions surrounding mailing come up in nearly every campaign at one time or another. On the plus side, mailing enables a candidate to target his/her message to a given subpopulation or to a geographic area with greater precision than virtually any other campaign vehicle. This has the effect of assuring a campaign director that he/she is not paying for the dissemination of a message to a nonregistered and nonvoting population. On the negative side, mailing is fairly expensive, especially if the campaign seeks to send a message to every registered voter in a subpopulation or a specific geographic area.

By sorting a registrant file so that the names of all persons in a household are printed on the same mailing label, one can reduce mailing costs by as much as forty percent. The average group of voter registrants will have 1.7 persons per household. Accordingly, one reduces mailing costs, and probably increases the effectiveness of the candidate's image, by sending *one* item to each household rather than inundating a multiperson household with unnecessary paper.

The computer program that generates household labels should first sort the names by zip code, since bulk mailing rates require that mail be sorted in this order. Other sorting should establish the household order. The next precaution that should be taken when writing the computer program is to check for the number of persons at a given address. If there are more than three or four registrants at one address, this may mean that a common address is being used by persons not normally associated with one another in household fashion. Possible examples of such places are senior citizens' centers, small mobile home courts without lot numbers, rural routes without accompanying box numbers, and boarding houses. The safest procedure is to have the program write individual labels whenever a given address has more than three or four registrants. This procedure may result in marginal inefficiency, but it can avoid major blunders.

Fundraising from multiperson household mailings

Some consultants tell you that you should not attempt to raise money from voter registration lists and, if one approaches this task in the traditional way—of sending one letter per registrant—the conventional wisdom is sound advice, indeed. However, we have found that if one sorts registrants by household and selects households carefully, it can be very cost-effective.

Multiperson households in which the members share important characteristics such as party identification, interest group and labor union membership, or where they have the same or a similar occupation, tend to reinforce one another's political predispositions. Through the social and psychological processes of selective perception and social reinforcement, residents of single-party households will tend to blame persons of the opposite party for everything—from bad weather to the 0–32 record of the local college basketball team! Meanwhile, registrants living in single-person households are less likely to receive reinforcement for their political and social views. At a minimum, the social reinforcement necessary for singles to articulate their political views is left, at least to some extent, up to chance, and, thus, they are more of a "risk" in fundraising terms. Accordingly, fundraising from voter registration lists can, if properly done, be very effective. It can also be more effective (how effective depends on a multitude of socioeconomic factors) if mail is sent *only* to multiperson households where the residents can be expected to share important characteristics.

Solving problems in voter registration data

Solution of the problems attendant to registration data requires the services of a sophisicated computer programmer and a mainframe computer complete with large disc drives and tape drives (7 to 9 track; up to 6250BPI), plus a full set of utility programs (i.e., file handling, sort-merge, etc.). In addition, it may be necessary, depending on the state, and jurisdictions within states, for the mainframe to be able to read and convert registration data on cards, diskettes, mini-cassettes, and any one of a number of other electronic data processing (EDP) media. It is wise to conduct an inventory of the types of EDP storage devices used in storing registration data for any state, jurisdiction, or geographic area of interest, as a first step; then, with needs ascertained, acquisition of the necessary reading and conversion services can begin. If you do not have good conversion services at your immediate disposal, you should contact a private computer services bureau in your area.

Conclusion

Voter registration data need not be the wasteland that many political activists have come to believe that they are. These data are useful for many purposes, *including* fundraising.

Despite the many potential uses of voter registration data, it is a safe assumption that not much of the potential is ever realized in most campaigns. The reasons are numerous. First, many candidates and their managers have been "sold" on the effectiveness of broadcast media and, thus, often choose to devote usually scarce resources to the electronic media. Second, some candidates and their staffs tend to be philosophically predisposed to think that computers and computer technologies are dehumanizing and are incompatible with their goals. Third, many so-called campaign organizations are not sufficiently organized in advance of the campaign period to be able to incorporate advanced technologies into their campaign efforts.

13

How Direct Mail Works

Larry J. Sabato

Most individuals greatly enjoy receiving mail. In one survey, more people (sixty-three percent) said they looked forward to the post than to any other of a laundry list of pleasurable activities on the daily schedule. Protestations to the contrary notwithstanding, most people even delight in the so-called junk mail they get, at least the political variety. One study indicated that three-fourths of the individuals who are sent a piece of political direct mail actually do read it.

It is this sort of statistic that has made political direct mail one of the most ballyhooed of the new campaign techniques, while remaining the least understood. Direct mail combines sophisticated political judgments and psychological, emotional appeals with the most advanced computer and mailing technologies. Used for two very distinct purposes (persuasion and fundraising), direct mail is considered a necessity by many candidates, but few know how and why it works. This article unravels some of the direct mail's mysteries by shedding light on the methods of the process.

The process of direct mail is a confusing one for the lay person, if only because at certain stages it often appears to be unprofitable and nonsensical. The accompanying illustration in Figure 13-1, depicting the fundamentals of a presidential campaign's direct-mail system, will serve to elucidate. The "eleven steps to raise $2 million by direct mail" revolve around two different kinds of mailings, "house" and "prospect." A "prospect" mailing is a general, mass mailing to suspected potential campaign donors, based on some characteristics or qualities thought likely to make them susceptible to a candidate's appeal for funds. Note that this propensity to donate is merely suspected, not proven. Those individuals who actually respond to the prospect mailing become members of the

prized "house list." They are proven donors who, having contributed once, are believed good possibilities for additional donations. As such they are the targets of repeated mailings during the course of the campaign, and normally such mailings are quite profitable—in contrast to prospecting mailings, which frequently lose money or manage to pay for themselves with a wafer-thin profit.

The illustration demonstrates the potential of a well-coordinated direct-mail program, where an initial investment of $200,000 can produce (under ideal conditions) a gross profit of over $2 million in a year or so and, far more important, compile a house list of over 200,000 individuals. Direct mailers go back and forth between prospecting and house (or "contributor") mailings, and during the early stage of building a reliable house list, all of the profits from house mailings are reinvested in additional prospecting. Gradually, the house list grows, as does the bank balance,

This article is drawn in part from Larry J. Sabato, The Rise of Political Consultants: New Ways of Winning Elections (New York: Basic Books, 1981).

even though the cost of later mailings increases because more persuasive material is sent in each letter and the response rates simultaneously decline a bit since the mailings are sent repeatedly to the same house lists. Yet as the election draws near, an interesting phenomenon can be seen: The response rate increases, as does the size of the average gift. The immediacy and impact of events, such as the growing excitement of a forthcoming election, significantly affect the willingness of individuals to give. This can be a bonanza for presidential candidates during the primary season, when another election is held almost every week (assuming a candidate is winning at least some of the contests).

Investment concepts

The direct-mail strategy just described is often referred to as the *basic investment concept*. An alternative *dual investment concept* is used by some direct-mail firms that do not rely so heavily on prospecting. Here only about a quarter of the profits are expected to come from the house list compiled by prospect mailings, while the other three-quarters is derived from a "master file" of past contributions to the candidate (and others like him/her) that is assembled from house lists of previous and current campaigns. This dual investment pattern ensures that profits are made much earlier and is thus less risky than the basic investment system, which can leave a candidate whose effort begins to flag before the final stages with little to show for all the prospecting investments. Table 1 presents an analysis of two direct-mail letters, one sent in a prospect mailing and the other to a house list. Both letters, signed by President Ford to raise funds for the National Republican Congressional Committee (NRCC), used the same text and were posted during the same general time period. The prospecting letter was mailed to almost 4.9 million people, while the contributor letter was sent to few more than 200,000. Yet the response rate—the proportion of those receiving a letter who make a contribution—was so much greater for the house mailing (11.7 percent to 1.8 percent for the prospect package) that the profit from the small mailing ($576,000) approached the level of the much larger mailing ($797,000). Prospecting produced almost three times the gross income ($1.8 million versus $636,000), but mailing costs were far higher ($1 million versus $60,000). This is despite the fact that each prospect letter, a rather impersonal "Dear Friend" item, was less expensive than the

TABLE 1 A Direct-Mail Letter from President Ford: An Analysis

	Prospecting Mailing[a]	Contributor Mailing[a]
Period of Mailing	Dec. 1975–June 1976	October 1975
Total Names Mailed	4,883,462	210,760
Number Responding and Contributing	86,596	24,674
(Percent Response)	(1.8%)	(11.7%)
Average Contribution	$20.72	$25.77
Gross Income from Mailing	$1,794,658	$635,934
Cost of Each Letter Sent	$ .21	Computer: $ .27
		Robotype: $1.04
Total Cost of Mailing	$998,126	$59,549
NET INCOME FROM MAILING	$796,533	$576,385

[a]Both mailings used exactly the same letter text. There were, however, several differences in the contributor cards and mailing envelopes.

Source: Letters and mailing data provided by the National Republican Congressional Committee.

FIGURE 13-1   Eleven Steps to Raise $2 Million by Direct Mail

1. Raise initial investment of $200,000 to pay for the first mailing.

"House" List	Bank Balance
0	$200,000

2. Use the $200,000 to pay for 952,381 letters at 21¢ a letter.

"House" List	Bank Balance
0	0

3. The mailing produces a response rate of 2.9 percent, meaning 27,619 letter recipients give a donation (at an average of $10.82 each). The mailing returns $298,838.

"House" List	Bank Balance
27,619	$298,838

4. The whole balance is used to mail again (1,423,038 letters at 21¢ each).

"House" List	Bank Balance
27,619	0

5. This time the response rate happens to be a bit lower (2.6 percent) but since a larger list was used, more new donors are produced (36,999). The average gift is about the same as before ($10.75), producing $397,739. All the new donors are added to the "house" list total.

"House" List	Bank Balance
64,618	$397,739

6. Now the "house" list of all previous donors is mailed. The letters are bulky (with personalized enclosures) and therefore costlier (38¢ per letter), but the response rate is a high 14.8 percent and the average donation is $13.10. After deducting $24,555 in mailing costs, the profit is $100,733.

"House" List	Bank Balance
64,618	$498,472

Larry J. Sabato

FIGURE 13-1 *(continued)*

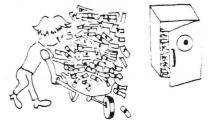

7. Empty the bank to prospect again. At 21¢ a letter, 2,373,676 letters are sent. Less reliable lists are used, and the response rate dips again (to 2.2 percent), but the largest mailing so far still yields the most new donors yet (52,221). The average gift of $9.91 adds $517,510 to the empty bank account.

"House" List   Bank Balance
116,839 $517,510

8. Take the whole sum and go prospecting again, buying 2,464,333 letters. With a 2.0 response rate this time and an average donation of $10.68, 49,287 new donors and $526,385 are produced.

"House" List   Bank Balance
166,126 $526,385

9. Since a month and a half have passed since the last "house" list mailing, send another one. At 38¢ a letter, the costs are $63,128. The response rate, though, is 16.3 percent with an average gift of $14.20. Thus the mailing yields a hefty profit of $321,380.

"House" List   Bank Balance
166,126 $847,765

10. Take about half the money ($425,000) for a final prospect mailing of 2,023,810 letters. The 1.9 percent response rate and average gift of $10.74 produce 38,452 more donors and $412,974 (or less than the cost of the mailing).

"House" List   Bank Balance
204,578 $835,739

11. With the primaries now underway, the political excitement and attention permit regular mailings to the "house" list (about every six weeks), and produce both a higher rate of return (an average of 22 percent) and a higher average donation (about $28). The first mailing (at these average rates) brings in $1,260,196 at a cost of only $77,740.

"House" List   Bank Balance
204,578 $2,018,195

computer or robotyped letter sent to the house contributors. The computer version had a computer-imprinted personalized address and salutation, and the addressee's name was invoked twice in the text (those lines being computer imprinted, with the rest offset). A facsimile of Gerald Ford's personal stationery was used. The robotyped letter, sent to contributors with the most generous donation records, was the most personalized of all— printed on a heavier bond, individually typed, and machine signed in real ink. There were five two-cent stamps on the return envelope and a large, attractive commemorative on the mailing envelope, and the return envelope was stamped "personal" in red ink, with the individual's name typed in the return address slot and the envelope addressed to Ford at the White House. (As we shall shortly observe, these items are not the insignificant details they seem.)

This sophisticated package proved to be exceptionally lucrative for the NRCC, with an unusually high rate of return on both packages, especially the house list. The presidential imprimatur was no doubt responsible, and the letter's text was kept noticeably bland (by comparison to most direct mail) in keeping with the dignified tone thought appropriate for a chief executive. A similar house list letter mailed out by the NRCC under Ronald Reagan's signature in February and March of 1976 secured a 6.4 percent response and netted $250,000—still good but far below the presidential letter's results.

Mailing lists: finding the committed

There is no more crucial stage in the direct-mail process than the assembling of mailing lists. Knowing to whom to send a letter is as important to the success of a fundraising effort as the message and the candidate. There are five basic types of lists: in-house, outside contributor, compiled, commercial, and universal. "In-house" lists are the most valuable, consisting of current and previous contributors to a candidate, the names of campaign volunteers, and records of individuals who have made inquiries of the candidate by mail and telephone. Past and present donors are always identified by the time of their last donation, the frequency of donations, and the amounts contributed.

A good past contributor list, if kept current, is an irreplaceable campaign resource. Members of Congress have a great advantage in the access they have to the correspondence and in the constituency contact files they have built up over the years. The average House member has between 20,000 and 30,000 names on file, which are periodically updated by his/her staff, and most senators have even larger voter reservoirs. Occasionally, a campaign can gain access to "outside contributor" lists, which record donors to various causes and other candidacies. Some direct mailers believe that people who are constitutionally inclined to give to charities, religions, and educational institutions are good bets to make political contributions as well, given the right incentive. And obviously, if an individual has given to a previous liberal cause or candidacy, there is every reason to consider him/her a possible donor to a new liberal product.

"Compiled" lists are basically group and membership rosters. Doctors, lawyers, businesspersons, labor organizations, alumni, gun owners, veterans, and scores of other professions and special-interest groups have rosters of one sort or another. Some of these lists are obtainable free from supporters, and others can be purchased. Another popular source for direct mailing is the voter registration roll. Most states permit voter registration lists, including the names and sometimes telephone numbers of all qualified voters, to be bought by candidates or campaigns. The National Republican Congressional Committee has found lists of registered Republican voters to be very productive in prospect mailings, and the cost of the lists when purchased from states or localities is generally far less than similar lists bought from list "brokers" or companies. On the other hand, such firms and individuals have an unbelievably wide range of "commercial" lists for sale, from magazine subscribers and all people who buy products or enter contests through the mail to lists of all deer hunters and trout fishermen in Arizona and all burley tobacco farmers in Tennessee. Magazine lists have proven popular with liberal and conservative candidates for prospecting, since demographic information on subscribers is usually fairly comprehensive. Liberals often mail to readers of *New Yorker*, *New Republic*, and *Mother Jones*, while conservatives pick *Human Events* and *The Saturday Evening Post*. "Universal lists" (such as telephone directories and social registries) normally are not profitable for direct mailings precisely because they are so diversified.

These are standard criteria for evaluating the worth of any mailing list to a campaign. If the individuals listed have a history of giving to campaigns (and possibly to anything), if they are politically active in some way, and if the candidate has had some previous exposure or relationship to them, the odds are good that the list will be useful for prospecting. The same holds true if the individuals are likely to agree with the candidate on some important issue or have a strong reason to dislike his/her opponent. Additionally, a record of contributing or purchasing by mail is a good indicator of direct mail's potential effectiveness.

Personalization and package design

Gimmicks and personalization are two of the most pronounced characteristics of the successful direct-mail package, and these qualities can be detected in each of the five pieces of a traditional package: (1) the letter; (2) the additional enclosures; (3) the contribution card; (4) the return envelope; and (5) the carrier or mailing envelope. In each part, the direct mailer attempts to attract and rivet the recipient's attention in some way, while making the approach seem as personal as possible. The overriding principle of direct

mail is intimacy. As a Republican party direct-mail expert once advised GOP campaign chiefs, "It would be best to have your candidate write a letter by hand to every name on your list. And every step you get away from that weakens the letter a little."

In keeping with these rules, the letter is usually printed on the personal or business stationery of the signatory, and brown or ivory stationery with dark blue or brown letterhead (rather than starchy, official white) is often preferred. The body of the letter is typed on a regular-faced typewriter in black, with short, indented paragraphs of variable length that are never more than six lines long and sometimes consist of just a single sentence. The signature is printed in fine-point blue ink, closely resembling a fountain-pen-signed name. If the letter cannot be properly dated because of the production or mailing schedule, then a designation of "Monday morning" gives the effect of immediacy. Surprisingly, longer letters generally produce greater profits than shorter ones. Letters should run a minimum of four pages (two pages front and back, single-spaced), and one of the most lucrative direct-mail letters ever sent—for George McGovern in 1972—ran seven full pages.

Direct mailers are especially careful about design and enclosures. Mass-produced brochures and literature are thought to be far too impersonal, and sending bumper stickers has been deemed a complete waste of money. Some consultants believe that enclosures are more effective for prospect mailings, when the recipients presumably appreciate additional information or it is needed to stimulate contributions. (A member of the house list is already convinced, and his/her letters should be kept uncluttered and direct, according to the prevailing theory.)

The enclosures contained in direct-mail letters indicate the range of creative gimmickry in the field. Letters for George Bush in 1980 included reprinted news articles with "personal notes" laser-printed in the top margins: "To Irving Potzrebie—I thought you might be interested in these recent clippings—G. B."

Several consultants reported that occasionally respondents return annotated clippings with notes such as "Thanks for lending this—I'm returning it because I'm sure you'll want to keep your copy."

When Texas gubernatorial candidate William Clements sent out money requests for television advertising, his direct mailer attached a list of all the reserved spots by city, station, and program so that the individual could see precisely what he was purchasing. A 1979 National Republican Senatorial Committee mailing let respondents target their money to the Democratic senators they most wanted to see defeated. Each respondent got to judge the Democratic incumbents on a "Danger Rating Scale" and was encouraged to scratch out, as viciously as he/she liked, the names of personal targets. There are all sorts of other "participation mailers," as letters including involvement devices are called. People are frequently sent "mock election" ballots to vote or "critical issues" surveys to fill out and return (along with a contribution, of course); the Republican party even charged a fee in 1979 to count a recipient's mock presidential vote. Individuals are also inundated with "status gifts." Ronald Reagan sent each of his "first supporters" a "commemorative edition" wallet-sized card emblazoned with his countenance and the supporter's computer-typed name. Multicolored plastic membership cards are also common enticements to "join" (i.e., contribute to) various Victory Funds, Eagle Clubs, and Stars and Stripes Forever candidates. Photographs are becoming quite popular as enclosures. Snapshots of the candidate and family or the candidate receiving an award or the acclamation of admirers are adorned by handwritten descriptive notes in blue pen ink on the back. The Republican party used three photos of President Ford to evoke sympathy and stimulate giving as he was leaving office. The highly successful piece, mailed on December 30, 1976, included poses of Ford in the Oval Office, at his swearing-in, and with his family.

Occasionally, large past contributors receive a worthwhile gift with a new solicitation, such as a superbly illustrated historical calendar. More frequently, respondents are made to feel as guilty as possible if they seem inclined not to contribute. The state and national Republican parties use the marvelous gimmick of a laser-printed "memorandum" from the party's finance director to the chair, bemoaning the absence of "key supporter" Irving Potzrebie of Jonestown from the contributor's list and vowing to "keep the books open" until he opens his wallet. Many times letters will also enclose a sealed envelope with the handwritten notation, "Read this please, if you have decided not to contribute," containing a desperate, breathless final pitch for money. For doubting Thomases, unconvinced of a candidate's electoral promise, direct mailers have a cure: an official-looking "excerpt" from a fictitious "Viability Study for Candidate X," concluding that, if the candidate can just get enough money from the person reading the note, victory is assured and the future of Western civilization is secure. No one else, though, has matched the number and sheer diversity of enclosures in Richard Viguerie's "state-of-the-art" direct-mail packages for the Conservative Caucus's anti-SALT treaty campaign and the National Tax Limitation Committee's drive to secure a budget-balancing amendment to the U.S. Constitution. No trouble is spared, as up to a dozen different items are packed into a booklet format with perforated tear sheets. There are gifts ("Christmas Seal"-like stamps with political messages on them), participatory devices (postcards expressing strong views on the subject at hand, preaddressed to the individual's representative), and a legion of persuasive materials—all in a package that is almost as much fun to go through as a box of Cracker Jack.

The contributor card is a crucial part of the direct-mail package, since once an individual has decided to contribute, he/she often determines the size of the gift while completing the card. Direct mailers have discovered that people tend to donate more when the suggested amounts listed go from greatest to smallest ($500, $100, $50) rather than the reverse and when a blank is left for even larger contributions at the higher end of the scale. The contributor is asked to sign a personalized statement as he/she donates: "Yes, Candidate X, I want to help you rid Washington of the superliberals. . . ." The reader is even asked to sign and return the card without making a contribution—if he/she can sign a statement only slightly milder than this: "Sorry, Candidate X. I'm afraid I cannot contribute to your crusade even though I know your defeat would condemn my children to a life of misery and enable Sodom and Gomorrah to prevail on earth." Richard Viguerie's shrewd anti-SALT package asked each respondent to signify a contribution decision by affixing one of two flags onto the reply card—either the Stars and Stripes or the "White Flag of Surrender" (printed on a blood-red background).

Even a simple envelope can be a useful tool in direct mail. The carrier (or mailing) envelope, after all, influences the recipient's decision whether or not to bother opening it. The more personalized is the address, the better is the chance that an individual will read the contents. If an envelope cannot be personally addressed (handwritten or typed), then window envelopes are generally used, allowing the typed address on the letter itself to show through. "Live" (i.e., real) stamps on the envelope are vastly preferred to either meter or bulk-mail, and colorful commemorative stamps are especially prized as attention grabbers. "Teaser copy" is sometimes printed on the carrier envelope as an enticement. A gun control group was very forthright ("ENCLOSED: Your first chance to tell the National Rifle Association to go to hell!"), while the sponsors of Proposition 13 were deceptive ("Your 1978 Property Tax Increase statement is enclosed . . . RESPONSE REQUIRED"). The return envelope is, if anything, even more carefully and attractively designed. Colors that contrast with the rest of the package are often used, and ideally the individual's name is personally typed in the return-address space. Sometimes a calendar appears on the envelope

with a date circled, as a reminder to the recipient that the candidate needs a gift by a certain time.

A bulk-mail indicia is frequently used in prospect mailings, but again, live stamps are more desirable, and for good reason. As an experiment, the National Republican Congressional Committee mailed the exact same fundraising package to two different samples of the same list, the only difference in the mailings being that one used a bulk indicia on the return envelope while the other had five two-cent live stamps. Incredibly, the mailing with the bulk indicia raised only $0.50 per name mailed, while the stamped mailing garnered $1.64 per name. It is a fascinating commentary on human behavior that our actions can be so easily manipulated, and this illustration serves to underline the subtle but substantial impact that consultants and the new campaign technology can have in politics.

Copywriting with emotional ink

Direct mail is a copy medium. On television, visuals supplement copy, and on radio sound effects can embellish, but direct mail has only graphics, stamps, and the printed word. Words unspoken cannot easily move, but direct-mail consultants have long known of a secret ingredient to stir the soul: emotion. "To raise money by mail you don't have an hour of explaining things across the table to someone," insists Democratic direct mailer Robert Smith. "You have to do it in a couple of pages of print. The message has to be extreme, has to be overblown; it really has to be kind of rough." Smith's axiom for the political left applies as well on the right. One antiabortion group, for example, sent out a "Stop the Baby Killers" letter in 1979 to 50,000 Catholics, Baptists, and members of other religious faiths, calling for the defeat of five proabortion "baby killer" incumbents in the U.S. Congress. The words "baby killers" and "murder" appeared forty-one times in the text of the letter. When someone in the antiabortion movement complained to Jim Martin, a former Viguerie employee, about the extreme emotionalism of the letter, he replied as a businessman who knew the role of emotion in direct mail: ". . . the bottom line in my business is to raise money."

The letter tone for in-house mailings, particularly to high donors, is usually softer, since these givers already have some sort of commitment to the candidate. But in prospect mailings, the tacit rule among direct mailers is that there are no rules—anything goes in the pursuit of profit. Direct mail, consultants insist, must make the quantum leap between belief and action—painful action (the parting with money). And only emotion can do that, they argue.

A candidate near the extreme ends of the spectrum can be himself or herself in direct mail, but for more centrist candidates, emotion must be manufactured, either by selective and exaggerated emphasis on a couple of issues or by sharp, personal contrast with the opponent. Involvement devices can also be useful for centrists. Robert Smith advises campaigns contemplating a direct-mail program to "Find your candidate a nasty enemy. Tell people they're threatened in some way. . . . It's a cheap trick, but the simplest." Events that generate their own emotion can also be harnessed with great effectiveness by direct mail. One of Smith's profitable letters for the prochoice National Abortion Rights Committee was mailed shortly after Congress cut off Medicaid abortion payments in response to a 1973 Supreme Court ruling liberalizing abortion laws. And one of his firm's best fund-raising letters for the American Civil Liberties Union came on the heels of the furor created by Nazi demands for marching privileges in Skokie, Illinois.

Almost every line of copy is related either to emotionalism or personalization. The letter is always in conversational (if ungrammatical) English, it is written from one person to another (not from one to thousands), and it is spiced with dozens of "you's" and "I's." The salutation is as personal as possible (individually typed to the addressee if possible, but "Dear Friend"

if not). The opening paragraph, the most crucial part of the entire letter, is usually succinct and breathless. It is designed to rivet the reader's attention and pique his interest immediately, explaining in an intimate or momentous way why the letter is written, what the common ground with the reader is, or how the candidate's election will be vital to the recipient's own welfare. Urgency is the mood most often created in the first few words, as these examples of opening lines indicate:

If you're like me, you've received literally thousands of pieces of mail this summer. But I urge you to pay special attention to this letter, the MOST IMPORTANT LETTER you'll receive this year.

I believe you've been waiting 25 years to receive this letter. . . . But unless you step forward . . . there may never be another like it.

I need your advice. And I need it right away.

This is the most urgent letter I have ever written in my life.

These same lines recur frequently in national direct mailings, since they have been found effective. As one consultant wryly reported, "We usually write about ten 'most important letter ever written' letters a year—but not to the same group, obviously. It's always good for one shot." There are other approaches besides urgency. Involvement phrasing is sometimes used: "You and I can save America" or "Will you go to the White House with me on October 1st?" Guilt is always handy ("The Republican party can't afford to lose people like you!"), and the personal touch can charm ("I need your advice immediately" or "Would you do a very special favor for me?"). Frightening the recipients can certainly work with appropriate lists. Former military personnel responded generously to a letter that began "If you and I don't do something immediately, our country's vital security interests will be sold down the river." California suburbanites were gripped into giving by a direct-mail piece that opened like this: "If a bloodthirsty criminal like Charles Manson had you or your family brutally murdered, that criminal would not face the death penalty under current California law. We can change the law."

The body of the letter is devoted to selling the candidate and his/her chances and closing the sale with a contribution. Boosting the candidate's electoral prospects usually comes first. A Republican party direct-mail manual advises campaigns to "think in terms of how your candidate's election will provide something for the reader that your opponent cannot provide. In selling terms—think of benefits to the reader." Testimonials and endorsements in the body of the letter can bolster a candidate's credibility and pave the way for the quarter of the letter spent in actually asking for the contribution.

In general, the reader is asked to make a specific contribution; the amount is computer- or laser-printed in the body of the letter and is based either on the recipient's contribution pattern or projected potential given the list from which the name was taken. Previous donors are never asked to give precisely the same amount as they gave before. Rather, the last previous gift is noted and gratefully acknowledged, and a percentage increment (ten to twenty-five percent) is added to comprise the new donation request. The pitch for funds is normally based on the campaign budget, which is identified as the minimum necessary to win, according to "the experts." The candidate explains an immediate need for a certain amount ($25,000 or less) to be used for a specified purpose (radio and television time being the favorite justifications). The recipient can even be asked to buy "four prime-time radio spots for $312.18"; the more precise the request, the better it is likely to be considered. Finally, adding to the sense of urgency, the reader is given a make-or-break deadline by which time the money must be in the candidate's hand.

All the while, the letter continues to make personal connections of various sorts. These are raw, scratchy "blue pen" underlinings, dashes, and checkmarks "personally" added by the candidate to emphasize parts of the typescript. If the letter was individually addressed, then the heading of all pages after the first reads, "Page two (three, etc.) of letter to Irving Potzrebie," and the addressee's name is parenthetically interspersed throughout the text in computer- or laser-printed lines ("And now, Mr. Potzrebie, let me turn to another matter of interest"). The phrasing is kept direct and simple with lots of conversational connecting phrases ("It would mean a lot to me personally," "NOW—here is the most important part," "But that's not all," etc.).

The final paragraph usually restates the candidate's greatest attractions and attempts to end on a dramatic and very personal note. Sample closing lines give the flavor of the climax:

Success in the 1980s will be measured by your support today.

When we meet in person, I'll be honored to shake your hand. And you—with good cause—will be proud of your actions today.

I need help from my friends. Can I count on you again, Irving?

The survival of America is on the line. Let me hear from you today!

The signature follows, usually that of the candidate, but occasionally of someone who is well known to the people on the mailing list (the president of the American Medical Association for doctors, for example) or who has special credibility on the issue stressed in the text (a retired general for a letter on national defense, for instance). Believability is important. The Republican party almost sent out a letter that would have been jointly signed by President Ford and Ronald Reagan at the time they were hotly contesting the 1976 GOP presidential nomination. But the party's fundraisers concluded after testing that average people simply could not conceive of the two sitting down together for any cooperative purpose at the time, so they scrapped the original plan and enclosed two separate letters, in the same package, one from each man.

Postscripts are standard devices on direct-mail letters, because people have been found to pay close attention to them. (A "P.S.," in the signer's handwriting, often follows the typewritten postscript for added emphasis.)

The requested donation and specified deadline are almost always repeated, along with still more phrases evoking guilt, urgency, patriotism, and hatred of the enemy:

If I fail to win your support . . . I'll begin to despair of success in 1980. I've figured and refigured our chances of raising dollars every way I can. There's just no way to make it without you.

I will be given a list of contributions soon and I certainly hope your name is on this list.

We are waiting for your verdict. As far as we're concerned, you'll be passing judgment on America's future.

But the emotionalism of direct mail is not always so hard and virulent. Conservative Richard Viguerie's ingenious "wife letter" is a good example of the soft sell, which pulls the heartstrings instead of pumping adrenalin. Written in longhand by the candidate's wife on personal, pastel stationery, the letter is an expensive, photo-offset production that is mailed in a ladylike envelope with full postage (no bulk reduction, and using live stamps). It is even shipped back to the candidate's hometown for a local postmark. In the four-page letter the wife gives a chatty rendition of her family history, children, and marriage, lightly connecting it all to her husband-candidate's concerns about inflation, taxes, energy, and other problems. The text is opened and closed with references to housewifely and childbearing duties ("The baby's crying so I must close for now," ended one), and a photo of the happy family, pets included, is enclosed with a "hand-scrawled" inscription.

The "wife letter" has been widely mimicked, but that is the fate of most effective direct-mail packages. Richard Viguerie himself discovered a 1980 Reagan fundraising letter that was almost precisely copied from one he had mailed for another GOP presidential contender fifteen months earlier. The same format, the same issues, and many of the same words were used; ten of the first eleven paragraphs were virtually identical. Direct-mail letters are not copyrighted, and the techniques are certainly standard. If direct-mail consult-

ants were as emotional as their letters, charges of plagiarism would often fill the air.

Production and mailing schedules

Artful, inventive wording can greatly increase the profit margin of a letter, as can the quality of the letter's production, and it is in this area that technological precision has made its most significant impact. "I started out typing envelopes, 500 a day, each of them individually stuffed with letters," recalled GOP direct mailer Bob Odell. "Now I'm at the point where I'm not sure I can keep up with the new technology." The added degree of personalization, which multiplies a letter's effectiveness, is a direct result of changes in technology. The first direct mail letters were unvarying, mimeographed copies in an envelope carrying a computer-printed label. Then window envelopes came into widespread use (with the label affixed to the inside letter). The computer-typed letter, at first in all uppercase type and then in more natural lower and upper was a major advance, since each letter was individually typed even if identical in message. Next came the computer "fill-in" letter, where the addressee's name was interspersed in the initial attempt at personalization. Simultaneously, advanced photo-copying and printing equipment was being developed, allowing continuous production and unheard-of quantities of letters to be mailed each day.

The latest generation of word processing machines is nothing short of phenomenal. Five or more items in a reasonably priced direct-mail package can now be personalized in some way, and the machines' operation is far more flexible than previously. Another marvel, a laser printer, uses a "burning" process to print 10,000 lines per minute (compared to the computer's 1,200 lines) and can print sideways and upside down. New package preparation machines easily convert the long printed forms into manageable, mailable packets with all enclosures neatly cut and properly folded.

The exact schedule for posting a direct-mail

package necessarily varies considerably from campaign to campaign. Generally, prospect mailings are done as soon as a list is available, so that house donors can be identified and added to the files as quickly as possible. Mailings to house donors, though, must be more carefully planned, and there are usually specific times during an election when awareness will be heightened or the sense of urgency and immediacy will naturally seem greater. Just before or just after a candidacy announcement, at the time of a major media broadcast or blitz, and shortly before the primary or general election are all dramatic entry points for direct mail.

Direct mailers try to avoid the summer period, when many people are away, and December/January, when many are financially drained from the holidays, but there are few other clear scheduling rules. Many of these rules are made to be broken; two consultants reported their most successful mailings are regularly sent in early January and around the Fourth of July, presumably because of the lack of competition from other mailers who have read the "rules" too carefully. Standard guidelines are also quoted, and often disregarded, about the frequency of mailings. Normally, the house list is mailed every thirty to forty-five days, but within a month or so of the election another letter is sent each fortnight. Generally, five percent of those on the house list will give with each mailing (averaging perhaps $25 a head). The most important job of each new contributor letter is to upgrade previous gifts, of course. The Republican party has had a lengthy program of trail-and-error testing to determine the percentage increase that is best to request for each category of donor. In general, there is just a small percentage upgrading for gifts of under $100, but for gifts of $500 and more, a major increment is added. It is helpful to thank the individual for the original contribution first, citing the amount and specifically what it bought for the campaign; for larger donors, some sort of certificate and memento might be sent along as a symbol of gratitude.

Occasionally, reminders are used to prod negligent givers. For robotyped letters to large contributors, carbon copies are kept and sent along with a new cover letter if a recipient has not responded to the original within a few weeks.

Concluding remarks

Because the art of direct mail is still inexact, and conditions and circumstances vary so greatly from candidate to candidate and election to election, there are few guaranteed techniques. Direct-mail consultants frequently contradict each other; what one thinks is a shrewd idea, another discounts as wholly worthless. The direct-mail industry, and the professionals who run it, like to operate on the principle "If it ain't broke, don't fix it," but most are insecure (and wise) enough to realize that last week's magic may not work for this week's candidate. Therefore, a testing phase is sometimes added to ensure that a mistake is not too costly. Testing requires taking a 1,000- to 2,000-person random sample from the mailing list and posting the prepared copy to this small group first. This adds four to eight weeks to the schedule, of course, but the adjustments and improvements can increase the profit margin substantially.

Indeed, given the primitive nature of the direct-mail "science" and the considerable financial risk involved in each mailing, it is surprising that testing is not almost universal. Many direct mailers foresee a time when they will commission extensive psychological testing of word patterns, colors, and approaches, and use focus groups and much more sophisticated list selection techniques. For the moment, though, direct mail is a decidedly trial-and-error technology, where professionals rely on instinct and whim as much as test results. One consultant cited an instance where he disposed of $10,000 worth of already printed letters because he had last-minute doubts about the mailing's success. Better to do that than mail at great expense a package that does poorly—which is exactly what very often happens.

The Telemarketing Center:
Nucleus of a Modern Campaign

David S. Boim

Increasingly, direct mail is being supplemented by telephone solicitation. A campaign's telemarketing program, as David Boim explains in the following article, can make a useful contribution to fundraising, voter persuasion, registration, get-out-the-vote, and other activities. More powerful than mail (but less so than door-to-door canvassing), telemarketing has the potential to be both an efficient and an effective component of a campaign's organization. It can also be enormously expensive and disastrously unproductive if not carefully planned and executed—and precisely tailored for each candidate's needs.

Is it possible? Through one system, is it possible to target campaign contributors, recruit volunteers and supervise their activities, take polls, and survey targeted voters on the issues? Is it possible for this same system to run a registration campaign, get the vote out, and gather endorsements for a candidate? And can it keep in contact with vendors, handle inquiries, and make direct mail more effective? One system to coordinate all activities and process data for all these functions? Is there a single answer to a campaign's organizing needs?

Telemarketing may be the answer. Simply using the telephone is not telemarketing. Telemarketing requires a *systematic* approach involving careful planning, good management, statistical research, targeted messages, and good recordkeeping. Telemarketing is a blend of telephone technologies and marketing techniques interfaced with computers, and it is being used effectively in the private sector,

bringing lower costs and increased productivity. It can make the difference between an efficient, cost-effective electoral campaign and one that is not. For many campaigns, it can be the difference between winning and losing.

Often the word *telemarketing* conjures up images of a "boiler room" filled with callers calling long lists of numbers. When candidates and their campaign volunteers dial those numbers, they are trying to spread a message, raise funds, or get out the vote. Sometimes it is "efficient" but not "effective." "Telemarketing" implies both.

Why telemarketing?

Phone communications enable a campaign to *target* groups of voters and get a message across in a more *personal* way than can the more mass-oriented electronic and print media. It allows for two-way conversation so the voter feels a *sense of shared ownership* in the message. Telemarketing is intimate. You enter the home of the citizen and speak directly into his or her ear. Telemarketing can be many times more effective than direct mail and can be

David S. Boim is Director of Marketing for Telemarketing Systems, Inc. of Fairfax, Virginia.

less costly than printed or electronic media in getting a message out and motivating people.

By setting up a Telemarketing Center, a campaign can take advantage of computers and their available compatible software, and build a people-oriented organization at the same time. The data collected during a campaign, direct mailings, and printed and electronic media messages should all revolve around an effective campaign telemarketing operation.

For example, if you run a television spot or newspaper ad, you must be prepared for immediate response. Your incoming telemarketing arm can handle inquiries about contributions and needed volunteers. Additionally, telemarketing can give a friendly answer to voters' questions about registration, about voting, and about your candidate. At the push of a button, an operator at a telemarketing workstation can call a variety of scripts up on the screen to prompt him, locate a contributor's record, update existing volunteer files, or create a variety of new files. Press another key and a follow-up letter targeted to a voter's particular interest is fed to a printer. The same person can take a call, enter data, and prepare a response in just a few minutes.

Case study: fundraising

"Boiler room" set-ups have been used for fundraising for many years. Scores of volunteers or "telemarketing firms" (with scores of "phone drones") call lists of past donors or prospective donors to raise money for candidates. On the surface, it seems all you need to do is order some telephones, acquire telephone lists, staff the telephone room, and you're on your way.

Sounds simple. It's not. The paperwork can be staggering. How does one keep track of each call, whether a contact was made, the result of that contact, and then compile meaningful statistics? Is there a system to recontact "no answers" and "busies"? Is there a system to schedule follow-up calls? And what about follow-up letters to donors?

The staff and hours necessary to coordinate the fundraising process defeat the main purpose: to "net out"—that is, to take in more than you pay out for the program. Hiring, training, and supervising personnel can be a nightmare. Turnover and absenteeism are burdensome. Lazy workers who "fudge" calls are a major problem. Quickly integrating the statistical sheets, individual pledge cards, follow-up letters, and the database is almost impossible. For most fundraising operations, a true database is nonexistent.

Enter the "Automated Telemarketing Workstation" (ATW). Do not let the hardware and software incorporated in the ATW make you anxious. Most people recoil in fear because they are unfamiliar with the new technology. Computers elicit images of great expense. The ATW hardware includes an IBM Personal Computer, a color monitor, a telephone modem, and a printer. Either hard disk or floppy diskettes may be used. The software is a unique telemarketing application package.

The ATW gives a user an easily accessed database. Each record includes the name, address, and phone number of the prospect. It also includes the name of a contact if you are going through a business or a spouse. The database will tell you whether prospects have contributed before or not. You can then assign a calling priority. Each record also includes the last date the prospect was contacted, how often she or he should be called, and when the call should be made (date and time). Other donor-specific data can be retained as well. Then when you need it, all this information can be called up on one screen.

Call-scheduling is tedious and time-consuming. But it is a simple task when you use a personal computer and file-management software that will list the prospects to be called and their priority, and record the date and time the call should be made.

With this information at hand, the operator merely goes to the data file and selects the prospects. Then all the operator has to do is press a key on the keyboard. An individual's record appears on the screen and the computer dials the number. When the party answers, the operator presses another key and a script comes up on a new screen. The operator moves through multiple script screens (up to eight) to respond to key questions or requests by the prospect. This process helps the volunteer deliver a smooth, professional presentation. At the conclusion of the conversation, the operator returns to the individual record screen, updates the record, and schedules a call-back if necessary. (Call-backs may be rescheduled immediately for no-answers, busies, and recording machines.) All pertinent information—pledges, address or phone number changes, and personal information— is immediately updated. The operator presses another key and the ATW becomes a word processor so a printer can begin to print out a letter or pledge card while the operator is already making another call.

The ATW eliminates time lag. It accomplishes four critical tasks. It is a database manager, a telephone, a script prompter, and a word processor. It maintains and updates files.

An operator plus ATW can do the work of three or four people and eliminates a vast amount of management and supervision time.

A key to ATW fundraising success: the script

Scriptwriting is the least understood and most important aspect of telemarketing. A professionally written script delivered by a trained operator will net the campaign thousands of extra dollars. Here's an example that shows the structure of an effective script.

Introduction
If you do not capture the prospect in the first fifteen seconds, your chances of success are substantially diminished.

Hello Mrs. Harmon,
I have a message that we think you, as an American, would think is important. The President needs your help to finish what he has begun. My name is David Boim and I am calling you to help President Reagan keep America a nation proud of its heritage and maintain its place in the world.
Do you think the President has put America back on the right path?

The question
This question serves as a transition to the text of the script. The text is a series of questions and statements with which a supporter or probable contributor to the President is likely to agree.

Well, the Democrats are trying to mount a serious challenge to what the President has accomplished.
Do you remember what inflation was under the previous Democratic administration?
The President has brought inflation under control.
Do you believe in a strong national defense?

The climax
Occurring before the conclusion, it leads to the close.

So does President Reagan. He has rebuilt the integrity of our armed forces. We think we need four more years of Ronald Reagan. Don't you, *Mrs. Harmon*?

The close
A direct statement asking for support, followed by specific requests or a series of "closing" efforts.

Last election you were able to help President Reagan's campaign effort. Can he count on your support again?
Can we count on you for $ _____?
Thank you, *Mrs. Harmon*. The President and all of us who support what he stands for appreciate your contribution. Let me confirm your address. We will send you a letter of thanks today.
©Telemarketing Systems, Inc.

This sample format for good scriptwriting has a tight introduction, allows the prospect to participate in the presentation and to feel a sense of ownership in it. Yet it leads the prospect to an inevitable conclusion. A good script incorporates these basic ingredients.

David S. Boim

Telecomputer systems

Telecomputer systems or "automatic dialers" will become invaluable tools in future elections. Their use is growing in many ways. For instance, they are being utilized by school districts for fighting absenteeism and by long-distance phone companies to audit their lines. These electronic marvels are voice-activated and can carry whatever message you wish to give the voter. And it allows them to respond. Telecomputer systems can aid in a registration campaign, recruit volunteers, seek campaign contributions, endorse a candidate, survey issues, and take polls three times faster than people at one-tenth the cost. Unlike any other form of communication media, telecomputers give you immediate feedback. These systems are easy to operate and only need an electrical outlet and modular telephone outlet to work.

If you are prey to an easy sale—beware. The telecomputer industry is new and is experiencing growing pains. For the most part the systems are marketed like Amway or Tupperware—that is, multilevel. There are hundreds of makeshift, unreliable systems on the market, sold by hundreds of individuals with little knowledge of computers or the marketing methods they support. There are only a handful of reliable and reputable systems and distributors out there.

Telecomputers come in three basic types: those that download, those that are stand-alones, and those that do both. The technology is rapidly changing, and lately more sophisticated and less expensive telecomputers are entering the market. All good telecomputers should be able to dial sequentially in targeted neighborhoods. The operator inputs a calling exchange (e.g., 225), a starting suffix (e.g., 0001) and an ending suffix (e.g., 9991). The operator may choose the sequence on some models (every tenth number, every fifth number, etc.). You choose the day(s) and time(s) you wish the calls to be made. Then you leave the telecomputer system to perform its task. It will turn itself on and turn itself off. Scientific random polltaking, messages about registration, and getting out the vote are accomplished at a minimum cost in a short period of time.

Campaign management can store specific lists. Some models can edit those lists. The telecomputer can call registered Democrats or Republicans with a special message from a party leader to endorse a candidate, take special polls, or get the vote out. You can solicit for volunteers and manage them by having your telecomputer remind them about assignments.

What to look for in a telecomputer set-up

1. Find a reputable distributor. This task is more important than price or system. If a dealer has made institutional sales to corporations or school districts and has good references from these institutions, that's important.
2. Purchase the best system available that meets your needs. Here is a partial list of important features
   - The ability to expand to multiple lines by purchasing additional "satellites" so that you won't have to buy telecomputer units to increase volume.
   - A reliable disconnect (hang-up) function.
   - The ability to dial from a file as well as sequentially.
   - A record-editing and word-processing capability.
   - Storage capacity—some units can store up to 50,000 numbers for a single dialing session.
   - An easy-to-learn keyboard.
   - Sensitivity controls.
   - The ability to generate a printout that logs calls; some units provide a multicolor printout that differentiates calling results.
   - Automatic insertion of MCI, Sprint, or other reduced-rate codes for long distance calls.
   - Flexible file maintenance functions.
   - Variable interval sequential dialing.
   - A variable voice activator.

FIGURE 14-1

The Core of a Campaign Telemarketing Center
Volume and Output per 8-Hour Day and 45-Hour Week
Six-Person Phone Bank • 1 Word Processor
• Three-Line Telecomputer • Two ATW Operators

Auto-dialer Telecomputer	Phone Bank								Automated Telephone Workstation	
Staff-1 person	Staff-7 people								Staff-2 people	
Manager	Word Processor	Phone Oper.	Phone Oper.	Phone Oper.	Phone Oper.	Phone Oper.	Phone Oper.		ATW Operator	ATW Operator
1,200 outgoing calls per day.	2,400 records inputted and 1,700 letters out per week	1,600 calls per day, 266 calls/operator per day.							750 contacts per day 375 contacts/operator per day	
One three-line system will make 7,200 outgoing calls per week and provide a hard copy of the results of each call made with totals. This output would require 5 people working at a phone bank.		A six-person traditional phone bank with a telephone logging system can process approximately 9,600 incoming and outgoing calls per week. A seventh person would handle wordprocessing.							Two ATW operators can contact 4,500 or more people per week, while performing data-entry, wordprocessing, call-scheduling and statistical functions at the same time.	
Eliminates the need to mail. Voter ID information, requests for voting and registration assistance, offers to volunteer, etc. could be recorded for approximately 6,000 contacts per week.		Data provided for approx. 9,600 people per week. 1,700 letters out per week per printer 5,900 records flagged per week for high-speed letter writing							Data entry for 4,500 records and letters to 4,500 per week	

Total Volume = 21,300 Contacts/week
Follow-up Letters Out = 6,200/week
Records Inputted = 6,900/week

PRIMARY CAMPAIGN USES OF EACH TELEMARKETING COMPONENT

SIX-PERSON PHONE BANK
To handle incoming calls:
- On issue positions
- For registration information
- To volunteer
- To contribute
- To ask for voting assistance
- To request and schedule candidate appearances
- Campaign inquiries

To make outgoing calls:
- For follow-up efforts
- For voter identification/to identify supporters
- For polling
- To handle ATW overflow and bolster high-volume calling efforts

TWO ATW STATIONS
Outgoing calls and follow-up letters for:
- Fundraising
- Voter identification
- Polling
- Management of vendors

THREE-LINE "AUTO-DIALER" TELECOMPUTER
Outgoing calls for:
- Registration drives
- Get-out-the-vote efforts
- Prospecting for volunteers
- Random sample and other types of polling
- Targeting message delivery
- Spreading the word about endorsements
- Coordinating efforts of staff and volunteers
- Voter feedback on key issues.

David S. Boim

- Attended or unattended operation capability.
- A programmable clock function.
- The ability to distinguish a recording from a live voice.

3. Once you have the right hardware and software, you need the right script. Scripts for a telecomputer operation are both directed and intimate. The tapes should be professionally done using a well-known or a professional voice. The following telecomputer script was used effectively to bolster a registration drive in Louisiana for a recent gubernatorial race.

Hello, I'm Jesse Jackson, talking to you via a recording made while in your city. By the way, can you hear me? [Responses to questions activate the recording to continue.]

Throughout the United States, we are registering black people to vote for our concern. A special effort is being conducted in New Orleans. Have you done your part? Are you a registered voter? That's important. Are all the members in your family registered? If you need registration assistance, please wait for the tone. Give us your name and telephone number [Tone]. We will contact you soon. If you are registered, please help us by making sure all of your friends and relatives are also registered. Please call us at 246-1938 or 246-1983 and give us a hand. Remember, you are somebody and your vote counts. There is a freedom train coming. When you register, you can ride [Tone].

Note that this highly successful script was recorded by a well-known personality who is immediately identified at the outset. Like the script for an operator at an ATW, it relies upon a series of questions to hold the attention of the party called, keep the party on the line, and prompt action. The voice of the person called activates the recording to proceed through its different segments reaching an emotional climax that minimizes resistance to an automated message. By targeting such recorded telephone messages to targeted audiences, your campaign can get results— a fact proved by the increase in black registration in Louisiana.

The Telemarketing Center

A Telemarketing Center utilizing the new phone technologies is the nucleus of a modern campaign headquarters. It is the hub through which a campaign can reach and involve large numbers of people. This center will bring needed centralization and organization to the most diffused (or confused) aspect of the campaign. It can have several automated workstations or telecomputers or a traditional phone center, or a combination of all three.

Computer hardware and software can be adapted to your operational needs. There are telephone systems for traditional telephone centers that will log calls, keep call statistics, even find the most cost-effective lines for long-distance calls. There are telephone modems that will dial numbers for you from most personal computers.

Keep in mind that your Telemarketing Campaign Center will be able to handle incoming as well as outgoing calls. All inquiries—from voter registration to volunteering to the vendors pounding at your door— can be easily incorporated into your center. You will need fewer volunteers, less space, and less money to run an effective campaign. This can be seen from the diagram showing what a *basic* telemarketing system can accomplish in a single week.

A fully integrated system like the one outlined there (utilizing the new telemarketing technologies and staffed by nine operators and one manager, working 45 hours per week) can contact and follow up calls to more than 85,000 people in one month. In a six-month campaign, a Telemarketing Center can process close to a half-million calls, providing a valuable database and targeting statistics.

A new campaign professional is emerging, one who understands the impact of telemarketing technology and is sculpting a new concept from it for political campaigns. This professional will be well-versed in the technologies of the future and will reshape the political campaign of today.

Geodemographics: The New Magic

Jonathan Robbin

The essential principle of political targeting was best expressed well over a century ago by Abraham Lincoln: "Find 'em and vote 'em." Just as Lincoln understood, the keys to victory in competitive races are to identify and locate as many of your supporters as possible and to get them to the polls on election day.

This simple idea is a monumental task in practice. No campaign—even the best funded—will have the resources to reach every citizen. Who should be eliminated from the campaign's effort to contact the electorate? Nonvoters and firm supporters of the opponent, obviously—but efficiently striking these individuals from the target list while retaining the candidate's supporters and the swing undecided (or "persuadable") voters is an elusive goal. In many states, the computerized tapes of registered voters can be bought and used for targeting, automatically restricting a campaign's contact to qualified voters. Determining which of this pool of registered people to concentrate on is far trickier. In making these judgments, campaigns usually rely on past precinct voting returns, current poll results, and the intuition of veteran party workers. These are helpful indicators, of course, but considerable inefficiency remains, and precious time, money, and volunteers are wasted contacting many unfriendly voters.

One new and advanced voter targeting methodology is described in this article by its developer, Jonathan Robbin. Robbin's Claritas Corporation has created forty separate "clusters" that together include all of America's tens of thousands of small geographic neighborhoods. Each cluster contains all the neighborhoods scattered across the United States that exhibit similar socioeconomic and demographic characteristics. This so-called geodemographic targeting can enable campaigns to determine (through random sample surveying of the political attitudes of each cluster) which neighborhoods are supportive, opposed, or undecided and which messages are most persuasive to each group. As the article following this one makes clear, Robbin's system has its critics, but his form of targeting is a fascinating one that deserves attention.

The essence of political campaigning is communication. A majority is built by repeatedly contacting voters and persuading them to register, turn out, and cast their ballot for the "right" candidate or side of an issue. Winning margins are not developed, however, by communicating at random. The campaign must bring to the polls the "favorable" portion of the electorate, while the opposing portion must neither be enlarged nor incited to vote the "wrong" way. The undecided portion must

Jonathan Robbin is Chairman of the Claritas Corporation, which he founded in 1971.

be convinced of the merit or benefit of voting the "right" way.

These precise objectives must be accomplished under the constraints imposed by limited resources of money, people, and time. The efficiency of a campaign depends on *accurate* delivery of *effective* communications. No resources should be squandered on convincing the convinced, attempting to convince the intransigently opposed, or trying to persuade the uncommitted with an inappropriate, irrelevant, or unimportant message. Each dollar spent on communication must have maximum positive and minimum negative impact to produce a win.

In the best of all possible worlds, the campaign would contact each voter one on one, face to face, and the following would take place:

1. The voter would identify for the campaign researcher his voting intentions as well as his particular combination of needs, demands, concerns, experiences, perceptions, convictions, loyalties, and attitudes toward the issues and candidates.

2. Next, the researcher would respond in appropriate political ways. He might secure a commitment to vote for his candidate. Or he might try to persuade the voter to support a candidate using compelling reasons consistent with the voter's most important individual interests or alignments.

In the real world, however, it is too costly to obtain this complete information about every voter. With limited resources, we can't even identify all our favorables, nor can we contact the entire electorate one on one.

Traditional approach to demographic targeting

Traditional targeting attacks the problem of effectively allocating communication resources through *aggregation* and *inference*.

First, rather than collecting complete information about each voter, a representative

---

Targeting, Clusters, and Politics

The Claritas Corporation's primary activities are to compile, analyze, interpret, and publish socioeconomic data, largely derived from the U.S. Census of Population and Housing, at the neighborhood level. The principal application of Claritas' resources, including databases, professional personnel, computer systems, and large-scale statistical models, has been the guidance of targeting decisions, i.e., the direction and evaluation of optional promotional investments when precise geographic concentration of effort is possible.

Over the last ten years, Claritas has been successfully creating action plans for major publishers such as TIME, Inc., and for numerous banks, insurance companies, communications media, advertising agencies, nonprofit and public-interest organizers, and government agencies.

A Claritas action plan is essentially developed along guidelines of determining "who" and "where." Claritas locates the optimum (lowest risk) small geographic areas **where** the people live **who** are most likely to respond to the message delivered in a positive or profitable way in the promoter's terms. The "who" part of the plan is determined when data showing certain outcomes, such as the purchase of a magazine or product, the donation of a contribution, or the stated preference for a political candidate, are correlated with the demographic characteristics of the buyer's, donor's, or voter's neighborhood. Hence the term "geodemographic targeting."

sample of voters is surveyed or polled and the results are aggregated. The proportions of voters who are pro, con, and undecided are summarized and related to a host of attitudes toward issues, perceptions of candidates, and demographic characteristics. If the poll is properly taken, it will fairly reflect the *aggregate* characteristics of the electorate for the entire geographic area surveyed (such as a state) or a few portions of it.

Second, data are collected (where available) to show certain aggregate characteristics of relatively small geographic areas such as precincts, wards, legislative districts, or counties. These characteristics primarily include:

- Registration statistics, including party membership.
- Electoral history of the region, showing the outcomes of recent elections and proportions participating.
- Census data, giving selected demographic characteristics of the populations residing in each small area.

Third, the traditional targeting process uses these two data sources *inferentially* and, for the most part, *one-dimensionally* to direct selective communications in an attempt to increase efficiency and effectiveness.

For example, a poll shows a candidate preference strongly tied to a party affiliation. The registration data identify the small areas with high proportions of the candidate's party members. A canvass is undertaken to register voters in these areas and a phone bank is organized to make calls to households listed on the targeted area streets to identify "favorables." A subsequent direct mail effort urges the favorables identified over the phone to get out and vote on Election Day.

This hypothetical selective communication effort ignores the opposition party and limits its contact efforts to the party voters because the poll showed a strong relationship in the aggregate between party affiliation and candidate preference. The *inference* was drawn

that the optimum use of campaign resources would be to make contacts based on the *single dimension* of party affiliation. The selection process sought compact populations of the desired type of voter by identifying small areas with high observed proportions of the same. Areas with low proportions were excluded.

This process also typically uses electoral history and census data in the same manner at a one- or two-dimensional level to apply poll results to target selective communications. For example, if the poll shows that persons voting for Candidate X in a past election lean toward favoring the current targeted candidate, areas of Candidate X's past majorities will be designated for concentrated efforts. The census data are generally used to identify concentrations of classical monolithic "blocs" or coalitions by age, race or ethnic status, occupation, and/or income.

Through a poll, an issue may be isolated that concerns blacks and that the candidate is "on the right side of." Direct mail, phone calls, or canvasses can then be directed to black wards as identified through the census data, and an appropriate message used to inform or persuade these potentially favorable voters. Similar efforts are made to reach wealthy, blue-collar, Irish, or elderly voters.

This technique of targeting is actually rudimentary "geodemographics." Data from a poll are tabulated to isolate the "favorable" or "persuadable" segments of the electorate in terms of certain simple, unidimensional demographics that can be observed through both the poll and census data at the level of a small geographic area. A message appropriate to each segment targeted is devised and delivered by selective means.

A key assumption underlying this traditional targeting is that the neighborhoods targeted on the basis of one demographic or electoral characteristic are homogeneous enough in others such that political attitudes are fairly well explained by that single demographic variable alone. However, in most real political situations, this assumption is rarely justified. Unidimensional geodemo-

Jonathan Robbin

graphic targeting, while headed in the right direction and *partly* explanatory or predictive, is weak compared to the more complete and realistic *multivariate* approach.

In other words, the standard demographic measures observed on most political polls cannot be combined by "crosstabulation" more than a few times before they are reduced to statistical noise. For example, if the poll has measured its respondents (numbering, say, 1,000) on five categories of income, ten categories of occupation, four categories of educational attainment, two of sex, two of race, and ten of age, the resultant possible combinations are $5 \times 10 \times 4 \times 2 \times 2 \times 10$ or 8,000, more than the total sample. The number of middle-income, skilled-laborer high school graduates who are male, white, and in their mid-thirties might appear either as a statistically insignificant and uninterpretable proportion, or might not appear at all in the extensive crosstabs needed to count such persons in the sample.

In traditional targeting, other important characteristics of the respondent such as home ownership, marital status and state in the family life cycle, years of residence, veteran status, ethnic background, history and direction of migration, etc., *cannot* be considered together with the aforementioned "demographics" to further refine the lifestyle variables associated on the poll with political attitudes. Thus they are rarely used for identifying geographically targetable concentrations of favorables or persuadables.

Thus, traditional targeting makes the essential linkage between current political attitudes and the characteristics of targetable aggregates by using only the shallowest of inferences. In most instances this results in only a faint intimation of the underlying facts. Such data may be misleading and result in misallocation of scarce campaign resources. Certainly, the *real* coalitions are not observed.

In their place, the targeter who uses traditional methods must substitute arbitrary caricatures defined by hackneyed custom. The voting public is sorted into one-dimensional pigeonholes such as "women," "blacks," "blue-collar," or "senior citizens." Communications are designed to suit these narrow segments. How useful are such crude categorizations in explaining the political orientation of individuals? Reviewing my own family, acquaintances, and colleagues, I find it difficult to make the big inferential leap on such sparse data. For example, my wife is a woman, white-collar, middle-aged, and of Italian extraction. Singly taken, none of these characteristics help me determine why she votes the way she does.

The task remains, then, of finding a way to fully measure the real and somewhat complex demographic determinants of political preferences and attitudes, and to discover the whereabouts of voters possessing the characteristics that are fully descriptive of these powerful mediators of voting behavior. The primary goal is to identify the persuadable voter in terms which, through the analysis of aggregate small-area census data, allow the targeter to find out *where* this persuadable voter lives for the purpose of selectively contacting him with the right message and through the right media. The answer to this crucial question is provided by *Cluster Geodemographics*.

The Cluster Geodemographics concept: natural human groupings

Humans group into natural areas where the resources—physical, economic, and social—are compatible with their needs. They create or *choose* established neighborhoods that conform to their lifestyle of the moment. The neighborhood or community can be viewed as the smallest unit of homogeneous population where adjacent households, and the individuals dwelling in them, make up a distinct social group that shares demographic and economic characteristics.

As people's lives change, they may move on to more accommodating surroundings. From 1975 to 1980, for instance, 47 million Americans made the economic and social decision to move. Mobility is typical of youth, and a large cohort of young people has contributed to the current trend of increased migration. As individuals grow older, they start families, rise in social status, settle down to a given occupation, move up through economic strata, and select their residences accordingly.

At each state in their life cycles, individuals join their peers in appropriate communities. In their twenties, they typically marry and choose relatively transient rental housing. In

---

Beyond the Census

The United States Decennial Census of Population and Housing is a definitive source of information about the American people and their neighborhoods and communities. Yet the researcher cannot directly use Census data to discover facts about individuals.

Individual data cannot be revealed by the Census Bureau or its personnel under penalty of law. In essence, the Census data are purposely adapted to aggregation and are released only as tabulated characteristics of geographically defined populations. These populations start as small as a city block and grow in size to include small collections of blocks (block groups or enumeration districts), areas combining block groups called tracts, wards, towns, cities, ZIP Codes, counties, legislative districts, states, metropolitan areas, regions made up of states, and finally the nation. For each of these populations, the Census counts distributions of a variety of attributes of persons, households, families, and the dwelling units housing them. Unlike an ad hoc questionnaire, however, the Census schedule is fixed in that Bureau professionals determine the items of information requested. Generally, these items satisfy the requirements for precise counts of political constituencies, measurement of the basic variables affecting population growth and decline, and supplying data to government agencies for planning and administrative purposes. However, Census data do not, nor will they probably ever, measure opinions, belief, religions, membership in political or fraternal associations, or attitudes and personal preferences on the part of the respondent.

For the most part, in spite of their limited purpose, the data collected by the Census measure a set of social expectations called statuses. Status reflects the place that an individual occupies In society by virtue of a number of personal attributes, either involuntarily possessed or acquired by chance or merit. Lifestyle is determined to a very large degree by these statuses and their social prerogatives. Level of affluence determines a level of expenditure and can indicate ideology and political heritage as well. Age, sex, marital and parental position, educational attainment, type of living quarters, property ownership, length of residence, occupation, industry of employment, and ethnic or racial background all mix to define the social expectations that configure a person's unique identity and guide his or her political behavior.

What happens, then, to these individual measures of social and economic status when they are added up into geographically defined population units? If the units are compact enough to define neighborhoods or small communities, patterns emerge that show remarkable homogeneity of status variables. The data show that the determinants and consequences of human grouping can be used to explain and predict individual behavior as it varies over different types of neighborhoods. The Claritas Cluster system uses this principle for creating estimates of neighborhood characteristics not measured by, but related to, the underlying Census data. Included among these characteristics are political variables key to winning elections.

---

their thirties, they buy homes suitable for raising small children. In their forties, they are launching teenagers into society, and in their fifties are settling down to increased community participation as their family responsibilities wane (there are proportionately more registered voters in this age group than any other). During their sixties and beyond, they seek out domiciles suited to leisure and retirement.

Simply speaking, a Cluster represents a number of small geographic areas containing populations that are homogeneous along a very substantial series of socioeconomic and demographic indicators. The mathematical technique of taxonomic analysis employed to sort these small areas into homogeneous groups also maximizes the differences between the groups. Claritas has assigned to Clusters the following small areas:

36,000 5-digit ZIP Codes

32,400 Census Tracts in Urbanized Areas

100,000 Sub-tract Census Block Groups in Urbanized Areas

142,000 Census Enumeration Districts in the Nonurbanized Balance of the United States.

The political applications of the Claritas Cluster system* generally use the Block Group/Enumeration District (BG/ED) model. The average size of the 242,000 BG/EDs is about 330 households or 890 persons each.

The Claritas Clusters show a vivid picture of American neighborhood lifestyles that will be immediately familiar to anyone who has taken a moment to observe his surroundings. Individuals, of course, change more rapidly than places. It requires a whole generation or more for a neighborhood to change its character. Areas do change, but over relatively long periods lasting twenty or thirty years. People move, but their houses stay put. The country can be considered a patchwork quilt of relatively stable neighborhoods or communities. New housing developments extend the borders of a neighborhood to create a larger enclave of similar style.

Census data describe the basic determinants of human groupings. Community differences can, therefore, be described parsimoniously by five basic sets of variables that measure the grouping phenomenon, called the domains of social structure. They are:

Social Class—the usual measures of affluence, prestige, and influence.

Housing Style—measures of urbanization, including type and density of housing.

Ethnicity and Race—measures that show concentration of black, white, and Spanish–American populations, as well as composition of foreign stock by country of origin.

Family Life Cycle—measures of age and family relationship.

Mobility—measures of the frequency, recency, distance, and direction of migration.

In order to identify these basic factors, Claritas performed an extensive multivariate analysis of its complete United States file of population and housing data at a small-area level. Five hundred-thirty-five variables for each small area were factor analyzed and reduced to composite measures. The resulting thirty-four uncorrelated factor scores explain over eighty-seven percent of the variance between areas (see Figure 1). We then sought to group similar communities, relating each area to every other one according to its profile of factor measurements. Claritas isolated forty distinctive types of American communities through a quantitative taxonomic cluster analysis of the factor scores for all small areas. The resulting forty Claritas Clusters describe the range of different community lifestyles encountered in the country. While certain Clusters or types occur more often in specific regions, generally each type can be found in all parts of the country.

Claritas Cluster Groups

Each Cluster Group is identified by a *Group Code* and a *Title*. Group Codes denote basic

---

*Registered trademark of Claritas Corporation.

neighborhood types, as seen below (the code letter is derived from the first letter of the last word in the description):

Metropolitan
U1–U3 (Center-City Urban)
S1–S3 (Fringe-Suburban)

Non-Metropolitan
T1 & T2 (Minor Cities & Towns)
R1 & R2 (Farm & Other Rural)

The forty Claritas Clusters are distributed across ten Cluster Groups (see Table 1).

Group Titles provide brief, thumbnail characterizations for Clusters within Groups. Each Claritas Cluster is identified by a *Cluster Number* (randomly assigned by computer during the creation of the clusters), a *Nickname* (designed to capture the essence of a cluster and trigger recollection), and a *One-Liner* (offering nine key demographic highlights, abbreviated for computer printouts). In addition, each cluster is given a "zip quality" score (ZQ), a weighted composite of education and affluence variables that permits clusters to be ranked and grouped according to recognized socioeconomic levels.

In any complex segmentation system, there will be a few stand-out examples that can serve to illustrate the entire system. Claritas calls them the *Exemplar Clusters*, of which there are eight (see Table 2).

These exemplars display every important demographic characteristic of America and run

FIGURE 1

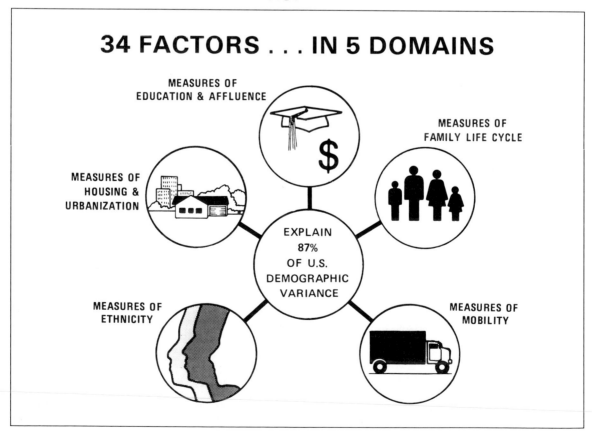

Jonathan Robbin

TABLE 1   Claritas Cluster Distribution

Cluster Groups	Within Groups		By Socioeconomic Levels			
	# Clusters	% US Households	Upper	Up-Mid	Lo-Mid	Lower
S1–S3 (Fringe Suburban)	10	27	7	2	1	—
U1–U3 (Central City Urban)	13	26	1	5	5	2
T1&T2 (Minor Cities and Towns)	9	29	—	2	6	1
R1&R2 (Farm and Other Rural)	8	18	—	—	2	6
TOTALS	40		8	9	14	9
% U.S. Households		100%	18%	28%	33%	21%

the full range, from near top to near bottom, on most of the index scales in the Claritas data base (see Figures 3–11—immediately following the text of this article—for a graphic representation and other demographic data on Clusters 1, 23, and 37).

The advantage of classifying neighborhoods is the great economy of scale possible in a model that achieves maximum explanatory power. The political researcher need not measure and search through hundreds of variables at large expense to discover the underlying combinations most predictive of demographic variance in a dependent variable such as voting preference. The Claritas Cluster model immediately explains most of that demographic variance directly.

Using this tool, we can approximate the

TABLE 2   Examples of Claritas Clusters (The "Exemplar Clusters")

Cluster No's	Nicknames
1	GOD'S COUNTRY
3	OLD MELTING POT
11	DIXIE-STYLE TENEMENTS
23	BUNKER'S NEIGHBORS
28	BLUE BLOOD ESTATES
29	COALBURG & CORNTOWN
37	BOHEMIAN MIX
38	SHARE CROPPERS

optimum efficiency of one-on-one communication. This breakthrough is made possible by the fact that the Claritas Cluster system is a sophisticated *multivariate* analysis of *all* underlying demographic voter identification variables.

Multivariate targeting: a new dimension

To take a *multivariate* approach means to consider simultaneously many variables in a single analysis. As noted above, the traditionally performed targeting process is severely limited in accuracy and meaningful application because small sample poll data are used to simultaneously consider only a few variables at most. In general, the more information that is brought to bear in any empirical explanatory model, the better the results. This is certainly the case in relating demographics to voting behavior.

Our approach to solving the problem of sparse demographic data in polls was simply to create a much more powerful *multivariate* explanatory demographic model through exhaustive analysis of the base data itself, i.e., the entire summary file of the United States Census of Population and Housing, at a small-area level.

Our data base gives us a cross reference to the Claritas Cluster neighborhood type for each of 242,000 Block Group/Enumeration Districts, or 36,000 ZIPs. A Cluster code is then attributed to individual poll respondents merely by using his/her address to identify the surrounding small geographic unit in which he/she resides. This information is then tabulated against the poll items that measure ideology, opinions, and perceptions of issues and candidates. The result is a set of robust relationships of neighborhood type to political attitudes that identify the "right" kind of *neighborhoods* for selective targeting. From Claritas files, small areas with the same Cluster classifications can be selected for repeated contact by phone, mail, or canvass. Knowing the Cluster composition of mass media

audiences, Claritas can evaluate these on an index of "right" to "wrong."

Cluster decisions translate directly into action. These actions are better informed than traditionally targeted efforts and correlate better not only with observed poll findings but also with actual election results. Certainly the vast scope of data analyzed—535 Census-derived neighborhood characteristics for each of more than 250,000 small geographic areas— is a primary reason for this increased accuracy.

The Cluster model's high efficiency even allows us to generalize the survey results geographically, projecting average behavior in each Cluster as observed in a sample to all clustered areas throughout the country.

Consequently, an area in which a political campaign is being undertaken, such as a single state, can be polled by a sample of about 1,000 to 1,500 voters and the results extrapolated through the Cluster system such that small component areas of the state will appear to have been completely polled. Accurate estimates of the proportions of voters who are pro, con, or undecided on candidate preference or attitudes toward issues can be made for all wards, precincts, legislative or congressional districts, counties, cities, townships, or media markets such as Arbitron's ADIs (areas of dominant influence) or Nielsen's DMAs (designated market areas). As a result, direct messages by mail, phone, and personal contact can be disseminated with a high degree of selectivity hitherto unknown.

Practicing the new magic

The communication targeting application of the Claritas Cluster system has actually been put to the test in several campaigns with excellent results.

The first such trial was undertaken for the United Labor Committee of Missouri in support of a campaign to defeat a right-to-work initiative on the ballot in that state in November 1978. The Committee represented the major units of the labor movement in

Jonathan Robbin

Missouri: the AFL-CIO, United Auto Workers, Teamsters, United Mine Workers, and various independent unions. Claritas was retained to perform the geodemographic targeting task as part of a team under the general direction of Matt Reese and Associates of Washington, D.C., which included Hamilton and Staff, a polling organization also in Washington. The Matt Reese organization designed and directed the voter contact systems and organized the campaign.

Early polls (July 1978) showed the right-to-work initiative passing by a sixty percent to forty percent margin. After labor's efforts using Reese-Claritas-Hamilton, the voters defeated the amendments by fifty-nine percent "no" to forty-one percent "yes."

During our efforts in Missouri, Claritas did the following:

1. A pre-geocoded list of 1,467,823 telephone households was obtained from the Metro-Mail organization.
2. Cluster codes were put in the computer and attached to each name and address according to its location in any of the 6,104 individually Cluster-typed BG/EDs in Missouri.
3. In a number of areas, lists of registered voters were matched/merged with the Clustered telephone file.
4. A random probability sample of phone names was drawn for polling such that each Cluster and specified regions of the state were adequately represented.
5. Polls were tabulated by Cluster.
6. Data were analyzed to isolate favorable and persuadable Clusters and to determine which issues and attitudes were to be dealt with in the messages delivered to voters inhabiting each Cluster group.
7. Phone bank call sheets were prepared for selected groups of Clusters containing predominantly favorables and persuadables, and 536,000 calls were made for voter identification and persuasion, and volunteer and block captain recruitment.

8. Nine message/Cluster groups were keyed in the file and, after the addition of voter identification data, eighteen different letter formats were developed and mailed to the keyed list.
9. Cluster composition of targeted areas (counties, wards, and precincts) were calculated for each one.
10. The poll was projected to these small areas, and maps were drawn showing areas of strength and weakness.
11. An index of attitude toward right-to-work was projected into television markets (DMAs) for rating their value as targets.
12. Using previously calculated Cluster profiles of the audiences of selected television shows (data derived from Simmons Market Research Bureau studies), the poll was projected by weighted Cluster proportions into estimates for each show.
13. A master file of telephone names was merged with codes designating voters' positions, and a "message group" determined by the Cluster was assigned to the voters' neighborhood. This file was then used to generate "palm" cards, poll-watcher cards, and a variety of statistical analyses for both strategic and tactical use.

Did it work? An empirical verification of the projection technique can be made by contrasting Claritas' estimates to the actual vote at the county level. Each county estimate was built up by weighting the proportions of population living in each Cluster in the county by the proportions of voters within each Cluster who favored, opposed, or were undecided about the passage of a right-to-work law, as observed on the September statewide poll. Within each county the "undecideds" were then split to the "opposed" category in the same ratio as "oppose" was to "favor."

The accuracy of this estimate is made evident by the strong correlation of the estimate to the actual results of the voting in November (see Figure 2). The actual "no" vote correlates

FIGURE 2

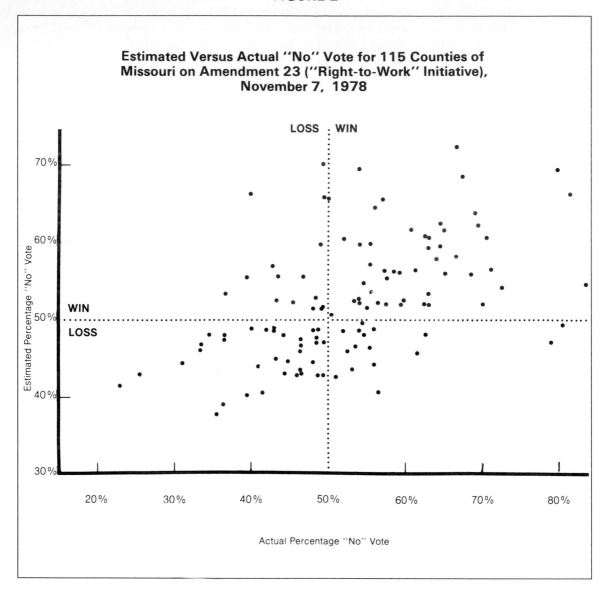

Estimated Versus Actual "No" Vote for 115 Counties of Missouri on Amendment 23 ("Right-to-Work" Initiative), November 7, 1978

0.628 (Pearson-r) with our estimates. We can also note that the counties estimated to vote over fifty percent "no" which actually did, plus the counties estimated to vote over fifty percent "yes" which actually did, sum to 83 out of 115, or a "hit" rate of seventy-two percent correct estimates. The political potential of geodemographic targeting is clearly great. Missouri is only the beginning.

FIGURE 3

EXEMPLAR CLUSTER NO. 1

NICKNAME:
GOD'S COUNTRY

A HIGHLIGHT:
REGIONAL PATTERNS

DISTRIBUTION OF
HOUSEHOLDS BY
CENSUS REGION
CLUSTER 1

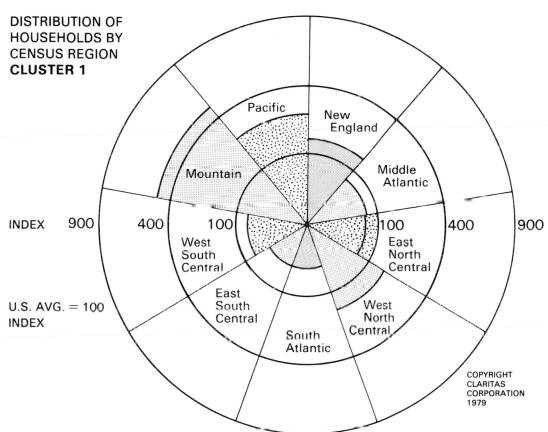

INDEX   900   400   100   100   400   900

U.S. AVG. = 100
INDEX

COPYRIGHT
CLARITAS
CORPORATION
1979

DESCRIPTION

Cluster 1 contains the most affluent communities that are located outside of major metropolitan areas. It also contains communities on the far edges of the country's major metropolitan areas.

Cluster 1 residents are primarily well-educated, well-paid persons of dominant English extraction in white-collar occupations. Minority ethnic presence is negligible.

Most significantly, Cluster 1 shows a marked skew towards America's most beautiful and sparsely populated mountain and coastal regions, hence the nickname "God's Country."

Cluster 1 is especially concentrated in such sparse western market areas as Billings, Boise, Butte, Casper, Cheyenne, Colorado Springs, Fargo, Idaho Falls, Missoula, Odessa-Midlands, and Yakima (see DMA map).

Reflecting the new American ethic of "quality" in lifestyle, Cluster 1 has led the nation in short-term population growth.

FIGURE 4

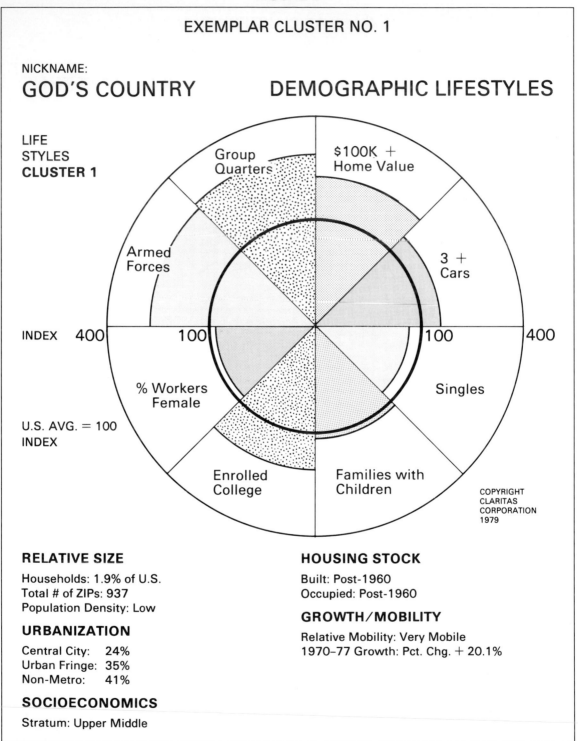

EXEMPLAR CLUSTER NO. 1

NICKNAME:
GOD'S COUNTRY

DEMOGRAPHIC LIFESTYLES

LIFE
STYLES
CLUSTER 1

Group
Quarters

$100K +
Home Value

Armed
Forces

3 +
Cars

INDEX   400   100   100   400

% Workers
Female

Singles

U.S. AVG. = 100
INDEX

Enrolled
College

Families with
Children

COPYRIGHT
CLARITAS
CORPORATION
1979

RELATIVE SIZE

Households: 1.9% of U.S.
Total # of ZIPs: 937
Population Density: Low

URBANIZATION

Central City: 24%
Urban Fringe: 35%
Non-Metro: 41%

SOCIOECONOMICS

Stratum: Upper Middle

HOUSING STOCK

Built: Post-1960
Occupied: Post-1960

GROWTH/MOBILITY

Relative Mobility: Very Mobile
1970–77 Growth: Pct. Chg. + 20.1%

Jonathan Robbin

FIGURE 5

RELATIVE CONCENTRATION OF CLUSTER 1 HOUSEHOLDS

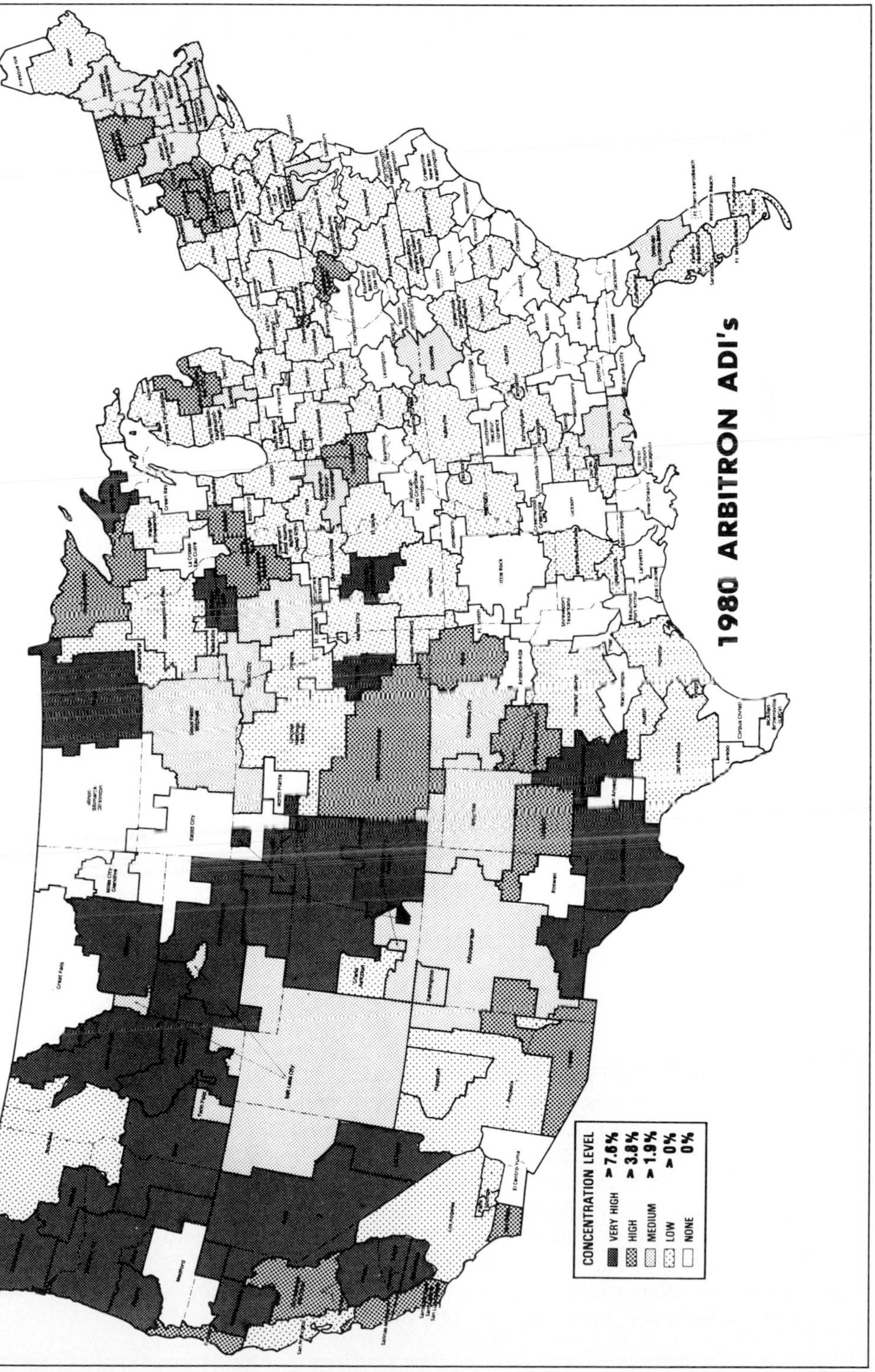

1980 ARBITRON ADI's

CONCENTRATION LEVEL

VERY HIGH	> 7.6%
HIGH	> 3.8%
MEDIUM	> 1.9%
LOW	> 0%
NONE	0%

FIGURE 6

EXEMPLAR CLUSTER NO. 23

NICKNAME:

ARCHIE BUNKER'S NEIGHBORS

A HIGHLIGHT:

OCCUPATIONS

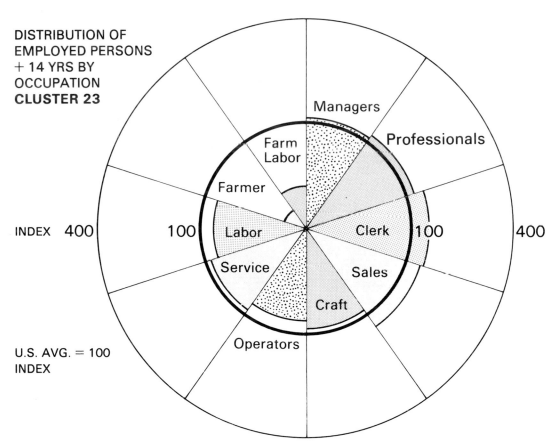

DISTRIBUTION OF
EMPLOYED PERSONS
+ 14 YRS BY
OCCUPATION
CLUSTER 23

INDEX 400   100   100   400

U.S. AVG. = 100
INDEX

Managers
Professionals
Farm Labor
Farmer
Labor
Clerk
Service
Sales
Craft
Operators

DESCRIPTION

Cluster 23 is a mix of urban, middle-class, backyard, row and apartment/house neighborhoods. It is seventh in concentration of persons of foreign stock (Irish, Russians, Italians, etc.).

It is our second largest Cluster (5.1% U.S. Households) and is found in 10–20% concentrations in such megamarkets as New York (Bayshore, Flushing, Yonkers, etc.), Miami (Tamiami, No. Miami Beach, etc.), Chicago (Elgin, Forest Park, Waukeegan, etc.), Los Angeles (Culver City, Glendale, Whittier, etc.), and San Francisco (Alameda, Daly City, Vallejo,etc.).

Cluster 23 often borders urban-fringe industrial parks, and residents are employed in well-paid, second echelon management and technical, as well as skilled blue-collar jobs. They are mobile, and the Cluster has shown no growth since 1970.

We have confidently placed Archie Bunker in a Cluster 23 ZIP in Queens and have honored him accordingly, but as to the address, our lips are sealed.

FIGURE 7

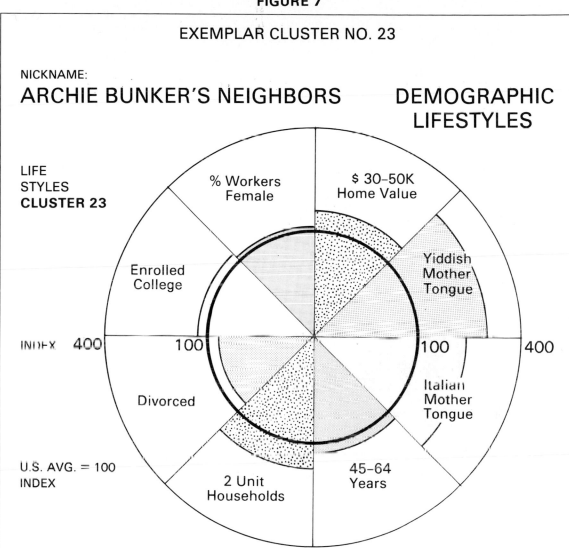

EXEMPLAR CLUSTER NO. 23

NICKNAME:

ARCHIE BUNKER'S NEIGHBORS

DEMOGRAPHIC LIFESTYLES

LIFE
STYLES
CLUSTER 23

% Workers Female

$ 30–50K Home Value

Enrolled College

Yiddish Mother Tongue

INDEX 400   100   100   400

Divorced

Italian Mother Tongue

U.S. AVG. = 100
INDEX

2 Unit Households

45–64 Years

RELATIVE SIZE

Households: 5.2% of U.S.
Total # of ZIPs: 313
Population Density: High

URBANIZATION

Central City: 56%
Urban Fringe: 39%
Non-Metro: 5%

SOCIOECONOMICS

Stratum: Upper Middle

HOUSING STOCK

Occupied By: Renters
Built: 1940–1959

GROWTH/MOBILITY

Relative Mobility: Mobile
1970–77 Growth: Pct. Chg. -0.2%

FIGURE 8

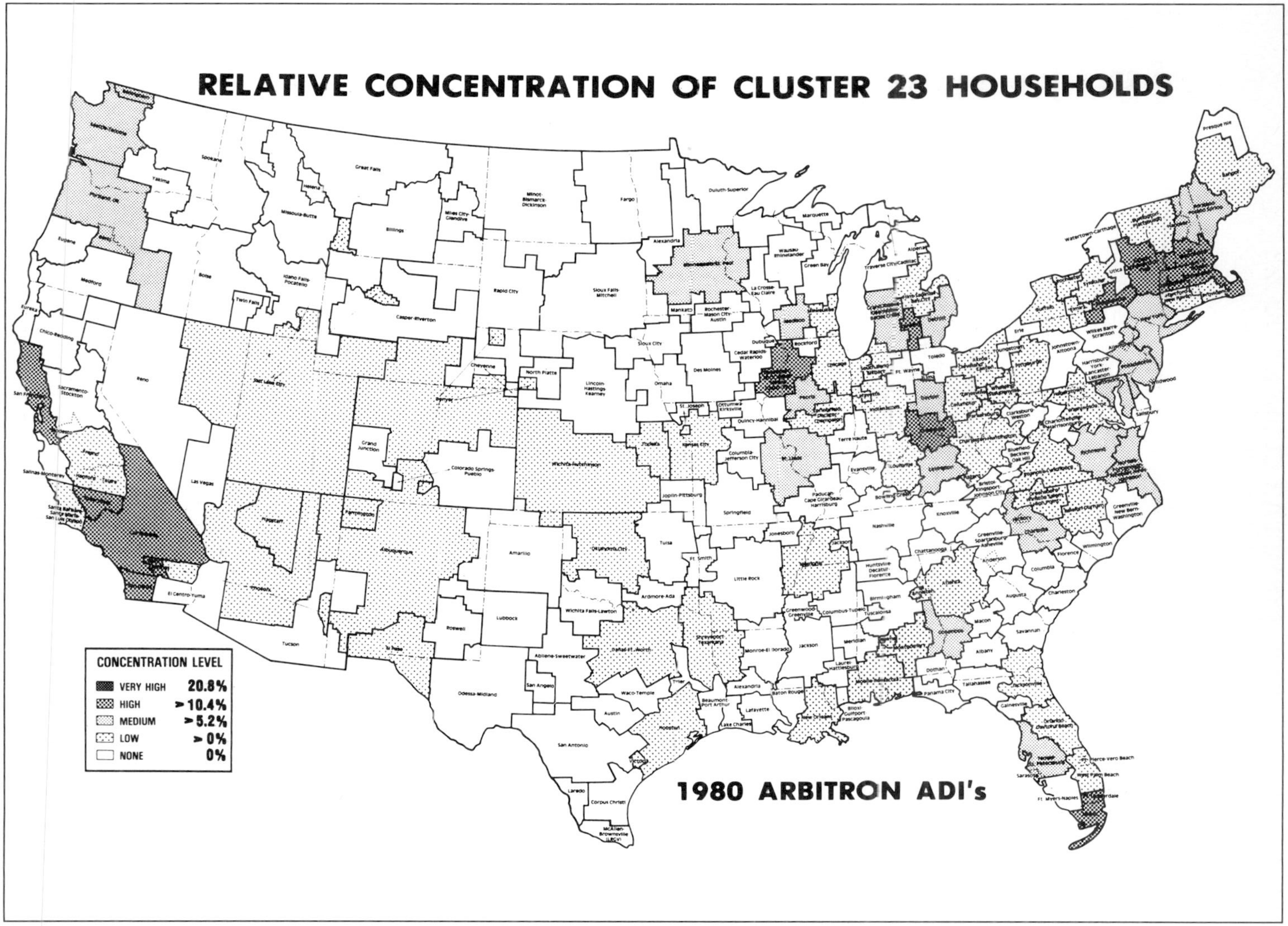

RELATIVE CONCENTRATION OF CLUSTER 23 HOUSEHOLDS

1980 ARBITRON ADI's

CONCENTRATION LEVEL	
VERY HIGH	20.8%
HIGH	>10.4%
MEDIUM	>5.2%
LOW	>0%
NONE	0%

Jonathan Robbin

FIGURE 9

EXEMPLAR CLUSTER NO. 37

NICKNAME:
BOHEMIAN MIX

A HIGHLIGHT:
HOUSING STOCK

DISTRIBUTION OF
HOUSEHOLDS BY
HOUSING TYPE
CLUSTER 37

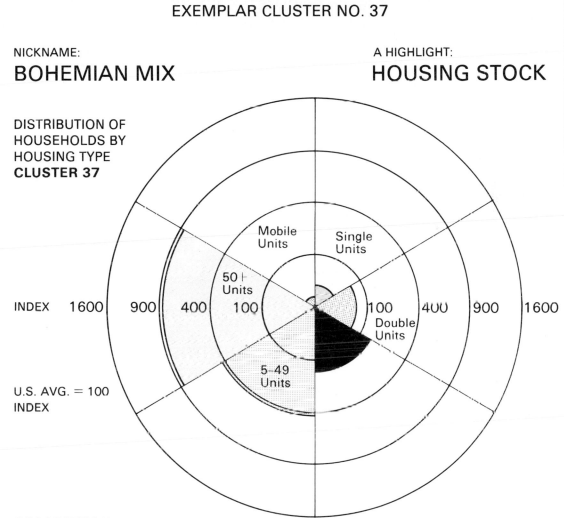

INDEX 1600 900 400 100   100 400 900 1600

U.S. AVG. = 100
INDEX

DESCRIPTION

Cluster 37 is clearly the closest America has come to a true "Bohemian" lifestyle. Cluster 37 is marked by well-educated, young adults with few children. These neighborhoods are frequently adjacent to center-city universities and show a correspondingly high college enrollment. Single renters predominate in 50+ unit, high-rise buildings.

Cluster 37 has a high concentration of people in the entertainment field and the graphic and communications arts, as well as students and educators. They also include mixed, downscale minorities, including the elderly (age 65+).

Cluster 37 neighborhoods are quite famous, including Old Town and Hyde Park in Chicago; Greenwich Village and Chelsea in New York; DuPont Circle and Capitol Hill in Washington, D.C.; Russian Hill and Haight-Ashbury in San Francisco.

Not even their notoriety, however, has been able to prevent some deterioration, and a corresponding 6% population loss in the 1970s.

FIGURE 10

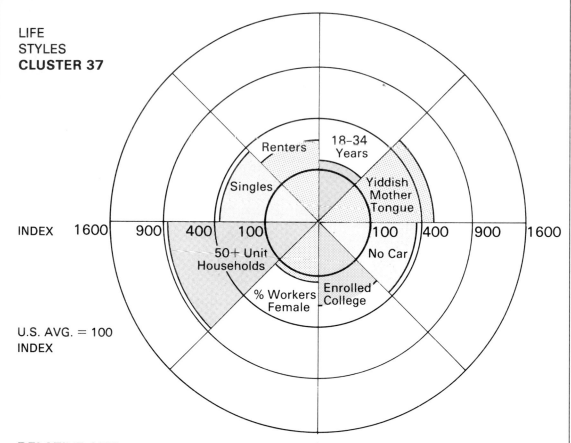

EXEMPLAR CLUSTER NO. 37

NICKNAME:

BOHEMIAN MIX

DEMOGRAPHIC LIFESTYLES

LIFE
STYLES
CLUSTER 37

Renters

18–34
Years

Singles

Yiddish
Mother
Tongue

INDEX   1600   900   400   100   100   400   900   1600

50+ Unit
Households

No Car

% Workers
Female

Enrolled
College

U.S. AVG. = 100
INDEX

RELATIVE SIZE

Households: 1.0% of U.S.
Total # of ZIPs: 46
Population Density: Very High

URBANIZATION

Central City: 94%
Urban Fringe: 6%
Non-Metro: 0%

SOCIOECONOMICS

Stratum: Upper Middle

HOUSING STOCK

Occupied By: Renters
Built: Pre-WWII
Occupied: Post-1970

GROWTH/MOBILITY

Relative Mobility: Very Mobile
1970–77 Growth: Pct. Chg. -6.0%

Jonathan Robbin

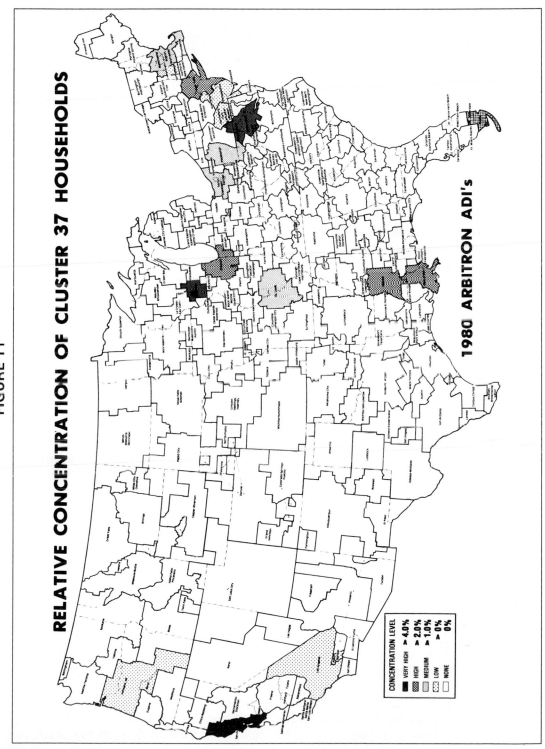

FIGURE 11

RELATIVE CONCENTRATION OF CLUSTER 37 HOUSEHOLDS

1980 ARBITRON ADI's

CONCENTRATION LEVEL

VERY HIGH ≥ 4.0%
HIGH   ≥ 2.0%
MEDIUM   ≥ 1.0%
LOW   > 0%
NONE   0%

Gambling with Elections:
The Problems of Geodemographics

Mark Atlas

The introductory essay in this volume asked whether the new campaign technology is "magic . . . or blue smoke and mirrors?" The previous article by Jonathan Robbin proclaimed the Claritas Clusters targeting system to be "the new magic." This article by Mark Atlas presents a very different perspective on Robbin's creation. Atlas critically evaluates the application of the Cluster system of geodemographics to political campaigns. Using the criteria and data supplied by Claritas, the author concludes that the claims made about the system's performance in a 1978 election in Missouri are unsubstantiated. The system was touted for its ability to turn a seemingly lost election into a victory and accurately to project what the final election results would be in each Missouri county. A reanalysis of the data suggests, however, that neither assertion is correct. The article also points out serious problems with the system's data collection procedures and potential difficulties with the quantitative technique used to process the data.

There is an old saying among the managers of Las Vegas casinos: "We welcome all gamblers coming to our casinos, but for gamblers with a 'system' we'll send them a free plane." Just as prospective gamblers may lunge too eagerly at "systems" that appear to offer the magic solution to their problems but that are in reality only sophisticated methods for losing their funds, so too political campaigners may grasp purported "revolutionary" improvements in campaign technologies too quickly for their own good. While no research methodology attempting to analyze political attitudes and behaviors can be perfect, it is crucial for the research supplier and the

client-candidate to be aware of the limitations of any technology used. Such an awareness can ensure the safe interpretation of any resulting data and enhance its usefulness in decision-making.

The purpose of this article is to examine the application of the Claritas Cluster system of geodemographics to political campaigns. After providing a brief description of the operation of the system, this analysis will follow the Claritas presentation through its major intellectual components, starting with an evaluation of the empirical evidence offered to verify the system's "magical" effect on a 1978 election, next considering the gathering and manipulation of the system's data inputs, and concluding with a discussion of the methodological underpinnings of the system.

Mark Atlas is a lawyer and researcher who has served on the staffs of several political campaigns.

As will be shown, the methodology underlying the system seems plausible enough to warrant further research to assess the procedure's validity. However, the methods for collecting and processing the data used, at least with respect to the 1978 "test" election, resulted in unreliable analyses. Furthermore, the figures provided allegedly proving the system's effectiveness actually show something quite different.

Overview of the Claritas Cluster system

A brief recap of the relevant parts of the system's structure and operation is in order. The system uses U.S. Census data as its initial information base. These data come aggregated into about 250,000 geographic units (called Block Groups/Enumeration Districts, or BG/EDs), each containing data on about 900 persons. Using factor analysis, a quantitative technique that combines a large number of individual variables into a smaller number of groups of those variables for easier analysis, 535 Census variables measuring the demographic characteristics of the people within each of the BG/EDs are divided into thirty-four groups (or factors) of composite variables. Then, using cluster analysis, a quantitative procedure that divides a large number of individual items (in this case, BG/EDs) into a smaller number of fairly homogeneous groups of those items, the 250,000 BG/EDs are divided into forty groups (or Clusters). Each BG/ED is mathematically assigned to a particular Cluster on the basis of that BG/ED's numerical values for the variables in the thirty-four factors previously generated. The end result, then, is that within each Cluster are Census geographic units from across the country in which people with similar demographic characteristics reside.

Therefore, on the basis of distinct demographic profiles, each of these Clusters could be thought of as containing neighborhoods in different parts of the United States wherein residents have unique demographic characteristics and—according to Claritas' theory—

a unique lifestyle, set of attitudes, and so on. Furthermore, every person in the country is assigned to a Cluster, by determining which BG/ED he/she resides in (by simply finding the person's address on a map of all BG/EDs) and then to which specific Cluster that that particular BG/ED has been assigned as a result of the original cluster analysis. Thus, a user could select a particular state, county, or electoral precinct and determine what general types of people inhabit it by analyzing the Cluster composition of the area (i.e., what proportion of the population in the area is in BG/EDs included in Cluster 1, in Cluster 2, etc.).

A major purported benefit of this process is that one could do a sample survey of people in a state (or nation) and then project the results of this statewide survey down to smaller geographic areas within the state. To do this one must assume that the *universe* of people actually residing in BG/EDs assigned to a particular Cluster would have responded identically to the survey questions as the *sample* of people who were actually interviewed during the survey. Thus, if a statewide survey showed that of those people actually interviewed who resided in BG/EDs assigned to Cluster 1 (assigned by the original cluster analysis done on all of the BG/EDs in the U.S.), 60 percent favored a particular ballot proposition, a BG/ED anywhere in the state assigned to Cluster 1 would be assumed to contain residents of whom 60 percent favored the proposition. Therefore, to project a statewide survey's results to a county, for example, one would first divide all of the statewide survey respondents into their respective Clusters, by using their addresses to locate the BG/EDs in which they reside and then determining the Clusters to which those BG/EDs are assigned. Next, one would calculate the overall response to each survey question within each Cluster, by simply cumulating the answers of all of the respondents who are members of a particular Cluster. Then one would merely assign each separate Cluster's sample survey responses to any of the Cluster's BG/EDs within that county. Finally, one would add up the resulting figures for each of the county's BG/EDs (weighting each BG/ED's responses by its proportion of the county's population) to derive the overall county total. This procedure could then be followed anytime when one wished to project survey results from larger geographic areas to smaller ones.

Obviously, any procedure that can accurately generate numbers detailing the opinions of small groups of people in relatively minute geographic areas by simply using a statewide survey, rather than accumulating a statistically acceptable sample from each area, has enormous potential. This is the potential that the Claritas Cluster system claims to tap, enabling campaigns to pinpoint very small population areas that, on the basis of *projected* survey results, seem receptive to campaign appeals. By clustering and projecting, one could allegedly pinpoint small areas where, for example, voters are less aware of the candidate's existence, where the candidate has only lukewarm support, or where a particular issue position could be exploited for votes— all of which after interviewing people from different parts of the state but not necessarily anyone in the particular geographic areas selected for targeting.

The ultimate question, of course, is whether the system as implemented actually delivers its promised benefits. Most of the empirical evidence Claritas offers to prove the system's effectiveness is from the 1978 election battle in Missouri over a right-to-work ballot proposition. To briefly summarize Claritas' stated role in that campaign, the company was brought in by Matt Reese & Associates, a political campaign management firm, to attempt to target on a very selective basis the geographic areas where there were voters who were susceptible to appeals to vote against the right-to-work proposition. A statewide survey was thereafter completed in September 1978 and questions regarding voters' stand on the ballot issue were then projected from the statewide survey down to Missouri's BG/EDs,

in the manner described earlier. These projected numbers were then used to pinpoint areas containing voters worthy of intensive contact, and subsequently direct-mail and telephone and door-to-door canvassing were used to try to persuade those people to vote against the proposition.

Evaluating Claritas' effectiveness: impact on the election

One of the two general criteria that Claritas used to assess the effectiveness of its system in Missouri in 1978 was the system's impact on the election results. This impact was supposedly shown by a comparison between the statewide percentage of voters opposing the ballot issue before the Cluster system's use in the campaign and the final election results after its use. Claritas claims that this comparison proves the system's powerful effect on the election since surveys in February and July of 1978 showed the ballot issue winning by about 60 percent to 40 percent, while the final election results had the proposition losing 59 percent to 41 percent. Claritas claims this "stunning turnaround" was at least partly its doing.

By examining Claritas' own data it is clear that, far from turning around the election, the system at best merely helped stabilize the status quo. Regardless of what earlier surveys indicated, the September 1978 survey shows that the right-to-work proposition was *already behind* by about 56 percent to 44 percent— nearly the margin by which it eventually lost in November. The clearest proof of the advantageous position of the anti-right-to-work forces is provided by Exhibit 1, a table reproduced from a sales document. That table displays what the attitude toward right-to-work was within some of the Clusters and, most importantly, the overall statewide situation according to the September 1978 survey. As the table's first column shows, 40 percent of the sample *opposed* the ballot issue (27 percent strongly plus 13 percent moderately), 29 percent were mixed, and 32 percent favored it (22 percent strongly plus 10 percent moderately)—far from the three to two margin *in favor* Claritas claimed existed before its system's use. In fact, if we then divide the 29 percent mixed in the same proportion as the opposed (40 percent) is to the favored (32 percent), the method used by Claritas in all of its predictions, the proposition loses 56 percent to 44 percent—strikingly similar to the final election result of 59 percent to 41 percent.

Another indicator of the strength of the early *opposition* to the ballot issue is provided in Exhibit 2, a graph reproduced from a Claritas sales document. The graph, again based on September 1978 survey data, plots each of the forty Claritas Clusters according to the percentage of the respondents in the Cluster that was opposed to the proposition (vertical axis) and the percentage that had mixed feelings about it (horizontal axis). Thus, for example, Cluster 29 is located at the intersection of 56 percent and 30 percent—56 percent of the respondents in this Cluster opposed the ballot issue, while 30 percent were mixed. Obviously, by subtracting each Clust-

er's percentages of opposed and mixed from 100 percent, the remaining portion is the percentage of each Cluster's respondents that favored the proposition. By carrying out this calculation for each of the Clusters, one can determine in how many Clusters and by what margins the forces opposed to right-to-work were ahead. The heavy line superimposed on the graph by the author (originating at the 50 percent point on the vertical axis and extending downward) serves as a dividing line showing each Cluster's overall position on the proposition—Clusters located above the line contain at least a plurality opposing the ballot issue, while Clusters below the line favor the ballot issue. Thus, as can be seen, right-to-work was *opposed* by voters in at least twenty-eight Clusters and favored by voters in only at most twelve Clusters, even before the system's "new magic" went to work.

Thus, the empirical evidence offered by Claritas does not support its claim of providing a "stunning advantage" to its users in Missouri; at best, it merely avoided squandering a substantial lead. Comparing the final election results to surveys done early in 1978 rather

EXHIBIT 1 Poll Results on Right-to-Work Attitude by Cluster

	State-wide	Cluster 24	Cluster 25	Cluster 26	Cluster 27	Cluster 28	Cluster 29	Cluster 30
Total Sample Size	1,367	66	24	24	56	24	28	104
Attitude on Right-to-Work Issue (Percent)								
Strongly Oppose	27	33	53	52	33	9	52	40
Moderately Oppose	13	10	9	11	11	21	4	7
Mixed	29	29	19	23	24	25	30	24
Moderately Favor	10	7	9	5	3	21	2	9
Strongly Favor	22	21	10	8	30	25	12	19
Pro-Union	23	24	46	46	23	6	58	31
Anti-Union	16	15	10	4	14	26	8	19

The anti-right-to-work people selected Clusters 25, 26, and 29 targets. The Cluster system then provided the campaign with the names, addresses, and phone numbers of people living in those Clusters. As a result, when the campaign contacted these people, they reached households that had respectively an 81 percent, 87 percent, and 86 percent likelihood of not being in favor of right-to-work.

**EXHIBIT 2   Targeting Chart of Attitude toward
Right-to-Work, Missouri, 1978, by Cluster***

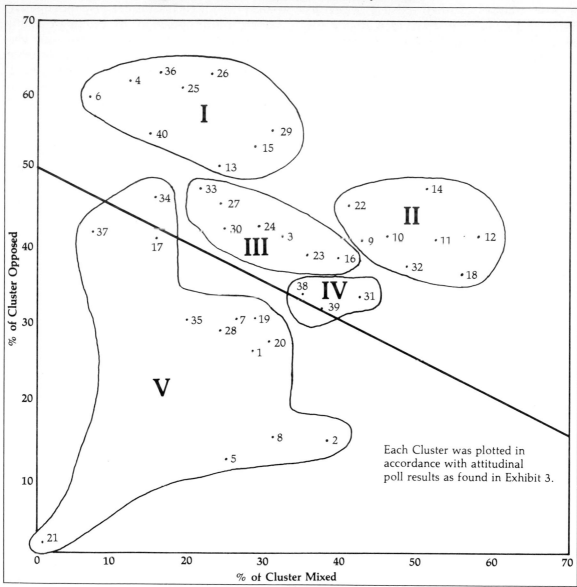

Each Cluster was plotted in
accordance with attitudinal
poll results as found in Exhibit 3.

V	Likely losers	
IV	Narrow margin for persuasion	II Wide margin for persuasion
III	Moderate margin for persuasion	I Likely winners

The Anti-right-to-work campaign targeted those people living in neighborhood/block groups in Group
II as highly persuadable since those Clusters polled high on both opposition to right-to-work and mixed
attitude toward (uncertain about) right-to-work.

*CLARITAS CORP. #5172, 9/28/78

than to surveys done immediately before the system was used in September serves only to mask the system's true impact. Why these early poll results differed so significantly from the September survey is beyond the scope of this article. Perhaps partial answers are data handling errors, changes in question-wording, or actual changes in people's opinions as time passed. The key finding, however, is that no sharp turnaround in voting behavior occurred after September that is disclosed by the data.

Evaluating Claritas' effectiveness: predictive ability

The second general criterion that Claritas uses to assess the effectiveness of its system is the accuracy of its projections of county election results. This was supposedly indicated by a comparison between the percentage of voters opposing the ballot issue in each county as projected from the September 1978 statewide survey and the actual final election results in each county. However, again by examining Claritas' own data, it is clear that the system did not produce exceptionally accurate estimates of county voting results. Claritas offers two items as its primary proof for the predictive ability of its system: (1) the system's ability to correctly predict which counties would have a majority oppose the ballot issue and which counties would have a majority favor it, and (2) the 0.628 correlation between the final election results and Claritas' projected vote totals for each of Missouri's counties (a correlation measures the degree of predictability that exists between two sets of data).

For the first point, Claritas claims that it correctly predicted which side would win the ballot issue in 83 of the 115 counties; however, this is an unnecessarily imprecise way of evaluating the county projections' accuracy. For example, if the actual election result for a county was 52 percent opposed to right-to-work, a Claritas projection of 80 percent opposed would thus be deemed more accurate than an estimate of 49 percent opposed, simply because the former projection was over 50 percent while the latter was under 50 percent, even though the 49 percent figure was much closer to the actual result. On the second point, the 0.628 correlation claimed by Claritas between the predicted and the actual county vote is not especially strong. By squaring this correlation, one obtains the "coefficient of determination," which is a measure of the percentage of the variance in the actual county election results that is explained by the Claritas projections and is, therefore, an indicator of the latter's predictive ability. By such a calculation, only 39 percent of the variance in the actual election returns is explained by the estimates—not a very substantial proportion.

Also, the whole process of producing the Claritas Clusters and projecting the results to individual counties seems hardly to be worthwhile from the viewpoint of enhancing predictive ability. If one calculates the absolute difference between the actual election results and the projected figures for each county, the mean prediction error over all counties was seven to eight percentage points. If one instead had foregone all of the clustering and projecting, but had simply predicted for ease and convenience that each county would have the same final election result as the September 1978 survey figure for the entire state (about 56 percent opposed), the mean prediction error for all counties would have been about nine to ten percentage points. Thus, all of the extensive processing techniques only raised the prediction accuracy by two percentage points, probably not enough to affect decision-making or to justify the additional expense.

Another criterion against which to measure the validity of a predictive technique is whether its estimates contain systematic biases—or, in other words, whether the accuracy of the predictions vary in some sort of pattern. Generally, it is desirable that the size and direction of any errors in predictions be randomly distributed among the predictions rather than displaying any consistent trends. By examining Claritas' own data presented in Exhibit 3, a graph reproduced from the previous article, it is obvious that very strong systematic biases occurred in its predictions. In the twenty-six counties in Missouri where opponents of right-to-work ultimately gathered *under* 45 percent of the vote, the Claritas predictions *overestimated* the vote percentages in twenty-four of those twenty-six counties (by a mean of about eleven percentage points). In the forty-seven counties where the opponents of the ballot issue finished with *over* 55 percent of the vote, the Claritas predictions *underestimated* the vote percentages in forty of those forty-seven counties (by a mean of about ten percentage points). Obviously, these are

extremely strong systematic biases indicating a flawed prediction technique. Only in those closely fought counties where the right-to-work opponents ultimately garnered 45 percent to 55 percent of the vote did Claritas' predictions split fairly equally between over- and underestimates.

Thus, on the whole, the empirical evidence offered by Claritas to prove its system's predictive capability shows instead that there exist within it strong biases, that the level of the statistical relationship between the predictions and the actual results is at best moderate, and that predictions of only slightly

EXHIBIT 3   Estimated Versus Actual "No" Vote for 115 Counties of Missouri on Amendment 23 ("Right to Work" Initiative), November 7, 1978

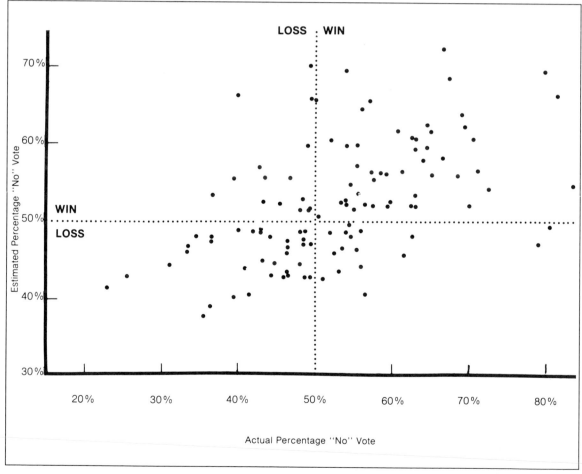

Mark Atlas

less accuracy could have been obtained without clustering and projecting the statewide survey results.

Data collection and decision-making

A major problem inherent in the manner of survey data collection and subsequent decision-making for the Claritas Cluster system is apparent in Exhibit 1. The first row of figures underneath the Cluster number headings shows the respondent sample sizes obtained for the Clusters and upon which the subsequent analyses and targeting decisions were based. The sample sizes shown are generally far too small to base reliable, quantitatively supported decisions upon. In fact, having forty Clusters to sample for and having interviewed only 1,367 people in Missouri, it is obvious that the mean number of respondents per Cluster was only thirty-four. Dealing with samples of this small size clearly crosses the line from quantitative to qualitative research. Statistically reliable results usable for decision-making are rarely attainable from just a few dozen respondents. For example, referring to Exhibit 1, Claritas selected Clusters 25, 26, and 29 as desirable because they "had respectively an 81 percent, 87 percent, and 86 percent likelihood of not being in favor of right-to-work." However, just due to normal sampling error, these numbers could be over a dozen percentage points too high (based on a 95 percent confidence interval) simply because there is a much greater likelihood of selecting an unrepresentative sample when only twenty-four or twenty-eight people are interviewed.

This finding has unsettling possibilities for the decision-making that was based on the Clusters' configurations shown in Exhibit 2. Since the Clusters that were targeted for intense contact were apparently selected on the basis of the numbers represented in the graph, it would have been important to keep in mind that due to normal sampling fluctuations a Cluster's position could actually be ten to twenty percentage points off (based on a 95 percent confidence interval) on the vertical and/or horizontal axis from where it would have been had an ideally representative survey been done. Thus, one should be extremely cautious when using such small sample studies for making decisions. What is doubly troubling is the notion that these possibly volatile small sample Cluster results were directly projected down to BG/EDs without identifying the potential error and were then used to predict county vote results. Even more troubling is the use of such small samples for designing advertising approaches adapted to each of the targeted Clusters—for something as complex as writing advertising appeals, samples of this size range are clearly inadequate and could yield very biased results.

One of the critical problems with using the Cluster system in politics is the need for enormous survey samples and thereby substantial survey costs. A general rule of thumb is that to analyze any subsample one generally needs at least fifty respondents to be contained therein, though the potential statistical error involved would be quite substantial even with fifty. If one tried, though, to ensure that each of the forty Clusters would have even fifty people in it, a total sample of 2,000 would be required—as would a large budget to pay the bill. While using forty Clusters may have generated adequate Cluster samples when Claritas was dealing with national marketing surveys of at least 15,000 people, changes need to be made for the procedure to be used effectively in politics. One obvious solution is reducing the number of Clusters by combining two or more very similar Clusters into new Clusters. While conceptually some degree of specificity would be lost, it seems better to have valid but more aggregated data than very finely differentiated data that cannot reliably be used for decision-making.

Claritas' methodological foundations

The Cluster system's methodology primarily rests upon its use of cluster analysis, both as a means of processing the Census data to generate distinct geodemographic segments and as a theoretical principle underlying the desirability of targeting on a multivariate basis. Unfortunately, very little information regarding the precise manner of clustering is provided in any of the system's literature; thus, evaluating the quality of the approach is difficult. Also, except for the 1978 Missouri election, there are few indications that any of the theoretical assumptions of the system have been tested, much less that any test results have been disclosed. Therefore, the following points address some of the issues surrounding the system's methodological foundations but generally will not—due to a lack of information—be able to decisively evaluate the quality of the analytic techniques and assumptions utilized.

One point brought out in Claritas documents that may give potential clients a false sense of security is the focus on the Cluster system explaining 87 percent of the demographic variance in the United States. This percentage refers not to the results of the cluster analysis that led to the forty Clusters, but rather to the factor analysis preceding it that combined the 535 demographic variables dividing a BG/ED into thirty-four composite groups. This is an important distinction because a "good" factor analysis result is a necessary, *but not sufficient*, indicator of a "good" cluster analysis since the latter segments the items through a different procedure and on different criteria. Also, the fact that 87 percent of the variance among demographic variables is explained is not surprising, since one would expect them to be strongly linked and since thirty-four factors—a fairly large number—are required to explain this percentage of the variance.

There are some additional aspects of cluster analysis that should be approached with caution, though it is unclear whether their associated problems affect the Cluster system. First, the number of clusters arrived at is fairly arbitrary—the user instructs the computer to divide the data into a designated number of clusters and then the user interprets the output. By trying different numbers of clusters (Claritas tried variations from twenty to one hundred) the user can then select the results that seem most interpretable, sensible, and usable; there is, however, no magic formula for determining the appropriate number of clusters. Second, most, if not all, cluster analysis computer programs can generate substantially different results even if only the ordering of the data used in the analysis is altered. For example, if data are processed in a clustering program in one order and results are obtained, the mere changing of the order in which the data are entered into the computer can cause a substantially different set of clusters to emerge when the data are processed again. Thus, the stability of the Clusters is always a matter of concern. Finally, one would expect that at least somewhat different cluster compositions would result from analyzing national data as opposed to data from a particular state or locality. Thus, the forty Clusters derived from the entire nation's Census data may be very different from the Clusters that would be generated if each state's data had been clustered individually. The degree of similarity of such sets of Clusters would indicate the generalizability of the Claritas Clusters. Given these potential problems that might undermine the efficacy of the Cluster system, it would be very useful for the results of any tests of the system's stability, validity, and generalization potential to be disclosed so that potential clients can evaluate the relative quality of the service offered.

Conclusion

As this article has demonstrated, using the same criteria and data supplied by Claritas, it is clear that the claims made about the Cluster system are not supported, and possibly are contradicted, by the facts. If added to this lack of proven effectiveness are the inherent potential methodological difficulties associated with cluster analysis, it is obvious that much more needs to be known and shown about the system before it can be used indiscriminately. The allocation of a campaign's resources is too crucial a task to be undertaken when there is substantial uncertainty about the targeting procedure's validity both in theory and in practice. Greater disclosure of the methodology used in clustering and of data from the system's use in other elections would help to either ease some doubts or clarify problems sufficiently to enhance their resolution. Also, it would be highly desirable to test whether projections from surveys done in larger geographic areas down to smaller areas accurately reflect the latter's opinions. (This could be done by comparing the results of such projections to the results of adequately sized surveys actually carried out in the smaller area, at the same time asking some of the same questions.) Finally, assuming that the doctrine of caveat emptor holds true in elections, it is the responsibility of political campaigners to closely scrutinize systems offered for their use, to demand proof for any claims, and to expect to spend considerable time verifying such proof.

Otherwise, such campaigners should always expect free planes to be sent for them.

New Techniques in Computerized Voter Contact

Frank Tobe

Another approach to voter contact is described by the author of this article. The old ward heelers, the key lieutenants of the city political machines, made it their business to know their neighbors and everything important about their lives. The decline of party organizations as well as sheer population growth have left a vacuum in the voter contact arena that consultants, using computers to compile extensive databases on each constituency, seek to fill. One of these consultants, Frank Tobe, explains how such a database can be constructed and how it can be put to use in a precisely targeted direct mail program. The author also mentions, and perhaps too quickly dismisses, the privacy concerns raised by some civil libertarians about voter database files.

All campaigns know the computer age is upon us and that it is up to them to learn how to control this new trend before it controls them. Most street-wise and aggressive campaigns these days are realizing that if they are not making the computer work for them, someone else is likely to make it work *against* them. This knowledge is the power and drive behind the emerging computer technologies of political database development, highly sophisticated targeting, and personalized voter contact.

As campaign costs have risen, new and more cost-effective methods of campaigning have appeared in the marketplace. In the last few years, new techniques in the fields of voter contact, direct mail, fundraising, constituency segmentation, and sophisticated targeting have become more cost-efficient *mostly* because of the use of computers. It is true that these techniques cost more to start (i.e., to develop the files to work with), but thereafter the costs are much less. Also, because of computer technology more campaigns can send highly personalized literature, target unique messages to different voter groups, and make more extensive get-out-the-vote and voter contact efforts.

Political databases

Computer targeting and database development have matured in the last few years into a sophisticated science. The near-term future promises evermore successful activities. Using political databases and today's other new campaign technologies, computers have made

Frank Tobe is the president and founder of Below, Tobe and Associates of Culver City, California, and Falls Church, Virginia.

it possible to select voters and voter households precisely and economically and to produce phenomenally successful response-provoking voter contacts that in turn provide further names and data to help win elections.

All candidates must decide whom to contact, what to communicate to those persons, how to deliver their messages, and how often to do so. In this light, the decision to build a comprehensive database can be crucial. What information the database should retain, how extensive it needs to be, what basic uses it needs to perform in order to justify its existence, and what publicity the computerization of the campaign should receive are all important factors to consider.

Campaign managers also need to be aware of the exciting new delivery products for campaign messages afforded by today's computer technologies and decide which are most relevant and cost-effective for the race they are working on. Some of these are: computer-prepared laser letters, pre-filled-in absentee ballots, computer-generated slate cards, tasteful and stylish response devices, urgent-looking (get-out-the-vote) messages, polished and authentic looking endorsement letters, and hundreds of other computer-prepared products all improved by some level of personalization far beyond simple inclusion of the recipient's name or city into the copy. (See Samples 1–4.)

Campaign computer systems (especially mainframe and micro-mainframe interfaced) permit hundreds (possibly thousands) of variations in persuasion and get-out-the-vote (GOTV) messages based on information within a database that provides some connection between the potential voter and the candidate. If an individual's occupation is known, a professional affinity can be discussed; if the recipient is retired, the candidate's ideas and policies regarding social services can be described; if the voter is young and living in an apartment, education, childcare, jobs programs, and home ownership can be topics that will make the recipient pay attention to the candidate and the rest of his/her message.

And if more than one "connection" can be made, the message can be tailored to address these multiple concerns.

The impact of these subtle personalizations may appear to be fleeting, but their effect is that extra fraction of attention to a candidate and to a message that it takes to win votes and elections.

It is insufficient now to identify voters and target them simply according to broad characteristics such as party and district. Instead, as voters tend to vote more independently, they require numerous customized persuasion and GOTV contacts specifically targeted and designed to motivate them. Unique and homogeneous voter groupings must be sorted, selected, and contacted based on:

- combinations of individual data already on the voter file
- additional data added to the file
- data derived from other files (census, voter's history)
- matched data (age, ethnicity, phone numbers)
- poll results (samples are taken, results appended to voter records, and comprehensive cross-reference tabulations of prime voters prepared).

Database development techniques

The details of political database development are fascinating. Consider this example regarding John and Mary Jackson. They live in a hotly contested district in a nice apartment in a moderate-income area. They're both 28 years old; he's a teacher and her occupation is unknown. They're black and both are Democratic. He's a member of the local school board (an elected job) and they're both members of the local Southern Baptist Church.

What a wealth of information! But how can you store all that in the computer? A coding system is the solution. For example, the code may specify the number 1 to mean Democratic, #13 to indicate ages between 25 and 35, #41

Under California Election Laws

YOU CAN VOTE BY MAIL

Simply sign and detach the attached

ABSENTEE BALLOT APPLICATION

and drop it in the mail.

INSIDE:
An IMPORTANT MESSAGE about Absentee Voting from Former Mayor DONNA ELLMAN

Citizens to Elect

300 North Swall Drive, #105
Beverly Hills, CA 90211

CAR-RT SORT   ** CR 02

Mrs. Joyce Doe
210 Main Street
Dallas, Texas 65390

ABSENTEE BALLOT APPLICATION
Beverly Hills Municipal Election — April 10, 1984

Here's your personal Absentee Ballot Application. California law allows you to vote by mail if you are registered but don't think you will be able to get to your polling place on election day.

All you need to do is sign your name in the shaded area below, detach the application and drop it in the mailbox.

You will receive your absentee ballot in the mail prior to election day — April 10th. When you receive your ballot, fill it out and mail it promptly.

Please send an absentee ballot to:

Mrs. Joyce Doe

Registered Address: # 210 Main St. Dallas, Tx.65390

Number and Street   **City, State and Zip**

Signature (Sign as registered)   **Date**

If you would like your ballot sent to another address, fill in the box.

Mail Absentee Ballot to me at:

Name _____

Address _____

City & Zip _____

DETACH AND MAIL TODAY
Application must be received by City Clerk by April 3.

PERMANENT ABSENT VOTER STATUS

Any voter who has lost, or has lost use of, one or more limbs, has lost, or has lost use of both hands, is unable to move without the aid of an assistant device (e.g., canes, crutches, walker, wheelchair), is suffering from lung disease, blindness, or cardiovascular disease, has a significant limitation in the use of the lower extremities, or is suffering from a diagnosed disease or disorder which substantially impairs or interferes with the person's mobility, may apply for permanent absent voter status.
You may request an application for Permanent Absent Voter Status from the COUNTY ELECTION DEPARTMENT

SAMPLE 1 Computer personalization makes it extremely easy for a California voter to file for an absentee ballot. The reverse side of this application was divided into two panels: a business reply card so the application can just be dropped in the mail on one, and a message from the candidate on the other.

Frank Tobe

Mailogram

```
              CAR-RT SORT ** CR 20
M/M John Doe
District Street
Long Beach, CA 90721

***************** YOUR POLLING PLACE IS *****************
          THE CUBBERLY SCHOOL AT 3200 MONOGRAM AV

GARY HART'S NEW LEADERSHIP BRINGS TO MIND THE ENERGY OF
THE KENNEDY YEARS. LIKE THE KENNEDY BROTHERS, HART OFFERS
NEW IDEAS AND NEW HOPE FOR AMERICA. AMERICA NEEDS HART.

IRA REINER IS THE DEMOCRATIC CHOICE FOR D.A. REINER HAS
THE STRENGTH AND INDEPENDENCE TO STAND UP TO THE SPECIAL
INTERESTS. HE WILL BE A GREAT DISTRICT ATTORNEY.

ALEX POPE HAS UNITED DEMOCRATS IN HIS CRUSADE FOR
SUPERVISOR AGAINST REPUBLICAN DEANE DANA'S BIG MONEY
MACHINE. ATTORNEY GENERAL VAN DE KAMP CALLS POPE "A REAL
FIGHTER FOR THE PEOPLE". DEMOCRATS -- VOTE FOR ALEX POPE
FOR SUPERVISOR.
          -- HARLAND BRAUN, CHAIRMAN
             CALIFORNIANS FOR DEMOCRATIC REPRESENTATION

P.S. REMEMBER -- DEMOCRATS VOTE YES ON 19 AND NO ON 24.
     THIS YEAR'S BALLOT IS CONFUSING--USE OUR PRIMARY
     SLATE.
```

SAMPLE 2 *This low-cost mailogram looks like an urgent telegram but is sent third-class bulk. The message is personalized with the voter's name and address; the delegates and candidates on the slate card are matched to the voter's address.*

Primary Slate for Democrats

Take This With You To The Polls

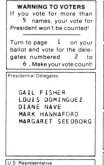

WARNING TO VOTERS
If you vote for more than 5 names, your vote for President won't be counted!

Turn to page 1 on your ballot and vote for the delegates numbered 2 to 6 . Make your vote count!

Presidential Delegates

GAIL FISHER
LOUIS DOMINGUEZ
DIANE NAVE
MARK HANNAFORD
MARGARET SEEDBORG

US Representative
GLENN M. ANDERSON

STATE SENATE
SUZANNE G. DISTASO

STATE ASSEMBLY
MARC A. WILDER

DEMOCRAT ALEXANDER POPE IS ENDORSED BY ALAN CRANSTON AND JOHN VAN DE KAMP FOR SUPERVISOR

Superior Court Judge
#20 Eli Isaac Chernow
#30 Sherman W. Smith, Jr.*
#33 Arthur (Art) Baldonado*
#38 Michael Tynan*

OUR FEATURED JUDGES ARE RATED "WELL QUALIFIED"

District Attorney
Ira Reiner*

SUPERVISOR
ALEXANDER POPE*

State Measures
16. YES   20. NO
17. YES   21. YES*
18. YES*   22. YES*
19. YES*   23. YES
           24. NO*

County Measures
YES on A,B,C

CITY MEASURE
YES ON N

Vote Democratic

KENNEDY

ROOSEVELT

TRUMAN

At every time of economic crises America has turned to the Democratic Party for leadership

Democrats!
YES
on
18, 19, 21,
& 22

GARY HART FOR PRESIDENT
Gary Hart is the only Democrat who can defeat Reagan in November. Like John Kennedy, Hart will give America the new leadership and new ideas it so desperately needs

DEMOCRAT IRA REINER — A COURAGEOUS D.A.
Ira Reiner is a strong and effective prosecutor who will be a great District Attorney. Reiner has the courage to stand up to the powerful special interests. He deserves your vote.

Democrats!
NO on 24
Reject
Extremism

Paid for by Americans for Hart and candidates and ballot measures marked with an [*] asterisk on the reverse side. Published by Berman and D Agostino Campaigning Inc. 14511 I.A. Cienega Blvd. Los Angeles CA 90035. Nonpartisan prices evaluated independent of party in consultation with Harland Braun Esq.

SMITH, BALDONADO & TYNAN FOR SUPERIOR COURT
Our featuring candidates for Superior Court have ALL been rated WELL QUALIFIED by the Los Angeles County Bar Association. They deserve the vote of every Los Angeles County Democrat.

---

for teacher, #28 to denote black, #81 for an apartment or for membership in a church group, #158 for a special interest in education (member of a school board), #112 to mean moderate income area, #89 for multiple person household—all Democratic, and #140 for an elected official.

Thus, John and Mary Jackson's computer record would be coded 1, 13, 28, 41, 81, 89, 112, 140, and 158. Simple! Our system can handle code numbers from 1 to 160 (see Table 1). Any individual can have any or all of these 160 codes, but the codes average fewer than 25 per person. (We've found the number 25 to be the high end for even the most fanatical database developers.)

Where does that information come from?

Much information is contained in the average computerized voter file acquired from the county registrar. Party, name and address, date of registration, precinct number, legislative districts, and in some cases, date of birth, occupation, phone number, sex, title, and whether the person voted in previous election(s) are information from that source.

By assigning codes for individual data such as party, age ranges, sex, title (e.g., Mrs., Ms., Miss, etc.), length of registration at the present address, and occupation, and then sorting the file into household sequence and identifying the type of the household (e.g., apartment, rural route, P.O. box, single family dwelling unit), the political registration of all the voters in the household (pure, split, two or more than

TABLE 1   Sample Assembly District—Voter Database Fields

1. Democrat	47. Armed Forces	93. R2
2. Republican	48. Teacher	94. RM2
3. Libertarian	49. Student	95. RD2
4.	50. Other Profession	96. RDM2
5. Minor Party	51. Civil Service	97. DM2
6. Decline to State	52. Misc. Medical	98. D2
7. American Independent	53. Show Biz	99. D1
8. Peace and Freedom	54. High Tech	100. M1
9. Pro-Candidate	55. Finance	101. M2
10. Moved	56. Aerospace	102. 2nd Supervisorial
11. Opponent's Supporters	57. Real Estate	103.
12. 18–25 yr. old	58. Pro-Rent Control	104. West Hollywood
13. 26–30 yr. old	59. Anti-Rent Control	105. Burbank
14. 31–40 yr. old	60. Mr.	106. Old 45th AD
15. 41–50 yr. old	61. Female	107. Old 24th CD
16. 51–64 yr. old	62. Mrs.	108. New 24th CD
17. 65+	63. Ms.	109. New 23rd CD
18. No age on file	64. Miss	110. New 26th CD
19.	65. No title	111. New 27th CD
20. Jews	66. Phone #	112. 20th SD
21. Italian	67. Education Concern	113. 22nd SD
22. Armenian	68. Crime Concern	114. 23rd SD
23. Hispanic	69.	115. 28th SD
24. Japanese	70. Candidate Met	116. Income Group A
25. Greek	71. Volunteer Met	117. Income Group B
26. Black	72. Observed Gay	118. Income Group C
27. Chinese	73. Liberal	119. Income Group D
28.	74. Conservative	120. Income Group E
29. Non-ethnic	75. Celebrities	121.
30. Other Asian	76. Unions	122.
31.	77.	123.
32. Philipino	78.	124. Miracle Mile/Park LaBrea Jews
33. Foreign Born	79.	
34.	80.	125.
35. Retired/Sr. Citizen	81. Apartment	126.
36. Business	82. Mail Address	127. Miracle Mile Mixed
37. Blue Collar	83. P.O. Box	128.
38. 9 to 5	84. Rural Route	129.
39. Law Enforcement	85. No House Number	130. Blax
40. Doctor	86. No Address	131. N. Hollywood Crackers
41. Dentist	87. Mobile Home	132.
42. Construction Trade	88. Condo	133. Mt. Olympus
43. Pharmacist	89.	134. Laurel Canyon
44. Lawyer	90. Black Code	135. Hollywood Hills
45. Social Worker	91. Gay Code	136. Shrecklach Hills
46. Accountant	92. R1	137. Lk. Hollywood

Frank Tobe

TABLE 1 *(continued)*

138. Park LaBrea	146.	154. East District
139. Toluca Lake	147. Schwab's	155. Hollywood
140. Hancock Park	148. Atwater	156. Cracker Households
141.	149.	157.
142.	150. Fairfax	158.
143. Wilshire/LaBrea Polyglot	151. Mixed	159.
144. W. Hollywood Polyglot	152. Flatland Valley	160.
145. Hollywood	153. Hills	

two persons in the household) and determining which sex heads the household, we have a wealth of information to begin a database with—and often enough to run a campaign with.

With some clerical help, we can also assign geographically derived identities such as homogeneous precinct groups (e.g., black areas, hillside areas, farms, areas with a particular community name, etc.) and voter historical data (propensity to vote Democratic, to swing the other way, to turn out in high numbers, etc.).

And with specialized programming help we can attempt to identify hard-to-find segments such as gay households, unmarried male/female couples living together, and people who have moved from one place to another within the district (to save valuable information collected previous to the move).

An example of this kind of programming may be helpful. Imagine a candidate running for mayor in a city said to have a twenty-five percent gay population (like San Francisco). Obviously, that's an important group which the candidate needs to reach (or exclude). In order to do so, he/she needs to identify them.

Here's how we would go about finding gays using our mainframe computer (and for complex selects on multiple criteria you need a mainframe or large mini). First, we identify a broad geographical boundary where a large portion of them are supposed to live. Then we start to eliminate households: married couples, unmarried male/female couples living together, and families—multiple male or female households with the same last name. From those that are left we count the number of two-person households of the same sex but different last names and where the age spread is less than twenty years (to eliminate parent/child combinations). Where the number is high, in comparison to heterosexual households, we encode the results as gays and we also encode the single households as possible gays (in those areas where the ratio of gays to non-gays is highest). This vastly increases the probability that the couples we identify are gay. Because of the geographical knowledge, moreover, we know that even if those individuals aren't gay, they are likely to be receptive to gay issues.

Finally, we can match a database file against various other available files such as the county assessor file (to get home values and other property ownership information); Census files (to get block-group information about age, home values, family incomes, percent white/nonwhite, and occupational data); union lists (to get occupational specialties and loyalties); driver's license files (to get dates of birth, other members of the household, and, possibly, race information); computerized files from the white pages of the phone book (to get phone numbers and additional members of the household); and, finally, dictionaries of prominent ethnic identity (e.g., Hispanic, Jewish, Italian, Japanese, Chinese, Irish, East European, etc.).

Put together, these bits and pieces of individual, matched, derived, and geographic information can be merged together into a very

Democratic Voter Guide

A COMPLETE GUIDE TO ALL THE OFFICES AND PROPOSITIONS
ON YOUR BALLOT. TAKE THIS CARD WITH YOU
TO THE POLLS.

WARNING TO VOTERS IF YOU VOTE FOR MORE THAN 7 NAMES, YOUR VOTE FOR PRESIDENT WON'T BE COUNTED! -- TURN TO PAGE 2 AND VOTE FOR THE DELEGATES NUMBERED 28-34. MAKE YOUR VOTE COUNT!!	**Judge of the Superior Court** #20 Eli Isaac Chernow #30 **SHERMAN SMITH** * #33 **ART BALDONADO** * #38 **MICHAEL TYNAN** *
Presidential Delegates **HERSCHEL ROSENTHAL** **MARCIA MEDAVOY** **GRAY DAVIS** **JANE NATHANSON** **SANFORD WEINER** **ROBERTA BENNETT** **STEVE SULKES**	**District Attorney** **IRA REINER** * **Supervisor** **ROSEMARY WOODLOCK**
	State Measures 16. YES 20. NO 17. YES 21. YES* 18. YES* 22. YES* 19. YES* 23. YES 24. NO*
"MONDALE OR HART BACKERS--SEND SEN. ROSENTHAL, ASSEM. DAVIS & THESE OTHER DELEGATES TO THE CONVENTION--THEY'LL BEST REP- RESENT OUR COMMUNITY'S VIEWS." --CONGRESSMAN HOWARD BERMAN --COUNCILMAN ZEV YAROSLAVSKY	**County Measures** **YES ON A, B and C**
U.S. Congress **ANTHONY BEILENSON**	**ROSEMARY WOODLOCK** OUR DEMOCRAT FOR SUPERVISOR. "ROSEMARY WOODLOCK IS EXPERI- ENCED . . . CONCERNED . . .
State Assembly **GRAY DAVIS**	HONEST. SHE'LL BE A GREAT SUPERVISOR." -- JOHN VAN DE KAMP ATTORNEY GENERAL
Democratic Central Committee Jill Le Clear Workman Patricia (Pat) Mac Neil Alan H. Friedenthal Toni Brown Kimmel Phyllis Kahan Elaine B. Strong Sondra L. Cohen	**VOTE NO ON 24** STOP THE REPUBLICAN POWER GRAB!

Paid for and authorized by Americans for Hart and candidates and ballot measures marked with an [*] asterisk. Published by

1435 S. La Cienega Blvd., Los Angeles, CA 90035   28   Non-partisan offices evaluated independent of party

***SAMPLE 3   This version of a low-cost slate card has
both offset-printed and computer-generated, laser-
printed delegates', party officials', and candidates'
names matched to the voter's address. Can you tell
the difference? (Sample one-half original size.)***

powerful database. Then, with the aid of specialized computer programs for tabulating and cross-referencing, we can count files and codes and report the results to campaign managers and strategists for their study and development into an overall campaign strategy.

Imagine the usefulness of highly detailed constituent files. For registration purposes, for example, you can know all the people who live in (most of) the residences in your district and which people are registered or not, *and* if not, the party registration of the other members of the household along with a wealth of other lifestyle data.

A brief discussion of voter files and list acquisition is in order. Voter lists come from registrars of voters in counties or cities and are most often available in data processing form at minimal cost. If not, they're available typed and can be converted to data processing form (at a not-inconsiderable cost). Driver's license, phone numbers, and Census data files are examples of more costly files that can be acquired and matched to the political database, if the cost seems justifiable, while many matchable lists come free, e.g., union membership lists.

The medium and the message

Using a political database, a campaign can specify various output products such as labels, lists, 3×5 cards, word-processed or computer-prepared mailers and letters, and the other products outlined at the beginning of this article. And the selection criteria can be so unbelievably articulate, using the codes described above, that the language of the resulting voter contact product can be customized for each segment selected. The language of the message can be strong and direct—provocative—because the user has confidence that the segment selected to receive the message is comprised of people with a direct affinity to that message (Democratic Jewish voters getting a partisan message about Israel, etc.). No more "mushy" letters having to say something for everyone!

Many new products lend themselves to variable messages. Quality laser printers produce 7,000 letters per hour; others can print at speeds approaching 12,000 per hour—each letter with the capability of being entirely different from the one before or following. Laser graphics, references to regional issues, local telephone numbers, issues of particular interest to the recipient—all these and other personalizations combine to compose a unique letter for each individual voter.

Working as a supplier to a Washington, D.C., consulting firm, we created one letter that had a response device for our targeted audience to mail to selected legislators. In order to make

Frank Tobe

the legislator's staff members think they were *not* receiving the product of a mass mailing, we mixed up one "response device" by changing paper color (six different colors), messages (thirty), type fonts (two), and layout of the device (six). *Then* we addressed it to the fifty legislators. That's over 108,000 combinations (or 2,160 possible variations to each legislator)!

New trends

One recent trend in the use of political databases combines the fields of polling and computerized database development and has proven quite successful in many recent California campaigns. A pollster, instead of asking demographic questions at the *end* of a survey, selects his or her sample from an already-computerized database and analyzes survey data based on the demographics contained in the database instead of the survey. This way, the resulting cross-tabs relate survey results that can be directly targeted using the political database. This process eliminates untargetable results and esoteric poll-determined population groupings.

Another trend involves refining the data in the database once the database is in place. Numerous additional information-gathering tasks can be initiated to increase the usefulness of the database. Door-to-door canvassing, phone bank operations, polling, direct-response devices (mail, coupon ads, call-ins), and other activities generate records of voters' attitudes that can be posted back to the database for later use.

Perhaps the most important trend in computerized campaigning, however, is the increasing use of micro-mainframe communications (interfacing) to develop sophisticated political databases, to reach targeted lists of all sizes and shapes, to link donor files and other data from different campaigns, to provide up-to-the-minute research information, and to assist with campaign housekeeping chores such as FEC reports, scheduling, and budgeting. Campaigns that intelligently utilize large

mainframe services suppliers for targeting and direct voter contact soon discover that micros can more economically handle direct mail to important targeted segments and other tasks. But a micro can't match the storage, processing, and speed capabilities of a mainframe. Communications software (such as Crosstalk) that ties a micro to a mainframe allows a campaign to fully exploit the capabilities of both.

Stand-alone or interfaced: common problems

Increasing numbers of political practitioners know how to utilize computers for the processing of massive amounts of campaign information and campaign lists. They under-

SAMPLE 4   Personalized petition to County Supervisor. (Sample one-half original size.)

stand how a computer can take data from voter lists, house files, and historical statistics, process those data, and come out with effective targeting information and campaign lists. They know good targeting saves time and money and are turning to the computer, computer suppliers, and consultants for that purpose.

But there is a great deal of difference between computer companies, products, and services available to campaigns, candidates, and political practitioners. It's quite important that candidates, campaigns, and political practitioners have an understanding of what is available so that they can be knowledgeable enough to decide whether or not to initiate a database development project, what is most cost-effective for their needs, and the extent to which staff and volunteers should be involved in computer applications. They need to know which files are in the public domain, which are proprietary, which cost the campaign money, which have restricted use(s), and so on.

Every campaign starting the process of database development is bound to be confronted with questions about the invasion of personal privacy; of computerizing what used to be personal effort from campaign volunteers; whether the database will (and can) be used honestly; and other questions of ethics and the ethical use of these new voter contact techniques.

As for the use issue, there is potential for some abuse. Most of our clients recognize that these techniques perform best through a positive connection, an affinity between the recipient and the candidate's stand on an issue. They are eager to use these techniques to inform, persuade, and encourage voters to vote *for* their candidates. We tend not to do many attack or negative campaigns as a result. Nor do we "misuse" these techniques to send out contradictory messages. But they *can* be misused. These techniques and products can easily let one letter say one thing to a business owner and another to a union member.

That's why I'm a firm believer in self-policing. There's a firm in California that practices what I call "desperate" politics. They charge an enormous amount to develop strategy for a candidate desperate to win at any cost. This firm has been known to do outrageous things using hardball tactics way beyond anything normal and just barely legal. They now have a reputation that makes *them*, the consulting firm itself, an issue in the campaign. Now there's an example of self-policing in action.

I think we can dispense with the privacy issue. Micros and databases in today's campaigns neither replace nor obviate the need for volunteers, personal contacts, and a well-meaning, intelligent, personable candidate. Nor do they invade a person's privacy. The information used is forthrightly acquired, in the public domain, and only used for campaign purposes. It is the same information carried on 3×5 cards and in the heads of staffers and volunteers in the past, but, because of larger district sizes, higher costs and declining voter turnouts, computer databases are essential for organizing, maximizing the effects of key campaign personnel, and motivating voters.

There seems to be less interest in campaigns today and fewer people involved in them. But political apathy is overcome through a personal connection with an awareness of candidates and issues. And computers are providing that connection as a tool for informing the public by performing the tasks that volunteers used to do and are not available to do today.

Fundraising by the PACs

Larry J. Sabato

More than 4,000 political action committees (PACs) have now been formed at the federal level by corporations, labor unions, trade associations, and other groups that seek to influence American elections by contributing money to office-seeking candidates. While PACs have always been with us in some form, the massive modern growth in their numbers was stimulated in part by the passage of reformist campaign finance legislation following the Watergate scandals in the early 1970s. By the 1986 midterm congressional contests, federal PACs raised $353 million and contributed more than $132 million of that total to U.S. House and Senate candidates, accounting for thirty percent of the approximately $450 million war chest spent by all the congressional contenders combined.

How do the PACs raise these enormous sums? Like the candidates themselves, political action committees have come to rely on the new techniques and technologies of mass communications and politics, as this article explains.

Every good advertising man knows that you cannot sell a steak without the sizzle. We learned that you don't just form a political action committee, send around a note on company letterhead announcing its creation, and expect big things to happen. You must merchandise the PAC.

—A spokesman for the Loctite Corporation's PAC

This PAC officer's instincts are widely followed in the political action committee community. Aggressive fundraising that utilizes all the technological tricks of the modern campaign is fast becoming standard practice among PACs. Before PACs can contribute dollars, they must get them, and the solicitation of donors has very rapidly become both an art and a science. Borrowing the political consultant's tools of direct mail,

This article is drawn in part from Larry J. Sabato, PAC Power: Inside the World of Political Action Committees *(New York: W. W. Norton, 1984).*

videotape, television, and telephone banks, PAC managers have increasingly and successfully sought to enlarge their committees' bank accounts, and thus their political clout.

Solicitation rules

The rules of solicitation are best described as a thicket, with somewhat different regulations applied to the different categories of federal PACs. Generally, a corporate PAC may solicit the parent corporation's administrative, executive, and professional employees, as well as stockholders, at any time and as frequently as it wishes. Additionally, a corporate committee may solicit the corporation's rank-and-file employees twice each year by mail to the employees' homes. In parallel fashion, a labor PAC may solicit its parent union's members without restriction and twice yearly may solicit nonunion employees and the corporation's administrative, executive, and professional

145

employees and stockholders. Trade association PACs operate under other strictures, and they must secure prior approval from their member corporations each year in order to solicit the executive and administrative personnel of those corporations. A member corporation is free to permit only a single trade PAC to solicit its employees and stockholders in a given year, and it may restrict both the solicitation pool and the number of solicitations made by its chosen trade PAC. Trade PACs have more flexibility in soliciting their noncorporate members—there is no limitation on frequency there—and trade PACs can of course freely solicit their own executive and administrative staffs. They have the same twice-yearly solicitation rights for their own nonexecutive employees as corporate PACs do. Finally, nonconnected PACs have wide latitude in solicitation; essentially, they may solicit the general public as often as they please for contributions.

How PACs raise money

Within this regulatory framework, how do the PACs go about asking money from those they can contact? The survey results in Table 1 suggest the answers. Over two-thirds (67 percent) of the PACs use various forms of direct-mail solicitation, with trade PACs and especially corporate committees wedded to this type of fundraising. Personal, face-to-face solicitation is the second most popular method (54 percent use it), although almost two-thirds of the trade PACs and 79 percent of the labor PACs select this device. Group seminars to promote the PAC are also relatively popular: 37 percent of the PACs choose this alternative. Telephoning is surprisingly rare; only 10 percent of all PACs use it, though close to half of the trade and nonconnected PACs do so. Labor PACs have a distinctive fundraising pattern: They are most likely to employ rallies and special events in addition to personal, face-to-face encounters to fill their coffers. Most notable is the fact that all categories of PACs use most or all of the solicitation methods listed in Table 1, and a large majority of individual PACs use two or more of the methods. Often one approach (say, a group seminar) is used to initiate contact, with a different approach (personal, telephone, or direct mail) used as a follow-up. The PACs with the highest response rates tend to use repeated follow-ups; if at first they don't succeed, or get only a pledge, they try, try again.

The most personalized solicitations are

TABLE 1   How PACs Raise Money

Solicitation Method	Category of PAC				
	All PACS[a] (%)	Corpo- rate[a] (%)	Labor[b] (%)	Trade[a] (%)	Noncon- nected[a] (%)
Personal, face-to-face	54	45	79	65	56
Direct mail/letters	67	82	36	73	56
Group seminars	37	40	36	27	22
Telephone	10	7	0	46	44
Other	20	12	46	19	11

Source: Survey question "What solicitation methods do you use?" from questionnaire for a random-sample survey of PACs. See Larry J. Sabato, *PAC Power* (New York: W. W. Norton, 1984), pp. 197–198 *n* 16.

[a]Columns do not total 100 percent due to multiple responses.

[b]For the labor PAC questionnaire only, another solicitation method was listed—"rallies and special events"—which 46 percent of the labor PACs reported using.

Larry J. Sabato

generally agreed to be the most effective. Many PACs, particularly labor but also some corporate committees, completely decentralize their fundraising in the belief that local officers, who know potential contributors on a first-name basis, are in a much better position to secure a donation. These PACs produce all materials for the fund drive in their headquarters or Washington office and then send them to each local union or corporate plant for face-to-face distribution and discussion. The next most personal form of solicitation is the small-group seminar. Both labor unions and corporations hold these, but the format is decidedly different. Labor's usual forum is the traditional local union meeting. David Sweeney, director of the Teamsters' DRIVE PAC, explained his operation:

> We have a staff of five guys who will attend local meetings and tell them "we need money to help your friends and defeat your enemies." We'll go with [congressional] voting records, legislative reports and we tailor each local presentation to what their interests are and what their bitches are.

The corporate PACs, by contrast, usually center their pitch around a short videotape presentation filled with praise for the PAC idea from leading politicians and climaxed by patriotic exhortations to get involved. Many of these sessions become PAC pep rallies, with a speech by the chief executive officer encouraging the audience to join up. The CEO is always the favored choice to lead such gatherings or indeed to sign the direct-mail letters. As a PAC official surmised, "If the CEO plays golf, everyone plays golf. If the CEO is involved in PACs, everyone gets involved in PACs." These seminars can be quite effective. After one such presentation for the Baltimore Gas and Electric PAC, including a showing of *BG&E PAC: Your Shot at Political Action*, a random-sample mail survey of participants indicated dramatic gains in awareness of the PAC and willingness to contribute to it. The organizers' aims were at least partially realized, for the PAC registered an 82 percent increase in contributors during the succeeding months.

Tricks of the PAC trade

Fundraising gimmicks of every stripe have become a PAC staple too. PACs have reported using "casino" nights, rummage sales, Hawaiian luaus, theater outings, and bowling, golf, tennis, and fishing tournaments to raise money—everything but bake sales. The Pennsylvania Dental PAC hired a shapely model to entice potential contributors to its booth at the group's annual association meeting. The National Committee for an Effective Congress secured the Washington comedian Mark Russell for a benefit concert. Television producer Norman Lear's People for the American Way PAC auctioned off Debbie Reynolds's promise to jump out of a birthday cake as she did in the movie *Singin' in the Rain*. Star-studded fundraising dinners are also popular. Senator Edward Kennedy snared a bevy of glitterati and all the declared 1984 Democratic presidential candidates for a $1,000-a-plate dinner for his Fund for a Democratic Majority. Tony Randall was featured at a brunch for Pamela Harriman's Democrats for the '80s, and Ginger Rogers performed for a National Conservative Political Action Committee (NCPAC) reception on the former presidential yacht *Sequoia*.

Adaptations are made for the special needs of each PAC. In addition to large dinners featuring Walter Mondale and Jesse Jackson, the gay-oriented Human Rights Campaign Fund held a series of "low-profile" cocktail parties for closeted gays in Washington, D.C., that netted $30,000. (Mike Farrell of *M*A*S*H* taped a film for HRCF that was shown at each party.) Many other fundraising gimmicks and tools are being adopted by PACs. For instance, rare is the PAC that does not invest its money in interest-bearing accounts, certificates of deposit, or money-market funds. An occasional PAC will even reach beyond the grave by accepting a bequest from the estate of a deceased member.

Another technique fast becoming standard is the creation of "high-donor" clubs and awards. Already more than a third (38 percent) of the PACs have at least one such group, with trade PACs leading the way. (Almost half the trade committees have established one or more of them.) A "high-donor" club is a special category reserved for contributors who give over a certain minimum. The Mortgage Bankers Association's PAC has a Capitol Club for $250 givers and a Chairman's Club for donors of $500 and over. The Workover and Well Servicing Action Committee (WOWSAC) has a Wildcatter Club with an admission price of $1,000 or $100 for each oil rig owned by the donor. These clubs are sometimes sold very simply. The National Association of Broadcasters' Television and Radio PAC (TARPAC) issues special colored pins to match the size of the contributions given by their "Red, White, and Blue Club" members. Average gift size increased considerably, according to TARPAC's Steven Stockmeyer, because "at our receptions everybody checks out everybody else to see what color pins they have on."

Whether they have donor clubs or not, most PACs establish contribution guidelines which, while never "enforced" and rarely adhered to, suggest to those solicited what they should be giving. Labor and large trade PACs usually just set a certain amount (most often $10) for all members, regardless of rank or salary. Corporate PACs are normally more precise, listing a range of gift levels corresponding to salary or position. In general, corporate PACs seem to hope for a donation of between 0.2 and 1.5 percent of an individual's gross salary. High-donor clubs and contribution guidelines are also useful in efforts to "upgrade" a contributor's donation. Every sophisticated PAC attempts to increase the size of each person's gift at renewal time, and donor's clubs can be a special inducement.

The use of direct mail

Direct mail,* as Table 1 indicates, is by far the most common method of PAC solicitation.

Direct mail is a generic term for mass fundraising through "personalized" letters.

PAC mailings range from the most primitive kind of mimeographed, impersonal note to highly sophisticated personalized letters with state-of-the-art enclosures. Labor PACs tend to have technologically the most inferior types of direct mail, although there are numerous exceptions. Some labor mailings, even when technologically unimpressive, have had excellent responses, such as the Machinists Non-Partisan League's mailings to its retirees. This rough, offset letter has consistently received a high response rate and a large return in contributions. Much corporate direct mail is not terribly sophisticated either. In part this is because corporations that use direct mail are simply looking for an easy and economical way to solicit, as one corporate PAC leader, Donald Cogman, suggested: "Most corporate PACs want to do [solicitation] the cheapest way with the least amount of trouble—and that's direct mail." By contrast, trade and nonconnected PACs usually produce the most effective direct-mail packages, possibly because they have fewer opportunities than corporate and labor PACs to convince potential contributors personally; thus, they must count on mail to a greater degree to get a donor's attention. Some of these PACs hire prominent political consultants with considerable direct-mail experience to conduct their campaigns.

But the most comprehensive and masterful use of direct mail is by the ideological membership and nonconnected PACs, which depend heavily (in same cases exclusively) on this means of solicitation. Pure emotion, lightening-rod issues, and "hot" names fuel the ideological PACs' search for funds by mail. Former Secretary of the Interior James Watt was a goldmine for environmentalist PACs; prominent use of his name in a direct-mail piece would usually increase the group's profit. Senator Edward Kennedy performs the same function for the right-wing PACs. NCPAC is particularly fond of citing Kennedy's "ever-present danger," and it featured him in several of its fundraising letters in the 1982 midterm elections. NCPAC has depended on direct mail since its inception in 1975, when conservative

Larry J. Sabato

direct-mailer Richard Viguerie mailed NCPAC's first appeal, signed by Republican Senator Jesse Helms. One of Helms's later letters for NCPAC is testimony of the emotionalism that characterizes ideological direct mail of all hues; the letter read in part: "Your tax dollars are being used to pay for grade school classes that teach our children that CANNIBALISM, WIFE-SWAPPING, and the MURDER of infants and the elderly are acceptable behavior."

Direct-mail packages for right-wing and left-wing PACs are often mirror images of one another. While the liberal National Committee for an Effective Congress was declaring in one of its 1982 letters, "Right wing extremists dominate the Senate . . . . throw the rascals out!" NCPAC was solemnly warning its mail readership that "At this very moment, we're facing a potential nightmare—Liberal domination of the U.S. Senate." The PACs also raise money by using each other as punching bags. NCPAC asked its contributors to dig deeper because of "the millions of dollars [the] new liberal pressure groups will be pouring into the 1982 election." Meanwhile liberal organizations asked for donations to "expose groups like NCPAC" and to fight "the NCPAC challenge."

Some PACs solicit not just individuals but other PACs, since PACs can give up to $5,000 to one another. The liberal PROPAC, under the signature of union president William H. Wynn of the United Food and Commercial Workers, has sent letters to labor union committees requesting the maximum gift. The Congressional Black Caucus's PAC (CBC-PAC) also has sought PAC support. In a 1983 letter to PAC officers, the CBC-PAC's executive director none too subtly wrote, "You have surely noticed that our PAC consists entirely of Congressmen," and portrayed the Black Caucus as a defender of the PAC movement despite the support of various PAC-limitation bills by leading black congressmen.

Other PACs are beginning to experiment with new forms of "direct-response" solicitation that technologically go beyond mail while operating on fundraising principles similar to those underlying direct-mail efforts. For example, People for the American Way, the PAC formed by Norman Lear in part to oppose the Moral Majority, produced a half-hour documentary on the "radical right" titled *Life and Liberty . . . For All Who Believe*. Hosted by Burt Lancaster, the film aired on cable channels and certain network affiliates from early October to December 1982; it concluded with a toll-free "800" number for contributors to call. Not only did the program generate enough pledges to raise most of the $525,000 costs of production and airing, but it added nearly 10,000 supporters to the group's membership rolls—a list ripe for additional direct-mail appeals.

The costly mail process

The costs of direct-mail campaigns, especially the personalized, sophisticated variety, are very high, and because of this nonconnected PACs spend an extraordinarily large portion of their operating budgets on the direct-mail process. Because "prospecting" for new donors—a task essential to building and maintaining a direct-mail contributor list—usually eats up all revenues produced by the mailings, many nonconnected PACs in their early years have virtually no money to spend on direct gifts to candidates. Even well-established PACs with large "house files" of proven direct-mail givers expend a considerable portion of new funds on mailing costs and direct-mail consultants. Through 1982, NCPAC had paid more than $4.7 million (out of a total budget of $17.7 million) to Richard Viguerie's direct-mail businesses; the National Congressional Club (associated with Jesse Helms) spends a minimum of 30 percent of its annual budget on mailing, and a larger percentage whenever prospecting is being done on a large scale. Many of the New Right PACs consider direct mail not merely a form of fundraising but a very useful and persuasive form of advertising and therefore an investment with important secondary rewards. Liberal PACs tend to discount this theory as excuse-making for low candidate contribution totals ("That's the Viguerie line, and I think it's horseshit," says Russell Hemenway, director of the National Committee for an Effective Congress).

NCEC is one of a number of PACs that have abandoned or reduced their direct mailing because of the financial problems associated with it. "We took a major bath on direct mail; we lost a lot of money," reported Hemenway. Direct-mail fundraising is often only marginally profitable, so PACs that depend on it too heavily can be damaged by even slight shifts of public opinion. As one conservative trade PAC manager ruefully noted, "The election of Reagan and a Republican Senate really did some damage to our direct-mail program. Our letter recipients said, 'What the hell is the problem? There's nothing to worry about now.' We're lacking a good boogeyman."

Direct mail has the lowest response rate (i.e., the proportion of the solicited who actually contribute) of all the forms of PAC solicitation. For the mass-mailing ideological PACs, tiny break-even response rates of 1 or 2 percent (and $10–$15 per donation) on prospecting are the norm, while mailings to the house list show a somewhat better response. The conservative Committee for the Survival of a Free Congress, for instance, posts a 1.5–2 percent return on prospecting, with a 5–8 percent house-list return rate. Handgun Control's PAC fares similarly: 0.9 percent on prospecting and 7–20 percent on the house list. Overall, as Table 2 indicates, nonconnected PACs have the lowest average response rate of all PAC categories (just 3 percent) because of their heavy reliance on direct mail. By direct-mail standards, the other kinds of PACs do a phenomenally successful fundrais-

TABLE 2 PAC Solicitation: How Much and How Often

	Category of PAC				
	All PACS	Corpo-rate	Labor	Trade	Noncon-nected[a]
Average donation to PAC (1981–1982)	$100	$160	$14	$81	$65
Number of individual donors[b] (1981–1882)	400	155	2,700	400	1,150
Average response rate[c]	25%	26%	23%	32%	3%
Frequency of solicitation					
More than twice a year	16%	5%	21%	18%	33%
Twice a year	22%	24%	0%	30%	22%
Once a year	47%	56%	50%	48%	22%
Once every two years	10%	12%	0%	4%	22%
Other	5%	2%	29%	0%	0%

Source: Drawn from responses to a random-sample survey of PACs. See Larry J. Sabato, *PAC Power* (New York, W. W. Norton, 1984), pp. 197–198 n 16.

[a]Nonconnected PACs were also asked how often they conducted repeat solicitations. The results: 33%—more than once a year; 22%—twice a year; 11%—once a year; 33%—less than once a year.

[b]Figures in this row are medians.

[c]The response rate is the proportion of solicited individuals who make a contribution to the PAC.

Larry J. Sabato

ing business. Between 23 and 32 percent of those solicited by corporate, trade, and labor PACs actually make a donation. However, their universe is much smaller, and many of these PACs are selective about which employees or members they solicit even within their permissible group.

While the average nonconnected PAC asks 141,000 individuals for money, the typical corporate PAC asks 900, and its labor counterpart PAC contacts 12,000. In a more intimate setting, even direct mail can produce a larger return, and most corporate PACs reported that their letters had between a 15 and 20 percent response rate. No other method could match personal, face-to-face solicitation, however; response rates for PACs utilizing the personal touch were usually well over 35 percent.

Conclusion

Overall, the PACs raised about 41 percent of their funds in the first year of the election cycle and the remaining 59 percent in the second year. They solicit fairly frequently: 38 percent of the PACs try to raise funds twice a year or more, while about half (47 percent) restrict themselves to once a year. The corporate committees are more infrequent in their fundraisers (to avoid irritating their employees, as they see it), while many nonconnected PACs are always on the hustings or in the mailboxes. (Only 5 percent of the corporate PACs solicit more than twice a year, while 33 percent of the nonconnected committees do so.) The amounts actually contributed by PAC givers are, on average, quite small—about $100 per donation. Corporate contributors are the most generous, averaging $160, while the usual labor donor's gift is just $14. Labor's large base and relatively high response rate, of course, enable unions to match the heftier but more infrequent corporate gifts. While, in light of potential membership, relatively few individuals participate in any PAC, PAC donors as a group form a mighty army: Fully 7 percent of all adult Americans report contributing to one or more PACs—as many as give to all candidate organizations put together.

Part Four

Case Studies: The Campaign Techniques at Work

White Knights, Dark Horses:
The Kentucky Governor's Race of 1987

David Beiler

Nothing excites the political world quite as much as the "Stunning Upset," a relatively rare but highly educational occurrence. One contest that certainly qualifies for this designation is Kentucky's 1987 Democratic primary for governor, when little-known businessman Wallace Wilkinson staged a phenomenal last-minute surge that carried him from last place to victory in a crowded and prominent field of candidates. David Beiler tells this remarkable story through the eyes of the campaign consultants, who used their technological tools to monitor and shape the unfolding developments. Note the limits of their powers, however. As Beiler reveals, the consultants can be slaves to their candidates' weaknesses, and technological wizardry is hard pressed to compensate for a politician's critical foibles or lack of vision.

It was Derby Day all spring long for Kentucky Democrats this year. Media consultant Bob Squier called it "a festival for consultants." A local political editor likened it to the Spanish Civil War, as major powers converged on a remote corner of the political landscape to test their latest weaponry.

But when the dust settled from a stunning stretch drive in the five-way Democratic primary for Kentucky governor, it was political newcomer Wallace Wilkinson's campaign that stood in the winner's circle, ready to provide a host of lessons for anyone seeking office in a multicandidate field. It also confirmed at

least three emerging axioms of campaign professionalism:

- It is better to have the reflexes of a political pinball wizard than the brilliant grand designs of a Bismarck.
- Those slow to counterattack will suffer irreparable damage.
- Only those candidates who give voters a reason to cast ballots *for* them can launch nonpyrrhic offensives.

These assertions go beyond what most pundits concluded after glancing at the Kentucky toteboard—that voters are losing patience with negative political ads and are looking more toward issues. Although ample evidence exists to suggest Bluegrass voters responded favorably to a "new ideas" outsider juxtaposing himself against battle-scarred

---

David Beiler is a contributing editor of Campaigns & Elections *and a senior partner of Democracy, Inc., a political communications firm in Washington, D.C.*

political veterans, Wilkinson's success appears to be more a matter of opportune timing and strategic decision-making than the result of a sure-fire formula. In Kentucky—as elsewhere—it took negativity to move the numbers.

At the starting gate

Bored and somewhat alarmed by the failure of Republicans to give serious opposition to U.S. Senator Wendell Ford's march to reelection, the Kentucky press corps spent much of last year speculating about the impending gubernatorial campaign. Media coverage was showered on Lexington attorney Larry Forgy, a telegenic two-time state campaign director for Ronald Reagan who never had run for public office. But when Forgy announced in January that he did not have the stomach to raise the huge campaign fund a Republican would need to win in this heavily Democratic state, the press abandoned all hope of a significant general-election campaign and focused on the Democratic primary.

Five serious candidates entered the sweepstakes for the Democratic gubernatorial nomination when the campaign season began in Kentucky:

- John Y. Brown, Jr., former governor (1979–83); Kentucky Fried Chicken magnate and husband of network-television personality and former Miss America Phyllis George; a moderate-conservative backed by the state's two major newspapers, virtually its entire financial structure, and roughly half the established politicos active in the campaign.
- Steve Beshear, lieutenant governor; former state attorney general; a liberal practitioner of coalition politics; backed by the AFL-CIO, the United Auto Workers, the Kentucky Education Association, and most active members of the political establishment not backing Brown.
- Grady Stumbo, former government official; Brown's choice as successor in 1983 when

he lost a three-way photo finish; a populist doctor with a base in the eastern coal country.
- Julian Carroll, former governor (1974–79); a political pariah after "taking the fifth" in testimony before a federal grand jury investigating alleged insurance fraud in his administration.
- Wallace Wilkinson, bookstore operator turned wealthy textbook distributor; political neophyte bereft of important supporters save 89-year-old "Happy" Chandler, patriarch of the state party's conservative wing.

The key to all early speculation was Brown, who held a ten–twenty point lead over his nearest opposition in published opinion polls. It was by no means widely assumed that Brown would even run—right up to his filing for the office at the February 25 deadline—so entrenched was his reputation for mercurial behavior. With Brown in the race, it was almost universally presumed that only Beshear would have a realistic chance of beating him. Stumbo's impressive strength four years earlier had been widely attributed to the Brown organization; he was unlikely to raise a sufficient war chest on his own. Carroll's early substantial support in the polls was written off to the inflated influence of name recognition in a campaign's initial stages; considered a political cadaver by the cognescenti, he was unlikely to attract much financial support regardless of whether the public could be convinced of his innocence.

The wild card in the hand was Wilkinson. A fresh face, he carried no political baggage— certain to be a distinct advantage in a state well known for rejecting political has-beens. Possessor of a fortune estimated at $50 million, he could outspend even Brown if he chose to do so. Moreover, that fortune had been amassed over a rags-to-riches career that would have made Horatio Alger cry, a powerful image for a people plainly self-conscious about their reputation for backwardness.

But Wilkinson already had been on the campaign trail for nearly two years (he officially

The Kentucky Governor's Derby: The Toteboard

Candidates	Media Consultant	Polling Consultant	Votes Received	Expenditures ($1,000s)	Dollars Spent Per Vote
Wilkinson	Sawyer/Miller	Information Assoc.	220,295	$4,084.	$18.54
Brown	Communications Co.	Hamilton, Frederick & Schneiders	163,013	$3,476.	$21.32
Beshear	Doak, Shrum	Hickman-Maslin	114,176	$2,906.	$25.45
Stumbo	Ken Swope	Harrison & Goldberg	90,087	$ 762.	$ 8.46
Carroll	Mike McClister*	Kitchens & Assoc.	41,916	$ 737.	$17.58
Others	—	—	8,247	$ 172.	$20.83

*Produced no media in 1987.

filed for the race on April 29, 1985) and had spent $2 million without raising a ripple in the polls. Whatever it took, Wallace Wilkinson didn't seem to have it.

The road from nowhere

Wilkinson by no means was without expert guidance. Campaign manager Danny Briscoe had guided Harvey Sloane to the mayoralty of Louisville before serving as state insurance commissioner under John Y. Brown. In 1984, he and Wilkinson had watched in dismay as Brown abandoned a projected race against U.S. Senator Dee Huddleston—Briscoe as the manager of that abortive campaign, Wilkinson as the chairman. Soon after, the two forged an alliance intent on winning the governorship, regardless of what their mutable friend might do.

By the fall of 1985, the duo had signed on longtime state-party chairman J.R. Miller to organize an extensive grass-roots network, while New York's Sawyer/Miller agency was engaged to produce the paid media. A year later, the first Wilkinson ads hit the airwaves— seven months before the election.

That initial flight of Sawyer spots alternated between two images. The first—featuring the uncharismatic candidate speaking to the camera about the state's economic and educational systems—sought to project the image of a knowledgeable outsider with fresh insights and solutions. The second was the Wallace Wilkinson "bootstrap" story, beginning with his career as a paper boy and shoeshine boy in high school, his family too poor to own a TV much less a car.

Local observers remained unimpressed by this early foray ("Laid an egg . . . . Too early . . . . Can't remember a thing it said.") and cited preference polls to prove their assertion it was a waste of money. But the primary objective of the ads was not to win support, though that did increase fivefold (to five percent). Rather, it began the task the campaign had set before itself: to establish Wilkinson as the only candidate representing a new approach—an approach that had led him from rags to riches and could do the same for the state—and to give voters a reason to vote for him. The stage was being set for conversions to Wallace Wilkinson's candidacy in dramatic numbers.

As spring loomed, however, the demand for more tangible results had begun to permeate Wilkinson headquarters. Miller left after losing a power struggle with Briscoe, and a campaign doctor was sent for.

The Cajun Cowboy

James Carville is a one-man wrecking crew. A self-described "cowboy," he snugly fits the bill of a political Clint Eastwood. He rides in alone, blows away the bad guys, then rides out again—for a fee. The townspeople are usually grateful, if warily so.

"We could not have won without James Carville," gushes Briscoe. "Working with him has been one of the great experiences of my life."

A native of Baton Rouge, Louisiana, Carville quit his law practice and started in political consulting with the Louisiana firm of Gus Weill and Raymond Strother during the late 1970s. By 1982 he was on his own, guiding Virginia Lieutenant Governor Dick Davis in a narrowly unsuccessful U.S. Senate campaign. In 1984 he moved his base of operations to Austin, Texas, and managed Democrat Lloyd Doggett's U.S. Senate campaign to two upset, razor-thin primary victories before being buried by Republican Phil Gramm in a conservative landslide in the fall.

The jive-talking, jeans-wearing Louisianan finally came to the attention of Wilkinson and Briscoe after taking Democrat Bob Casey to an unexpected victory over the GOP's well-heeled William Scranton III in the 1986 Pennsylvania governor's race.

When Carville came aboard the seemingly stalled Wilkinson bandwagon on February 1, 1987, $1.5 million had been spent, and the candidate's support stood at five percent. Soon, the character of the campaign appeared to shift. In contrast to Miller—the man he replaced in the Wilkinson hierarchy—Carville is almost disdainful of organization. His specialty is the delivery of a well-defined message, partly crafted through paid-media design, but primarily the product of carefully manipulated "earned" media.

Wilkinson, thus far, had earned no media to manipulate. The press was studiously ignoring him, casting the race as a contest between the personality politics of John Y. Brown and the coalition politics of Steve Beshear. The campaign had to attract attention in a dramatic way that would accentuate its central theme of a new approach to government. The avenue chosen by Carville and company promptly delivered these goods by startling political observers with its audacious disregard of conventional wisdom: Wilkinson blasted the arrival of the biggest single employment generator in state history—a Toyota automobile plant.

Definition from a different drummer

The administration of incumbent Governor Martha Layne Collins was not a popular one in Kentucky; some polls showed her job

---

The Horse Race: Changes in Candidate Preference

1987 Polls: Candidates	Early February (Mason-Dixon)	Mid-March (Courier-Journal)	Early May (Hickman-Maslin)	Early May (Info. Assoc.)	Election Results (May 26)
Wilkinson	5%	8%	13%	15%	34%
Brown	26%	35%	31%	29%	26%
Beshear	15%	17%	24%	14%	18%
Stumbo	9%	11%	9%	7%	14%
Carroll	15%	10%	7%	7%	7%
Other	9%	—	—	—	1%
Undecided	22%	19%	16%	28%	—

David Beiler

disapproval ratings to be as high as two-to-one. The source of this dissatisfaction is not clear-cut, but the electoral atmosphere in the state had a decidedly antiestablishment cast as a result.

Bringing a Toyota automobile plant to the state was probably the accomplishment of which the governor was most proud: It promised to provide 2,000 new jobs to a state long plagued by high unemployment and economic underdevelopment. No public figure had dared question the policies that had landed this plum until Wallace Wilkinson, the forgotten gubernatorial candidate, made headlines across the state by ripping the deal to shreds at a March 26 news conference.

The state had given away the farm to land the plant, Wilkinson charged, providing concessions worth $136,000 per job provided. He went on to claim that money could have been more wisely invested in entrepreneurial small businesses, although he emphasized he still welcomed Toyota and was not criticizing the Japanese automaker for having the good business sense to engineer the most advantageous deal it could. To make sure the point had not been missed, the second flight of Wilkinson spots—including an attack on the Toyota deal—hit the airwaves immediately following the conference.

The camps of the other candidates were soon chortling over this seemingly ignorant move. Some are still sneering, even today. Beshear pollster Harrison Hickman claims the tactic caused Wilkinson's negative rating to rise to a seventeen percent tie with his positive. References in the ads to the "Collins–Beshear Administration" also backfired, according to Hickman, who polled for Collins in her 1983 race.

Although Wilkinson pollster Mark Mellman contradicts Hickman's conclusions, almost all key observers of the race concur in the belief that for every Kentuckian who sided with Wilkinson on the Toyota issue, there was at least one who did not. But the relative unpopularity of the stand should not obscure the fact it was a public-relations breakthrough

of critical importance. For the first time, the press and public had taken notice of Wallace Wilkinson and seen him as an innovative battler against the status quo, the only such person in the race and a stark contrast to the easygoing front-runner.

The Glamor Boy glimmers

When one considers Kentucky's persistent image as a socioeconomic backwater, it is not difficult to fathom the political appeal of John Y. Brown. A handsome *bon vivant*, he is reputed to have a midas touch in business, if not at the Las Vegas gaming tables (where he dropped more than a million dollars in a single night during his term as governor). Married to a woman who is regarded as something of a national sex symbol, Brown leads the sort of life people love to fantasize about—especially if they have an inferiority complex about their own environs.

Not all Kentuckians have been mesmerized by Brown over the years; he won only twenty-nine percent of the vote when he was nominated in 1979, a victory that was pretty much tantamount to election given the weakness of the Republican competition. Many pundits have speculated that there is a fairly static "glamour vote" in the state of twenty-five to thirty percent that "John Y." has a lock on but can't move much beyond. This year, he did not even attempt to.

Mandy Grunwald, a Sawyer staffer, wryly sums up Brown's message during the campaign: "I was a great governor. Now I'm back. Aren't you lucky." Bob Squier, the former governor's media man, does not seem to quarrel: "John's problem in the campaign was he really didn't believe he could lose the race. . . . We were for John being in the dialogue; John was not. John's feeling was he could ride above the fray. He wanted to run something more like the Reagan [reelection] campaign: talking in generalities with pretty pictures."

For a while it appeared the "feelgood" strategy might win by default. Still regarded as the only real threat to Brown by the news media, Beshear spent late March and early April trying to emphasize his tenure of service in public office, a tactic of questionable wisdom, given the antiestablishment mood of the state. His television spots, produced by Doal, Shrum of Washington, D.C., seemed to emulate formats used in several 1986 campaigns: accenting the sibilance of the candidate's name for subliminal recall, playing basketball with kids, the black-and-white service record documentary. The images were pleasant enough, but nothing really registered.

Nevertheless, Beshear was creeping up in the polls (largely because of his steady harvest of endorsements and the effect they were having on media coverage), but so was Brown. By early April, the front-runner had reached forty percent in his own surveys and appeared to be maintaining his fifteen-point lead. The still lightly regarded Wilkinson continued to edge up virtually unnoticed, while the media-bereft duo of Carroll and Stumbo began to fall away.

The campaign's first debate, broadcast over Kentucky's educational-television network on April 13, opened the first obvious chink in Brown's armor. Repeating a little-known position he had held for some time, the conservative former governor indicated he favored the repeal of state House Bill 44, which severely restricted the property-tax powers of local governments. Brown quickly defended his stand by explaining he favored shifting more responsibility for government to the local level and that the Federal Tax Act of 1986 promised to shrink local government revenues. But the lid was off. He immediately fell under attack from Beshear and Wilkinson, with the latter suggesting the tax burden be lightened with a state lottery.

The day following the forum, Mrs. Wilkinson went stumping for votes in the foothills with her sister and a female party official in tow. She had covered much the same ground with her husband only a week before, finding little enthusiasm for the election. But this day was quite different. Talk of the debate and Wilkinson's revenue proposal greeted the women everywhere, and the consensus was fervently in favor of the lottery.

When the women returned to the Wilkinson house that evening, they found Carville and Briscoe discussing the day's strategy sessions. After listening to the exciting report from the hinterlands, the two men looked at each other. They had seen poll figures saying the voters preferred a lottery to new taxes by a seven-to-one margin, but had bought the conventional wisdom that its support was soft while the Bible Belt-based opposition was adamant. Yet, the numbers had not really communicated the depth of feelings.

The Wilkinson managers went into the house, called Sawyer in New York, and ordered a spot that contrasted the lottery proposal with Brown's position on House Bill 44. "New ideas—not new taxes," proclaimed the new ad when it began airing on April 21. The effect on Brown was accentuated by the fact he was playing "rope-a-dope" with Beshear, sustaining eleven days of withering attacks without responding.

The Battering Boy Scout

Steve Beshear had started the campaign season with positive ratings five times his negatives, the best ratio of any candidate in the field. His early media stressed a "good guy" image—the man always willing to help out. Yet in the weeks following the first debate, Beshear's image was drastically transformed.

Making slow progress with the electorate, but unable to close the gap on Brown's platitudinous campaign, Beshear's operatives grew frustrated and began to look for an opening to go on the offensive. When the debate provided such an opportunity, the gloves came off. But bare knuckles soon gave way to brass knuckles as if restraint had lost its way in the smoke of battle. What had started out as an attack on Brown's casual attitude toward higher property taxes soon drifted to more personal fronts: his gambling in office, his jet-set lifestyle, and finally, insinuations that linked the fun-loving ex-governor to cocaine.

Even with the gloves off, Doak, Shrum's media for Beshear continued to exhibit a trust in the tried-and-true formulas of past campaigns. Highlighting Brown's gambling had been effective for Dee Huddleston in his brief 1984 confrontation with Brown, driving up the challenger's negatives so efficiently as to escort him from the race. Another tactic employed was the "lifestyle ad," a mini-parody of *Lifestyles of the Rich and Famous*, narrated by a Robin Leach clone. Its familiar phrasing cynically summarized the Browns' campaign motivations: "No longer on the 'A' list, the fab couple now seeks a return to the Governor's Mansion to recoup their lost social fortunes."

"We'll pay to keep that Robin Leach ad on the air," Bob Squier publicly insisted at the time, perhaps knowing a similar ad had done little for Republican Henry McMaster in his 1986 attempt to unseat Senator Ernest Hollings (D-South Carolina). Privately, however, Squier was worried and exasperated: "Once he [Brown] had taken the onslaught from the Beshear people and sat there and watched a negative commercial run against him for eleven days without response—despite the fact we had produced a commercial within three or four days to respond to it—his negative rating started to slide. Then he finally responded. But the problem was he never understood that he had suffered a blow that you don't recover from. . . .

"Given the changes in Kentucky politics since 1979," Squier continues, "I think everyone was expecting those attacks on John—*except* John. I frankly think he was stunned."

Even before Squier was allowed to unlimber his big guns on Beshear, the lieutenant governor's negatives had begun to climb in reaction to the free-swinging attacks. Some fault the technical aspects of the Doak, Shrum ad campaign as much as its content.

"Beshear clearly was behind," says University of Kentucky political scientist Malcolm Jewell. "He had to do something to challenge the front-runner. But he could have run a stronger positive campaign than he did at the outset and distanced himself from the attack when it came. . . . For some reason, Beshear was much in evidence onscreen during that negative property-tax spot."

Thus, according to Jewell, two cardinal rules of political campaigning were violated by the Beshear campaign:

- Don't ask people to vote against someone else until you've given them a compelling reason to vote *for* you.
- Don't let the candidate carry his own attack in paid media.

Picking up the pieces

Derby Day, May 2, passed festively at Churchill Downs; the traditional signal for Kentuckians to start paying attention to their primary campaigns had been given, and the Squier counterassault had just begun in earnest. Grim ads painted Beshear as a desperate, irresponsible politician bent on destroying others, a tool of special interests whose grab-bag of promises would lead to ruinous taxation.

With their man's negatives starting to soar and his support beginning to waver, the Beshear campaign convened a vital strategy session. Hickman laid out two alternative courses. The first called for a return to soft, positive material, which he felt would guarantee at least a second-place finish—with a faint chance of victory should Brown sink with the ponderous weight of his no-vision campaign. The second course called for intensifying the attack on the front-runner, which might destroy Brown, Beshear, or both—the latter result leaving an opening for the still-distant Wilkinson. Beshear opted for escalation.

As the even more stridently anti-Brown ads started to air during the second week in May, the voters appeared to turn off to Beshear in massive numbers. When even Hickman's surveys asked which candidate was running an "unfair and negative campaign," respondents fingered Beshear over Brown by a nearly two-to-one margin. Beshear's soft support began to fall away, and though his media soon abandoned the attack, it was clear he was dead in the water. Still, content to study dated polls, most of the press continued to treat it as a Brown–Beshear race, as if any other possibility were beyond its frame of reference.

Although Brown's support had stopped falling precipitously as soon as he launched his counterattack, his negatives had now climbed to record levels. By a six-to-one margin, the voters were convinced he intended to raise taxes. With the front-runners thoroughly sullied in the public's eye, Wilkinson began to make his move to the inside.

In what is now usually cited as the key commercial series of the campaign, Sawyer juxtaposed stills of Beshear and Brown ads and quoted each attacking the other on taxes. "Aren't you fed up?" a voice asks, "Then speak up! . . . Vote for Wallace Wilkinson." Another spot first aired at this time begins with a graphic saying, "Steve Beshear says John Y. Brown will raise your taxes," then flips the names. "They're both right," an announcer intones, "and that's wrong. Brown and Beshear would fund their programs by raising your taxes." Wilkinson then adds, "We have a choice: higher taxes or a lottery."

Still unbeknownst to those who declined to put their ear to the ground, the Wilkinson campaign was making its stretch run toward the nomination right on schedule.

John Brown's mouldering body

At this point, Brown began "measuring the windows of the Governor's Mansion," in the words of one reporter, so completely did he dismiss the political acumen of Wallace Wilkinson. "John underestimated the man," says Squier, "and was going on his personal assessment of his opponent, rather than what the numbers were showing."

Brown's guard was plainly down again by the time he appeared in the second debate on May 12. When a panelist asked why he

had not involved himself in public issues during his years out of office, Brown nonchalantly replied, "I dabbled around some in business but really didn't find that that interested me. I really miss being governor." With Wilkinson's "bootstrap" ad starting to penetrate down the stretch, the contrasting images could not be more clearly defined. James Carville made sure the "earned" media painted the same picture.

Wallace Wilkinson had been an indefatigable campaigner for nearly two years, but his push in the final week was herculean. The campaign staged sixty-five media events in that brief period, including one stretch that had the candidate pressing the flesh in a much-publicized twenty-four–hour day. By contrast, Brown appeared to be at leisure in the climactic days of the race: taking in a Cincinnati Reds baseball game, playing in a celebrity pro-am golf tournament, and watching the Hardscuffle Steeplechase from a $3,000 box.

Carville, for one, was not surprised: "They did the same thing in [the gubernatorial race in] Pennsylvania. People just have a tendency to lay back the last ten days. It's amazing! . . . If I've learned anything in this business it's that earned media is awesome ten days out until Election Day."

The issues as well as the images were beginning to break Wilkinson's way at the end. The Thursday before the election, the *Louisville Courier-Journal*, the state's dominant newspaper, ran a banner story across page one declaring the race was becoming a Brown–Wilkinson contest turning on the lottery–tax question. Wilkinson's tracking polls already showed he had picked up ten points of support in the previous week. Brown suddenly began to panic and approved the airing of a response spot targeted at Wilkinson that Squier had been urging on him for days.

But only a holiday weekend remained before the voting. "By then almost no one was watching," Squier recalls. "Those that were had probably made up their minds."

The attack on Wilkinson aired at saturation levels and carried the same ominous tones

Lessons for Candidates and Consultants Campaigning in a Multicandidate Field

What are some of the lessons to be learned from the five-way race in the Democratic primary for governor of Kentucky? A sampler:

- **Define the race for the voters.** Give a readily grasped reason to vote for you and not the others. Emphasize what sets you apart. "In a democracy, campaigns are adversarial," says Wilkinson strategist James Carville. "People understand that. Footage of the candidate walking in the woods with his dog doesn't tell them [anything]. They want you to draw a distinction between yourself and the field. . . . Whoever gets to define the race will generally win it."

- **Trust hard facts, not established truisms.** A willingness to challenge the conventional wisdom—if you have indications it is faulty—will not only attract needed attention, it will give you a leg up on your conventional opponents. "If you take the time to really look at the data," insists Wilkinson pollster Mark Mellman, "you'll often find that the conventional wisdom is way off base."

- **Don't rest on your laurels.** No matter how successful a previous tour of duty may have been, voters hate being taken for granted. Give them an idea of what you're *going* to do for them and appear to be eager for the opportunity to do it. As Brown pollster Bill Hamilton observes, "In this day and age, we no longer annoint our leaders—they have to work for it."

- **Don't hestitate to counter a serious attack.** An opponent's unanswered negative adver-

tising can inflict irreparable damage on your credibility if it registers with the electorate. Brown media man Bob Squier knows first-hand: "I think if we had done it [countered Beshear] earlier, we could have dealt with Wilkinson earlier, and you would have seen a different result."

- **Emphasize a fresh image.** Voters are looking for new ideas and approaches and admire someone who'll go into the lion's den and rattle the cages. According to Wilkinson media consultant David Sawyer, "The voters' desire for new approaches in government will be the key factor in elections across the board in 1988."

- **Shoot for a plurality, *not* a consensus.** Attempting to please all of the voters all of the time makes Johnny a dull candidate. In a multicandidate no-runoff primary, you need not heed majority opinion; you just have to turn out more voters than everyone else. Taking a marginally unpopular stance could leave a positive impression and produce a needed cadre of support. "Attacking the Toyota deal was not a winning issue for us," recalls Sawyer of a turning point in the campaign. "But it made people begin to take notice of Wallace by presenting something different."

- **Don't play the heavy.** In a multicandidate race, if you pound too hard too long only on the most formidable opposition, his disaffected support is likely to move on—but not to you.

---

that ran behind Squier's anti-Beshear material, but the copy basically followed the "who is this guy?" approach that had been successful for Walter Mondale in his 1984 primary battles with Hart. Aside from being too little too late, the spot unintentionally might have served as a clarion call to the anti-Brown vote.

"That ad attacking Wilkinson made it clear to anyone paying attention that Wilkinson was now the one remaining serious threat to

Brown," assesses Malcolm Jewell, "so the anti-Brown vote shifted to him."

Thus, the race had been defined: Choose between a man who had grown up dirt poor and a man born to leisure; between a man who had made a dramatic success of his life through the dedicated application of his rare talents and a man who loved to fritter his time away at casinos, racetracks, and golf courses; between a man who had worked furiously for two years to seek support and a man who had filed at the last possible moment and had yet to explain why he was running at all; between fresh outlooks, approaches, and ideas and a rerun of years past; between a painless lottery to raise needed revenues and more burdensome taxes.

The result was what Mark Mellman calls "the rarity in politics: the landslide upset," though the real mystery is why it came as such a surprise.

A postscript: As the biggest loser in this Derby, John Y. Brown, Jr., bears compelling testimony: "I never dreamed that of all people, John Y. Brown would ever be beaten by an opponent's endorsement of gambling."

[Editor's Note: Wilkinson won another landslide victory in the November general election and is now serving his term as Kentucky governor.]

David Beiler

Running for Mayor with a Micro:

How Computer Volunteer Training Paid Off in Charlotte

Allyn McGillicuddy • Vernon L. Robinson

Harvey Gantt, a three-term city councilman from Charlotte, North Carolina, made his initial bid to be the first black mayor of Charlotte in 1979 and was narrowly defeated by fellow Democrat Eddie Knox When Knox decided four years later to run for governor, Gantt ran for mayor again, this time without primary opposition, and he won the general election with fifty-two percent of the vote. Here you learn how an Apple II microcomputer—the same one used by many high schools and colleges—was integrated into the Gantt campaign organization for his second attempt and utilized for a get-out-the-vote (GOTV) effort that led to victory. The volunteer training required to sustain a campaign computer operation is also examined in depth. The authors tell a methodical yet inspiring story of how modern technology was used to mobilize grassroots support to elect an underdog black candidate in a majority-white Southern city.

While Harvey Gantt had run three times citywide in council races, his previous campaigns had not used computers. We approached his campaign management group with a proposal that outlined the useful applications of large computers to political campaigns. A second section discussed possible uses for a microcomputer in the headquarters.

In the presentation to the campaign steering committee, we recommended buying a tape from the County Board of Elections with the entire voter registration list for the City of Charlotte. The campaign contracted with Jim O'Reilly of Calumet Associates, Durham, North Carolina, to generate voter lists from the tapes.

O'Reilly produced voter registration lists and mailing labels sorted by street, by precinct, by zip code, and by various demographic characteristics (age, race, sex, etc.). The campaign also received four-part printouts sorted by street and precinct for Election-Day GOTV operations in targeted precincts.

The Gantt committee also approved the use of a microcomputer in the campaign head-

Allyn McGillicuddy was the headquarters coordinator for the Harvey Gantt for Mayor campaign. Vernon L. Robinson is a faculty member at Winston-Salem State University in Winston-Salem, North Carolina.

quarters. (A system was donated to the campaign, reducing the required capital outlay.) The management decided not to acquire specialized software such as "Campaign Manager" because we were able to modify general software to meet campaign requirements.

The assembled system included an Apple II Plus 64K computer with monochrome "green" monitor, two dual-side diskette drives, and an Epson RX-80 printer. VisiFile®, the electronic filing system, was used extensively throughout the campaign. AppleWriter II, also available, was not used before Election Day. After Election Day, this word processing software was used in conjunction with an Apple letter-quality printer to produce several thousand thank-you letters and mailing labels.

The Gantt campaign used the Apple computer in a variety of ways. In addition to word processing, the campaign maintained a database with a 600-record volunteer file; specialized mailing lists; over 500 yard-sign locations, and 150 contributor records from a direct-mail effort. On Election Day, more computer applications proved helpful. The campaign had placed precinct workers at each polling place in addition to drivers in targeted precincts to take voters to the polls. The targeted precincts were primarily in the black community, where voter turnout in municipal elections was traditionally very low. Each precinct worker was given a four-copy list of registered voters from the precinct. As people cast their votes, their names were crossed off the list. Four times during the day, runners picked up one of the copies of the precinct lists and returned them to the closest GOTV headquarters. Drivers and drivers' assistants used copies of the lists to locate and pick up voters who had not yet voted.

Eight times during the day, runners also picked up vote counts and called them into the GOTV headquarters. The vote counts allowed the local headquarters to reallocate drivers and drivers' assistants at regular intervals to precincts with the lowest percent-

age of turnout. Similarly, the counts were reported to central headquarters. The counts were entered into the GOTV file, which included a record for each precinct. Using computed fields, VisiFile® compared the vote count to the total number of voters in the precinct, automatically calculated the percentage of voter turnout for each precinct, and used the tabulated information to reallocate GOTV resources throughout the city.

Using the sort function, the precincts were listed and printed out in order of percentage of voter turnout, with the lowest precinct on top of the list. The list allowed the staff to decide where to redeploy vans, cars, and 350 volunteers for the maximum effect in twenty precincts. In the last hour of the campaign, several teams combed the precinct with the lowest turnout for registered voters who had not been to the polls.

Computer concepts and campaign management

As confidence in microcomputers rises, more low-budget campaigns will use computers to support decision-making with timely information. Successfully integrating the computer into the campaign requires merging computer concepts with campaign management principles. Volunteer training, methods of enhancing accessibility, and establishing adequate controls are the means of accomplishing this integration. A substantial volunteer training program was required to support daily operation of the headquarters computer. The program was designed to quickly train a volunteer cadre that could later support an ongoing training program.

By the end of July, nearly 200 people had volunteered to work for Harvey Gantt's November election. Some had called twice, offended that nobody from the campaign had contacted them. The headquarters were not yet officially open, and lack of work for volunteers threatened to alienate them.

The headquarters coordinator of the 1979

race listed information required from each volunteer for use throughout the new campaign. The list included whether each wanted a yard sign, wanted to work in the headquarters, to do precinct work, or to work on Election Day. It asked what hours of the day each was available, and which days of the week. We added two questions: "Can you type?" and "Would you like to work on the computer?" We based the makeup of our volunteer file records on this list.

A volunteer information sheet was designed to match the format of our file records. Volunteers were invited to an organizational meeting at the beginning of August. Of the 200 who had volunteered, about 130 attended. The campaign manager outlined the jobs to be filled by the volunteers, and the volunteers completed their information sheets according to preference.

Approximately twenty-five volunteers answered "yes" to both the questions, "Can you type?" and "Would you like to work on the computer?" After manually extracting these volunteers' names from the pile of papers, we invited them to a computer training session.

Volunteer training

A four-week period was barely long enough to complete effective elementary training. The goal was to train fifty volunteers. It was our hope that training a large segment of the headquarters volunteers would ensure that there would always be someone in the campaign office who could retrieve and enter information. The trained volunteers could also teach other volunteers rudimentary file management operations.

Each week in August, four training sessions were held. The volunteers were invited to an introductory session and a session on "advanced functions." A grassroots leadership trainer, Barry Greever, developed an outline for the introductory training session. There were four objectives. The first was to familiarize volunteers with computer terms they couldn't live without such as menu, floppy disk, booting a program, and others. The second goal was to establish physical familiarity with the hardware. Each volunteer had to learn how to handle and insert diskettes, how to boot a program, and the location of special function keys on the keyboard. Third, each had to learn how to enter and inspect a record in the campaign volunteer file. Finally, and perhaps most important, each volunteer had to learn how to recover from any confusing situation that would arise while using the computer.

We scheduled ten to twelve volunteers for the first two sessions, assuming correctly that about six would actually attend. More than six per computer is too many because volunteers become bored when they have to wait too long for a turn at the keyboard.

Apple has developed a delightful introduction to the Apple 2E called "Apple Presents Apple." Parts of the presentation are adaptable to the Apple II Plus. The program directs attention to the function keys on the keyboard, explains the concept and use of menus, teaches the editing functions built into the keyboard, and describes other basic computer functioning in a most entertaining fashion.

The volunteer who came early was rewarded by starting immediately with "Apple Presents Apple." By the time all the volunteers had arrived, half of them had run through the short, computer-based introduction.

We arranged chairs in a semicircle round the computer so that everyone could view both keyboard and monitor. We began by encouraging the volunteers to ask all the questions they had always wanted answered about computers. We wrote the questions on a large sheet of paper taped to the wall, and promised to either respond to every question by the end of the session or to find an answer after the session.

An hour of lecture on command keys, devices, and computer terminology could have driven the most dedicated volunteer away, perhaps forever. The trainer's challenge, then, is to make computer education engaging. Our strategy was to make the session brief, fun, and to maximize personal involvement in the training. We were alert to the inevitable presence of that unwelcome guest at any computer training session—fear.

Barry began with a personal story about his own first encounter with a computer. He subsequently asked each volunteer to relate to the group any experience she or he had with computers. To our surprise, almost all of the volunteers had some experience, and some had programming experience.

Most businesses use computers, and many campaign volunteers can be expected to have interacted with them to some extent on the job, especially volunteers who can type. For this reason, we began to screen computer volunteers based on the question "Can you type?" instead of "Would you like to work on the computer?" We found that the greatest obstacle to computer use is the inability to find one's way around a keyboard. For the advanced computer user of large systems, our little Apple and limited software seemed cumbersome and frustrating. So we looked for the volunteer who could type and who had little opportunity to play with computers at work. These volunteers proved to be the most motivated, persistent computer volunteers.

Nevertheless, there is nothing more boring than watching somebody hit keys on a keyboard for an hour. Instead, we asked the volunteers at the training session to take turns at the keyboard. Each person began with a cold machine and diskettes in the box. For example, he or she would cold boot the machine, load the diskettes, and move from the main menu of VisiFile® to the section of the program in which records can be added to the data file. Then he or she would enter his or her own record, using the volunteer information sheet previously submitted. Having completed the record, the individual would move back to the main menu, remove the diskettes, and turn off the equipment.

At the end of the introductory session, we taped large sheets of paper on the wall behind the computer so that anyone sitting at the computer could look up and see them. In very large colored markers, we wrote our first version of system documentation. Beginning at step one, a volunteer could go from a boot-up to add a record, and then return to the main menu. For every screen the volunteers might see on the computer, a corresponding picture was drawn on the wall sheets. The next step was explained beneath the drawing. Thus, a volunteer could figure out how to add a record by using the wall sheets if he or she forgot what had been covered in the introductory session.

After two introductory sessions with different groups, we began to ask some of the volunteers to conduct part of the training sessions. After two weeks, several volunteers conducted entire training sessions, and they continued to teach volunteers throughout the campaign.

In the second training week, we held our first "advanced functions" session. The volunteers were already familiar with the program, the main menu, and the control keys. Some had entered a hundred or so records into the file. So the second session was easy. The trainers never touched a key, and the volunteers took turns at the keyboard. We chose menu items that had never been chosen in the previous session, such as "sort" and "print." At the end of the first advanced training session, we introduced the first real system of documentation.

Readable system documentation

The purpose of the users' manual is not to teach a volunteer how to use computer functions. Rather, it is to refresh his or her memory so he or she can quickly figure out what to do next. The 200-page book that comes with VisiFile® is not useful for this purpose. We wrote our own manual after consultation with a long-term microcomputer user. Following her advice, each page in the manual had three columns of text. The middle column was entitled "Computer Request." This column referred to the system prompt, i.e.,

Allyn McGillicuddy • Vernon L. Robinson

what is on the computer screen at any given point. The column to the right of "Computer Request" was entitled, "What You Do." These two columns provided a quick reference for the trained volunteer who couldn't quite remember what came next (see Table 1 for a sample page of the manual).

By scanning the columns, users could find their place in the program and determine the next step. They could also see whether and how far they had strayed from the proper course for the function they were attempting to execute. The leftmost column of the users' manual was entitled "Comments." This column briefly described what was going on in the program at each point. For example, the comment to the left of "Main menu is displayed at the top of the screen" read, "You are expected to select a function of the program, such as 'PRINT' or 'BACKUP' or 'DONE.'" This quick reference was vital for volunteers who came into the headquarters to work once every two weeks, or at three-week intervals.

We planned to open the headquarters to the public at the beginning of September. By the end of August, forty-two volunteers had attended at least one training session, and about thirty had attended two. To six reliable volunteers, we assigned file management functions, such as backups, printing reports, and updating indexes. These volunteers became the backbone of the headquarters during the rest of the campaign.

The computer training provided a means of engaging volunteers long before the campaign really got underway. It arrested dissipation of early enthusiasm, allowed volunteers to form friendships early in the campaign, and established early on a pattern of working in the headquarters on a regular basis. Thus, when the headquarters began to gear up, a group of people were in place to train others and to help create order.

Throughout the campaign, a wide variance in volunteer computer facility persisted. Nevertheless, the computer became a convenient file cabinet, rather than a campaign icon

worshiped by a corps of computer "priests." Widespread training made it possible to enhance the utility of the computer and to increase the accessibility of information stored therein.

While training is the most important step toward computer accessibility, other procedures must be followed, and pitfalls must be avoided. The greatest problem one confronts is computerphobia: Many people are simply afraid of computers. They are afraid they will break the expensive machinery or wipe out important data.

Others are supremely confident. This group includes a number of people who, because they have worked on one computer, assume they can use any computer without assistance or training. Our previous experience has taught that it is not possible to scare the overconfident volunteers into observing controls and accepting supervision. By attempting to do so, one succeeds in scaring the already terrified into refusing to touch the computer. However, effective controls *are* necessary and must be observed by everyone in the campaign headquarters.

System controls

Controls are an integral part of any campaign computer operation. Controls help avoid inadvertent or unauthorized action that could have a negative impact on the campaign and are especially important when a microcomputer is being used by volunteers. The Gantt campaign controls may be divided into four areas: procedures, physical controls, information security, and privacy.

Procedural controls

Backup procedures are critical to any information-handling system. The data encoded on diskettes are extremely vulnerable to damage. Diskette backup is accomplished by making a copy of data diskettes and by saving a copy of all the input since the last backup was made.

Program diskettes, on which applications

TABLE 1 Printing a Report

Comments	Computer Request	What You Do
1. You are expected to select a function of the program, such as "PRINT" or "BACKUP" or "DONE."	Main menu is displayed at the top of the screen.	PRINT (Use spacebar to move highlight to Print and hit Return key.)
2. You must select whether you want to print a report, mailing labels, or get out of the print function of the program.	Print menu is displayed at the top of the screen. REPORT LABELS DONE	REPORT (Use left arrow key to highlight and hit Return key.)

3. You must select a report definition, which is the way the information is going to be printed out. For example, a list of names and phone numbers, or a list of names and addresses. The Report definitions have already been defined, but you choose one.	REPORT DEFINITION
	  Yardsign
	  Applers
	  Districts
	  Projects
	  Voter Reg
	  Autos
	  Create Definition
	Select Done
		WHAT REPORT DO YOU WANT? See next page for a list and description of the available report definitions. Choose the one that seems closest to what you need. Choose by using the spacebar to highlight your choice, and then hit the return key.

4. The printer must be on and have paper in it. It should be lined up so that the perforation is just above the print nose.	READY PRINTER	Check printer to see if the Ready and Online lights are on and the paper is in the printer.
5. The report is done and the computer needs the next instruction.	INSERT PROGRAM DISK	Remove data disk and insert program disk.
6. You are back at the Print Menu. You must decide to either print out another report or to get out of the print function of the program.	Print Menu is displayed at the top of the screen. REPORT LABELS DONE	DONE (Unless you want another copy of the report or a different report.) Use right arrow to highlight Done and hit return key.
7. You are back at the Main Menu. You must choose to get into another part of the program, or to end it altogether.	Main Menu is displayed at the top of the screen.	DONE (Unless you have another job for the computer to do.) Using the right arrow key, highlight "Done" and hit the Return key.
8. You are about ready to turn the computer off. The computer is allowing you to leave the program and either use a different program or to write a program or to shut the computer off.	DO YOU WISH TO LEAVE VISIFILE?	YES (Move highlight to yes and hit return key.)
9. You have left the program. The computer has no program in it and it is waiting for you to tell it to do something.	]■	Turn the machine off. Don't forget the monitor, too. Store the diskettes in their boxes, and fill out the computer log.

software such as VisiFile® are encoded, are also vulnerable to damage. The campaign should have timely access to backup copies of the program diskette. Most of these diskettes cannot be copied, and should not be copied unless the user is so licensed by the software manufacturer. Many software vendors will provide backup copies for a minimal charge. Most require registering under a "user support plan" to have program diskettes replaced. The program diskette used in the Gantt campaign was damaged a week before the election, which caused many problems and great consternation on the part of the headquarters coordinator, who had to scramble on a deadline to find a replacement copy.

The Gantt campaign made weekly backup copies of the data files at the onset of the computer operation. As a greater volume of data was processed, backups were made more frequently. In addition to regular backup procedures and the retaining of primary documents, a listing or printout of the data diskettes was made on a regular basis. Five times during the campaign, diskettes were damaged or lost. It would have been difficult, if not impossible, to restore the lost data if backup procedures had not been in place.

Simple procedures pertaining to handling input data were also developed. Data to be entered on the computer were placed in an in-basket. A volunteer indicated the name of the correct input file on the upper right corner of each document. After the data were entered, it was placed in an out-basket and dated to indicate how long it should be held for backup purposes.

Several reports were generated from the data on a regular basis. These reports included new volunteer contacts and yard sign locations. Procedures were developed to enable the reports' intended recipients to easily find the reports in the headquarters. A location was designated as the report repository for each campaign committee head.

A computer log is a written record of who has used the computer and which application programs were used. This log is an invaluable method of control. The campaign management team can use an accurate log to determine which tasks have been accomplished, whether established deadlines are being met, and who is working on the computer.

A list of computer volunteers was posted on the wall, initially to buttress the volunteers' confidence. The computer log was tacked to the wall beside it. If the log is maintained, the headquarters coordinator can identify volunteers who consistently make errors on the computer and retrain them in a timely manner. Fortunately, the volunteers' error rate was minimal.

Physical controls

Physical controls over the computer area are also important. These controls are designed to reduce the negative impact of inappropriate or unauthorized activity on computer operations. Physical controls include creating a diskette library, providing insurance protection, and prohibiting food and drink in the computer area.

A strict prohibition on eating or drinking near the computer *must* be maintained. Pizza and soft drinks are commonplace in campaign headquarters. Computer components and diskettes can be badly damaged by tomato paste, Pepsi, and the moisture from other foods. Keeping these items away from the computer area is the best way to reduce the risk of unnecessary damage.

Most campaign headquarters look like disaster areas. A lost diskette can severely hold up operations. A secure place for computer supplies as well as for the diskette library should be created early at headquarters to reduce the chance of disrupted operations caused by poor housekeeping.

The Gantt headquarters sought to involve volunteers with the computer to the maximum extent possible. This consideration outweighed concerns about the large number of people who would have access to a fairly expensive system. The risk of loss from theft or damage is always present in this kind of environment. It is advisable to acquire both a hardware maintenance agreement and insurance to protect the campaign from substantial cost to replace stolen or damaged equipment.

Security and privacy

Controls must also be developed to address the problems of information security and privacy of the individual. Certain information should not be in the public domain. Information that reveals timing or strategy obviously should be protected. Polling and targeting information can be generated using microcomputers. This type of strategic information and the generation methodology should be closely held by the campaign staff. The way to "secure" information is to put the sensitive information on a separate diskette and limit access only to those who must use it. Another means of securing data is to use customized software with passwords to limit access to the terminal. The resources of the campaign will dictate which method or methods should be used.

Perhaps less obvious but just as important, information on volunteers and contributors should be used for official campaign purposes only. One campaign worker commented, "With all the phone numbers of these volunteers, I'll never go without a date." At the time, everyone thought the comment was humorous, but action was taken to remind campaign personnel of the importance of privacy with regard to information stored on the computer. The caveat was written into the user manual, which stated that this information was for campaign use only.

The most effective way to counter comput-erphobia is to damage-proof the system. If all precautions have been taken, the volunteers can be assured with confidence that nothing they can possibly do can cause the slightest damage to either the hardware or the software. The worst that can happen is that a slight inconvenience might have to be endured for a short period. We encouraged the volunteers to make mistakes, stating that greater learning occurs while attempting to recover from an error. For example, during training sessions, we often said, "How about hitting the wrong key right now just to see what happens." Although we didn't use it in the campaign, we had an AppleWriter II learning diskette in the office, and we encouraged volunteers to come in during their spare time and play with the word processing program to foster experimentation with the computer.

Conclusion

In order to use a microcomputer effectively in a low-budget campaign, the campaign must train a large number of volunteers. Normal campaign volunteer attrition requires an ongoing, systematic approach to training and procedural controls. All other things being equal, the low-budget campaign that successfully integrates this approach with sound campaign management principles will enjoy a decisive advantage over an opponent employing standard campaign techniques.

[Editor's Note: Harvey Gantt was less successful in 1987, when he was narrowly defeated for reelection to the mayor's post.]

Allyn McGillicuddy • Vernon L. Robinson

Computers, Control, and Communication:

How 30,000 Volunteers Beat the California Gun Initiative

Dennis Jensen

The initiative process, whereby citizens propose and secure a place on the ballot for issue propositions, is a familiar one for Californians, who regularly vote on a host of matters from tax relief to AIDS policy. In 1982, state residents who sought to enact controls on some kinds of firearms succeeded in getting Proposition 15, a pro-gun control initiative, before the voters. The public's initial reaction was favorable, to judge from a number of public opinion surveys, but opponents of the measure quickly went to work to reverse that trend. Capitalizing on the intensity of opposition felt by many gun owners, the anti-initiative forces ran a textbook computerized campaign that efficiently attracted and utilized 30,000 volunteers. Computer lists and careful detail work marshaled an army of activists who produced overwhelming defeat for Proposition 15 in the final vote. Note that almost every aspect of the modern campaign—from fundraising and press relations to research, canvassing, and direct mail—was nicely fitted together using computer technology as the invaluable mediator.

In March, 1982, California's Proposition 15, a pro-gun control initiative, led in the polls by two to one, yet went down to defeat in November by a margin of sixty-three percent to thirty-seven percent. One of the reasons for the overwhelming turnaround was the coordinated activity of the anti-initiative campaign's more than 30,000 volunteers, one of the largest grassroots campaigns in California. This grassroots effort was made possible by the use of a computer firm to coordinate the activities of the volunteers. While other aspects of the campaign, especially the media effort by George Young & Associates, deserve more credit for the defeat of the initiative, the volunteer effort was an effective arm of the campaign.

Dennis Jensen is a political consultant and was the volunteer coordinator for Citizens Against the Gun Initiative.

Identifying the volunteer organization's computer requirements

The campaign committee for the Citizens Against the Gun Initiative was made up of a coalition of six of the major gun-owner organizations in California, including the National Rifle Association (250,000 California membership) and Gun Owners of California (250,000 membership). There were at least 350,000 individuals belonging to one or more of the coalition organizations, and because of this, it was estimated that there would be anywhere from a few thousand to possibly tens of thousands of volunteers for the campaign against the gun initiative by November. It was imperative to keep the volunteers busy on activities that would substantially contribute to the campaign, in order to avoid any dissatisfaction by supporting member organizations that might otherwise feel the campaign wasn't doing everything possible to fight the initiative.

It was obvious, therefore, that a computer system would be needed to coordinate the large numbers of expected volunteers. Furthermore, while the major thrust of the campaign would have to be in the media, it would be a mistake not to use such a large resource of volunteer time if it materialized.

With these considerations in mind, the campaign identified the following requirements for a computer system for the volunteer operation:

1. The ability to store the names, addresses, and volunteer information on tens of thousands of volunteers and to retrieve this information in any type of format desired.
2. A need to quickly process large numbers of volunteers into a computer system— possibly up to ten thousand or more names per week—getting each name on the system within four days after it was given to the computer firm.
3. A short turnaround time to produce lists or mailing labels of volunteers in any of the categories desired, preferably within two days from the time of the request.
4. The ability to transfer and integrate other computer lists into the campaign's computer system, and to eliminate the duplication of names efficiently.
5. The necessity to meet all of the campaign's computer needs at a reasonable cost.
6. The use of a local computer firm to avoid delays caused by shipping and any problems of materials being lost in the mail.

Chart A was drawn up to determine what types of names and lists would be added to the computer system and to aid in the design of a procedure to get them on the computer. Chart B was made to determine what volunteer information should be gathered and sorted in order to make certain the computer system would be able to sort names and produce the types of lists that were likely to be needed. As shown in Chart A, the campaign expected volunteers to contact the office by both phone and mail, and to receive additional names of potential volunteers from people who contacted the office seeking more information on the initiative. Another responsibility of the volunteer organization was to coordinate the processing of campaign contributions and collect the names of contributors, many of whom were also volunteers, and put them on the volunteer computer system. Other types of lists needed in the campaign included a media list, a speakers' bureau list, and a list of gun businesses and gun clubs that would be used to recruit volunteers, to distribute literature, and to solicit money.

Computer requirements for fundraising

One of the basic tenets of political campaign fundraising is that the best fundraising list consists of past contributors and people involved in the campaign. The next best list is probably that of people who have something to lose on Election Day if the vote goes the wrong way. The campaign decided to put both a contributor list and a potential donor list on the computer for easy access. Two fundraising requirements were identified that

CHART A

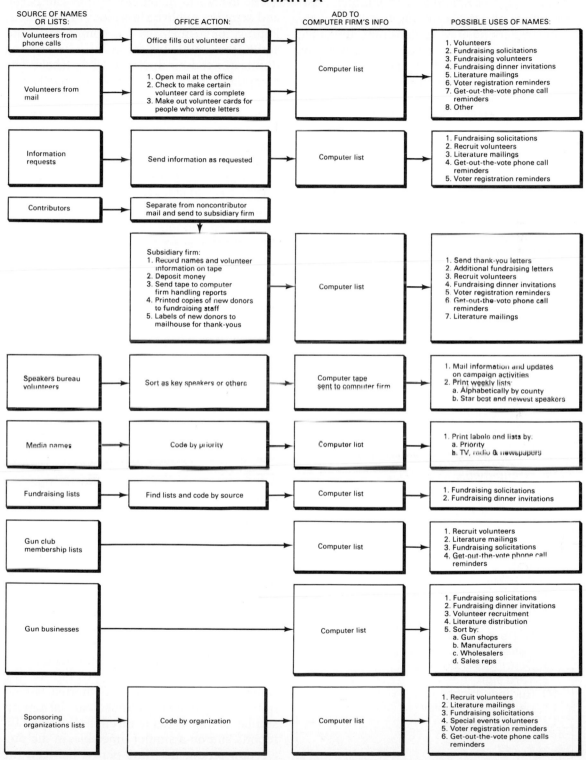

SOURCE OF NAMES OR LISTS:	OFFICE ACTION:	ADD TO COMPUTER FIRM'S INFO	POSSIBLE USES OF NAMES:
Volunteers from phone calls	Office fills out volunteer card	Computer list	1. Volunteers 2. Fundraising solicitations 3. Fundraising volunteers 4. Fundraising dinner invitations 5. Literature mailings 6. Voter registration reminders 7. Get-out-the-vote phone call reminders 8. Other
Volunteers from mail	1. Open mail at the office 2. Check to make certain volunteer card is complete 3. Make out volunteer cards for people who wrote letters		
Information requests	Send information as requested	Computer list	1. Fundraising solicitations 2. Recruit volunteers 3. Literature mailings 4. Get-out-the-vote phone call reminders 5. Voter registration reminders
Contributors	Separate from noncontributor mail and send to subsidiary firm		
	Subsidiary firm: 1. Record names and volunteer information on tape 2. Deposit money 3. Send tape to computer firm handling reports 4. Printed copies of new donors to fundraising staff 5. Labels of new donors to mailhouse for thank-yous	Computer list	1. Send thank-you letters 2. Additional fundraising letters 3. Recruit volunteers 4. Fundraising dinner invitations 5. Voter registration reminders 6. Get-out-the-vote phone call reminders 7. Literature mailings

Speakers bureau volunteers	Sort as key speakers or others	Computer tape sent to computer firm	1. Mail information and updates on campaign activities
			2. Print weekly lists:
			  a. Alphabetically by county
			  b. Star best and newest speakers

Media names	Code by priority	Computer list	1. Print labels and lists by:
			  a. Priority
			  b. TV, radio & newspapers

Fundraising lists	Find lists and code by source	Computer list	1. Fundraising solicitations 2. Fundraising dinner invitations
Gun club membership lists		Computer list	1. Recruit volunteers 2. Literature mailings 3. Fundraising solicitations 4. Get-out-the-vote phone call reminders

Gun businesses		Computer list	1. Fundraising solicitations
			2. Fundraising dinner invitations
			3. Volunteer recruitment
			4. Literature distribution
			5. Sort by:
			  a. Gun shops
			  b. Manufacturers
			  c. Wholesalers
			  d. Sales reps

Sponsoring organizations lists	Code by organization	Computer list	1. Recruit volunteers 2. Literature mailings 3. Fundraising solicitations 4. Special events volunteers 5. Voter registration reminders 6. Get-out-the-vote phone calls reminders

would have to be handled by a computer. First, the campaign was beginning to acquire lists of gun owners, businesses, gun clubs, and other potential contributors. Many people were on two or three lists, and to mail without first eliminating the duplicates would be a significant waste of money. Potential contributors who were sent two or three identical solicitations would also be very concerned

CHART B

Volunteer List Information

Information on Individuals

1. Source code
2. Name
3. Address
4. City
5. State
6. Zip
7. Home phone: area code & prefix included
8. Work phone: area code & prefix included
9. Employer's name
10. Employer's address
11. Employer's city
12. Employer's state
13. Employer's zip
14. Occupation
15. Date person put on computer file

Campaign Information & Volunteer Info:

1. General volunteer & special events
2. Speakers bureau
3. Fundraising volunteer
4. Headquarters volunteer
5. Phone bank volunteer
6. Get-out-the-vote volunteer
7. Contact neighbors
8. Distribute literature
9. Yard sign
10. Bumper sticker
11. Use name publicly
12. Contributor

---

about the waste of money by the campaign, and therefore might be less likely to contribute. Putting the names on the computer would serve the dual function of eliminating duplicates and producing mailing labels. The computer would also be able to match new names and lists against those people already mailed a solicitation, so that future mailings could avoid sending the same person the same letter.

The second fundraising requirement was the need to have the names of contributors readily available for sending thank-you letters, asking for more money, and inviting them to fundraising dinners and other events. Since each of the campaign's sponsoring organizations were soliciting their own members and then turning the money over to the campaign, there was no way to estimate how many people would directly contribute to the campaign. If each contribution averaged ten dollars, 10,000 contributions would have to be processed for every $100,000 received. The $5.2 million dollar budget for the "No on 15" campaign called for about $1.7 million to be raised by the campaign, with the remaining $3.5 million to be raised by the sponsoring organizations. Meeting the $1.7 million goal would mean the campaign would have to process over 100,000 contributions in the last three or four months before Election Day. As it turned out, the sponsoring organizations generated the bulk of the contributions, but the campaign did end up processing more than 30,000 contributions.

Computer requirements for the campaign reports of contributors

With a $5 million campaign and the possibility of tens of thousands of contributions, it was apparent that the campaign would have to use a computer to keep track of contributions and produce the contribution portion of the campaign financial report. California law requires campaigns to submit financial reports similar to the Federal Election Commission reports and on a similar timetable. In the pre-election report, the time period between the

cutoff date for contributions and the sub-
mission of the report was only five days. The
computer system would have to quickly record
contributions and produce campaign reports,
and at the same time record volunteer information for use by the campaign.

Selection of a computer firm

With the magnitude of tasks needed to be
performed by a computer system, it seemed
neither practical nor economical to set up a
computer system within the office. The input
of thousands of names weekly would require
several keypunch operators and the investment of tens of thousands of dollars in a computer system and several terminals. There was
also no time to find a suitable software program
or to train people to run the computer. Furthermore, since the names going into the system
would likely come in spurts (after a mailing
or a large fundraiser), hiring steady employees
would not be economical, since there would
be days when they had little to do. Part-time
employees, on the other hand, would result
in constant turnover and never-ending personnel problems. After looking into costs, the
decision to turn over the work to an outside
computer firm was an easy one.

The choice of a computer firm came down
to a choice between a large firm with several
large IBM computers and printers and offices
in several cities, or a local computer firm with
one computer which was eager for the
campaign's business. The large firm had
backup computers in case one broke down,
and it had dozens of major corporate clients
who were apparently satisfied with its work.
The smaller firm promised a two-day turnaround in putting names on the system, as
opposed to four or five days for the large firm.
The costs were about the same for both firms,
and they both used the same type of computer
system, an IBM 4331 Model 2. Both firms could
meet all of the campaign's requirements for
everything except processing contributions
and producing the state campaign reports,
which neither firm was equipped to do. The

smaller firm also promised a one-day turnaround on most sets of lists and labels, while
the larger firm promised two days. In the end,
the cautious approach of choosing the larger
firm with backup computers was made. Over
2,000 initial volunteer names were shipped
off to the firm, and the campaign was told
the system would be operational within a week.
Four weeks later, still without any lists from
the firm, the large firm was fired and the small
computer firm took over the work. Apparently
the large firm treated the campaign as a small
client, and only the sales representative in
charge of the campaign's account would
answer questions or talk to the campaign.
Since he was usually out of town three out
of five days a week, daily communication was
impossible.

The decision to change computer firms at
the beginning of the campaign was a fortunate
one. There was time to make up lost ground
since the election was still three and a half
months away. The smaller firm, Wayne
Systems in Torrance, California, provided the
best computer service the staff had seen. After
switching firms, it took about a week to get
the system fully operational. Wayne Systems
always met the two-day turnaround time for
putting names into the system, and they
produced the lists and labels on time. They
even provided mailing labels on one or two
hours' notice during the final days of the
campaign when a crisis developed and a
mailing had to go out *that day*!

The campaign reporting system proved to
be the most difficult operation to set up. The
law firm of Dobbs and Nielsen was handling
the campaign reports for the Citizens Against
the Gun Initiative, but they were not equipped
to handle the large volume of contributions
expected by the campaign and to turn those
names back to the campaign staff with the
volunteer information contained on the
donation cards.

One major firm initially agreed to process
the contributions for the Citizens Against the
Gun Initiative, but changed its mind because
of a potential conflict of interest. After a few

weeks of searching for a firm to process contributions and put the names on a computer system, the operations of accounting and computer processing were split between two firms. One firm was hired to provide the accounting functions, including depositing money and recording contributors and their volunteer activities on computer tapes. This information was transmitted daily by telephone to a computer firm in Sacramento (SAS) that was experienced in producing campaign reports. SAS had the capability to produce lists of contributors quickly in a form acceptable to the California Fair Political Practices Commission. On a weekly basis they sent Wayne Systems a computer tape of all new contributors with the volunteer categories coded on it. These names were immediately put on the Wayne Systems computer and duplicate names were eliminated, with all nonduplicative information merged onto a master tape. For example, if a person had initially volunteered to pass out literature and then later contributed to the campaign and asked for a bumper sticker, the computer would add the contribution and bumper sticker request to his file, and the duplicate file would be eliminated. In order to send thank-you letters to contributors with a request for more money, the Sacramento computer firm would print a set of mailing labels for new contributors every week, and the labels were sent directly to a mailhouse that processed and mailed thank-you letters on a regular basis.

The problem of setting up a system to process contributers and get their names on the volunteer computer system took nine weeks and was solved only five weeks before the first campaign report was due. Once operational, it proved very effective, though the time required to get a name on the volunteer computer system after a contribution was processed varied between five and twelve days, depending on what day of the week the contribution was received.

The computer operation for the volunteer organization cost approximately $14,750 for the entire campaign, or less than .3 percent of the entire campaign expenditures. The cost of putting 65,000 names on the computer file was about one-third of this cost. About 40,000 of those names were transferred to the system from computer tapes, and the remaining 25,000 were keypunched by the computer firm. The remaining $10,000 paid for over 120 separate computer orders, which included more than 200 sets of lists and mailing labels, some of them as large as 35,000 names. Considering the types of uses the campaign made of the lists and labels, the overall cost of the volunteer computer operation was a bargain.

The cost of accounting to process contributions and record the contributor information on computer tape was over $20,600 for more than 30,000 contributions, or somewhere over sixty cents a contribution. Production of the campaign reports by the Sacramento computer firm cost about $6,500. Probably $1,000 of this cost was to facilitate the volunteer computer operation and print labels for thank-you letters, and the rest was used for the campaign reports. When one considers what the campaign would have had to spend without a computer system to do the same things the computers did, the costs of the computer operation saved the campaign money.

Adjusting volunteer and contribution forms to fit the computer's format

In order to facilitate transferring information to a computer system, all of the volunteer and contributor forms used in the campaign needed to be standardized so that information requested of people was the same and was asked in the same order. At the time the major campaign effort against the Gun Initiative began, several different types of volunteer cards and contributor response devices were already in circulation. For example, the initial campaign brochure had a tearout volunteer coupon with six different categories, and the first volunteer card had ten volunteer categories. In addition, the NRA had sent out its own volunteer cards to members in the spring with volunteer categories different from the campaign's. The difference in forms could have created major problems for the computer keypunch operators who had to type the information on the forms. This was because they typed only one letter or number to designate each volunteer category. If the same volunteer category was first on one card, third on another, and last on a third, it would be very likely that there would be a large number of errors. Because the keypunch operators would also have to slow down in order to adjust to different forms, this would have cost the computer firm more money to type the volunteer information, which in turn would have cost the campaign more money.

The campaign quickly standardized all of the volunteer forms, which affected over fifteen different pieces of literature and response devices. (See the sample volunteer card in Figure 1.) Standardization of the volunteer card and contributor information solved the problem of people who had received the campaign's literature and had used it to respond, but it did not solve the problem of people who called one of the campaign's two major headquarters and eleven regional offices, or anyone who wrote to the campaign and did not include a volunteer or contributor

card. The solution was to print a Request Form (Figure 2) in pads of one-hundred to be placed by each phone. Every time anyone in the office took a request for literature or talked to a person interested in volunteering, he/she filled out the form.

The large number of literature requests led the campaign to develop a shipping department, consisting of two staff members and most of the volunteers in the headquarters. As they filled the literature requests, they initialed and dated the Request Forms and put them in a designated box to be taken to the computer firm. It became imperative to get requested literature mailed as quickly as possible, since the campaign found that a person would wait about ten days to two weeks for literature to be delivered, and then call the office. During the final six weeks of the campaign, the Los Angeles office received between 200 and 300 telephone calls a day for literature or for bumper stickers. Any type of system using names scribbled on scratch paper would not have worked either for getting literature requests filled, or for accurately transferring the names in the computer system. During the four months prior to the election, approximately 2,000 large literature requests (UPS shipments ranging from one to thirty boxes) and 5,000 small requests were mailed from the Los Angeles office alone.

FIGURE 1

Yes! Count on my help to defeat the California Gun Initiative.
(please print)

Name _____

Address _____

City _____ State ____ Zip _____ County _____

Phone(____) home (____) work

Signature _____

Employer _____ Occupation _____
State law requires this information with a contribution.

Here is my contribution

for $ _____

Sign me up for:
☐ Passing out literature.
☐ Contacting my neighbors.
☐ Working on special events.
☐ Public speaking.
☐ You may use my name publicly.
☐ Putting up a yard sign.
☐ Working at Headquarters.
☐ A bumper strip.
☐ Working on a phone bank.
☐ Getting out the vote.

Citizens Against the Gun Initiative. 1543 W. Olympic Blvd., Ste. 526, Los Angeles, CA 90015 / (213) 381-2551

A procedure similar to the literature requests was followed for incoming mail, which during the final two months of the campaign ranged anywhere from two to ten mail bags daily. The shipping staff and volunteers would open the mail and sort it into business mail, contributions, literature requests, and volunteers. A Request Form was filled out by an office volunteer for any nonbusiness mail that did not have a volunteer or contributor card. The Request Form would then be stapled to the letter with the person's name and address circled so that it wouldn't need to be copied on the Request Form, and it was put in a "Literature Request Box," a "Volunteer Box" (for the computer firm), or in the case of contributions, sent directly to the firm handling the contributions. Eventually the contributions overwhelmed the office, and any mail with a check in it was just sent on without

a volunteer or Request Form being completed, which was then done by the accounting firm.

Recruiting volunteers and collecting lists for the computer

A computer system to keep track of volunteers is of no value unless it has volunteers. As the computer system was being set up with the capacity to transfer lists of names to the campaign's computer, it became apparent that the campaign would not be allowed access to any of the lists of members of the sponsoring organizations. This created a difficult problem of how to find and communicate with potential volunteers for the campaign. It was obvious that there were several thousand potential volunteers, just based on the size of the sponsoring organizations' membership and on the nature of the issue. By June the campaign

FIGURE 2

Volunteer & Information Request Form

Date In: _____

NAME _____ HOME PHONE (___) _____
ADDRESS _____ WORK PHONE (___) _____
_____ CITY _____ STATE _____ ZIP _____
Request Taken By: _____ Office: LA   SF   SG   OC

Information Requested:

_____ "PROTECT YOUR RIGHTS"
_____ VOLUNTEER CARD
_____ NEWSPAPER
_____ BUMPER STICKERS
_____ VOTER REGISTRATION CARD
       (not after October 2nd)
_____ ATTORNEY GENERAL'S ANALYSIS
_____
_____
_____
_____
(INDICATE MATERIAL SENT & DATE SENT): _____
SENT BY: (Initials) _____

Volunteer To:

_____ PASSING OUT LITERATURE
_____ CONTACTING NEIGHBORS
_____ SPECIAL EVENTS
_____ PUBLIC SPEAKING
_____ USE NAME PUBLICLY
_____ YARD SIGN
_____ HEADQUARTERS HELP
_____ BUMPER STICKER
_____ PHONE BANK
_____ GETTING OUT THE VOTE
_____ FUND RAISING

office was already receiving dozens of calls daily from people offering to volunteer, and most of them were complaining that the campaign wasn't doing anything because they hadn't heard directly from the campaign. Many of the volunteers just wouldn't believe that the campaign had not been given access to their names by their organizations. As the number of calls and complaints to both the campaign office and the sponsoring organizations increased, it became apparent that the campaign would have to find some way to communicate with persons interested in volunteering to fight the gun initiative. Doing this would also help avoid the accusation by the membership that the campaign wasn't doing its job. While hundreds of activities were going on simultaneously, it was impossible to explain this to a volunteer. Furthermore, the campaign needed volunteers, so the problem became one that had to be solved quickly.

The campaign decided to solve this problem by holding a series of rallies or volunteer meetings in August throughout the state, which would recruit all of those in attendance as volunteers and at the same time show everyone that the campaign was organized and active. Most of the sponsoring organizations had committed themselves to doing at least two mailings to their members on behalf of the campaign, and one of those mailings became a notice of the volunteer meetings. Included in each letter was a volunteer card to be mailed back by those who couldn't attend one of the meetings. Four of the organizations, including the NRA, mailed the letter and volunteer card to their *entire membership*, one put a notice of the meetings in a newsletter, and Gun Owners of California sent out a letter to 50,000 of its key members.

The results of the mailings were impressive. Over 7,200 people attended the thirty-one weeknight meetings throughout the state, with at least three volunteer meetings drawing over 500 people. The campaign also raised about $14,000 in contributions at those meetings and distributed thousands of pieces of literature. An additional 4,000 to 5,000 volunteers sent in volunteer cards, and a large number also sent contributions with their volunteer cards.

The volunteer meetings accounted for about 10,000 of the campaign's volunteers, but other methods were also employed to recruit volunteers. In July a series of full-page newspaper ads were run in a few of the major newspapers to begin educating the public on the complex issues of the initiative. Included in the ads was a volunteer/contributor coupon to be sent in by anyone wishing to oppose the initiative. This generated several hundred responses plus phone calls to the campaign offices in Los Angeles and Oakland.

The campaign also contacted and recruited volunteers through the distribution of materials to the gun stores and gun clubs throughout the state. Each of the 1,400 gun stores and 750 gun clubs were sent the campaign's newspapers, which included a volunteer coupon, and several thousand volunteers and contributors returned the campaign's newspaper coupon. An interesting fact to note is that a large number of the volunteers and contributors sent in more than one card or coupon. Many of those who attended the volunteer meetings and filled out a card at the meeting also had previously mailed in a volunteer card before the meeting. Many of the contributors who checked volunteer activities on their contributor cards had also previously mailed in a separate volunteer card. A rough estimate would be that by Labor Day the campaign processed about 8,000 more volunteer cards than there were volunteers. The literature Request Forms were also filled out and routinely sent to the computer firm unless it was apparent from the phone call that the person was already a volunteer. Probably sixty percent of these people were already on the volunteer list. Eliminating duplicates with the computer saved the campaign thousands of dollars in postage, not to mention the uproar that would have been caused when the volunteers called the office to inform the campaign that they had received duplicate mailings. The results of all of these efforts produced about 16,000 volunteers by Labor Day, with another 8,000 to 9,000 individuals who were contributors but not volunteers. The final total of volunteers on Election Day numbered over 30,000.

Types of lists the campaign maintained in the computer

The campaign computer maintained a variety of lists that were divided into two major categories: (1) the volunteer list, consisting of individuals who contacted the campaign (volunteers, contributors, and individuals who requested information); and (2) the business list, consisting of people and businesses whom the campaign had a need to contact during the campaign. This list consisted primarily of gun businesses, a press list, and potential contributors and volunteers. Each list had the person or business identified by one or more source codes that indicated where the name and address was obtained, and if a name was obtained from more than one source, both were listed.

The major part of the volunteer list consisted of anyone who had volunteered to work on the campaign, and each name was coded by what activities the person was willing to help on. A letter code was also used to designate individuals who were sent certain mailings, such as those who had received a precinct walking packet. In this way, subsequent volunteers who hadn't received the packet were identified and called by the phone banks to see if they wanted to pick one up at a regional office.

The volunteer list also contained contributors who, when combined with the volunteers, were the recipients of the monthly campaign newspaper. The amount of each contribution was also put into the computer so that mailings could be sent to people who contributed above or below a certain amount.

The third category on the volunteer list consisted of approximately 4,200 supporters. This list was made up of people who called or wrote and requested information or literature on the campaign. These people had not contributed or volunteered to help, and the campaign was not certain that they would all be actual supporters since some of them may have been requesting the information to help them make up their minds on how to vote on the initiative. People who requested a bumper sticker or an amount of literature indicating that the person would pass it out to his/her friends (usually over two pieces of literature) were not put on the supporter list. Instead they were classified as a volunteer who was passing out literature or wanted a bumper sticker. The computer was programmed so that people could not be supporters as well as contributors or volunteers, and if at a later date they contributed or volunteered to help in the campaign, the computer automatically took them off of the supporter list and recorded them as a volunteer, contributor, or both.

The second major category on the computer was the business list, which accounted for about forty percent of the 65,000 names on file. The list included:

Gun Shops (California only)	1,415
Gun Clubs (California only)	755
Gun Manufacturers	593
Gun Wholesalers	675
Gun Importers	59
Press (California only)	1,295
Potential large contributors	2,654
Mailing lists of other gun owners	18,000

This list was used primarily for producing mailing labels. To the surprise of nearly everyone associated with the campaign, a complete list of gun shops, gun clubs, manufacturers, and wholesalers did not exist. It took the campaign nearly two months to build a complete set of these lists. Mailing list companies who were contacted had lists that were badly outdated and were about half the size of the lists the campaign eventually ended up with. The campaign acquired ten partial gun shop lists and five gun club lists from various manufacturers and salesmen. All of these lists were put into the computer and the duplicates were eliminated. The gun shop and gun club lists were used at least seven times to mail literature to them for distribution, and on several other occasions they were used for fundraising and other purposes. The manufacturing and wholesaler lists were used mainly for fundraising and were gathered primarily from convention attendance books, along with some names from donated mailing lists.

The business list also included the press list, sorted by television, radio, and newspaper. This was used to produce mailing labels for the press department. Another list consisted of potential contributors, which was made up of large political contributors in California, as well as wealthy and influential individuals associated with either conservative causes or the gun industry. This list was used for major fundraising solicitation and dinner invitations.

The remainder of the business list consisted of several different mailing lists of gun owners. These included gun club members, subscribers to magazines, and other lists of likely contributors and volunteers. These lists were donated by individuals and organizations in order to help the campaign get access to likely supporters.

Uses of computer lists by the campaign

One of the most valuable features of the computer system in the campaign was the ability to quickly sort names into different types of lists. Since there was no way to predict every type of list that might be wanted before the campaign was underway, the computer system was set up to make every conceivable type of list. Names could be sorted by volunteer categories, or by excluding certain categories. A list for any town or group of towns could be made from a town's name, or zip code numbers for an area to be used for the same purpose. The zip codes were especially useful when a list of volunteers was needed for a couple of dozen little towns scattered in an area. Phone numbers could also be sorted by

area code and prefix, volunteers by occupation, and by using the source codes, the campaign could determine, for example, which of the volunteers contacted the campaign through the NRA cards they mailed in.

The ability to produce these types of lists provided an inexhaustible variety of possibilities, and one of the problems was that many of the staff members didn't fully realize the possibilities they had to save time and money by using the computer and being able to do things that were otherwise not possible. A part of the author's time in the campaign was spent talking to people about what they were doing, and discovering ways to save the staff time and to help them do additional projects.

Volunteer organization

In a campaign with thousands of loyal, active, and vocal supporters, it is important to communicate with them on a regular basis. The campaign produced and mailed a monthly newspaper (two during October) to all of the volunteers and contributors, and sent each gun shop and gun club fifty copies for distribution to customers and members. This let the volunteers know what the campaign was doing, and it educated them on exactly what the California Gun Initiative would do and how it would affect them. As a result of this continuous flow of information, the volunteers were able to discuss the initiative with friends and relatives from an informed point of view, and they were more likely to stress the arguments given to them in the newspaper, which were the ones that the campaign's polls showed were most influential with undecided voters. The newspaper also helped to show the volunteers that the campaign was making progress, and it encouraged them to actively help the campaign. Sending out the newspaper was simply a matter of ordering a set of mailing labels for the volunteers and contributors and another set of labels for the gun shops and gun clubs, and sending them to the mailing house along with 100,000 copies of the newspaper.

One example of the effectiveness of communicating with volunteers was the response to one of the articles in the newspaper. In California, television and radio stations are not required to sell advertising time to either side of a ballot proposition, and many stations refused to sell time unless both sides bought air time in order to avoid being forced to give one side free time under the fairness doctrine. This created a problem because the "No on Proposition 15" campaign was behind in the polls and needed the media time. The refusal to sell advertising time had even more of an impact because the campaign was attempting to air a thirty-minute documentary narrated by Charlton Heston, and the major television stations were refusing to sell the campaign any time slot for it at any price. In order to encourage the stations to air the documentary, the August campaign newspaper described the refusal of the networks to sell the campaign time and listed the stations, their addresses and telephone numbers, and the name of the station manager. About a week after the newspaper went out, the campaign heard that one of the Los Angeles television stations had received over 300 calls one morning complaining about their refusal to sell the campaign advertising time. Most of the stations received similar numbers of calls from the "No on 15" campaign supporters. Eventually, many of the stations allowed advertising purchases, including some time for the thirty-minute documentary. The response from the volunteers illustrates the point that volunteers do read the mail sent to them by a campaign and they do respond. The ability to have quick and easy access to the volunteers and contributors was the reason for the success of the effort to influence the media.

As the press began making the initiative a major issue, many of the volunteers were anxious to begin working before the phone banks opened up and the precinct walking began. The campaign offices were being besieged by phone calls from volunteers asking what they could do immediately, and each phone call was taking five to fifteen minutes of a staff member's time. In order to utilize the volunteers who couldn't wait for the campaign to gear up, the campaign sent a letter to the entire volunteer and contributor list. The letter listed several projects for them to do on their own, such as registering all of their friends to vote and recruiting more volunteers for the campaign. Communication with the volunteers in this case solved the problem of putting anxious volunteers to work on productive projects, and it stopped the increasingly large number of calls to the office about how the volunteers could help.

Headquarters help

One of the surprising aspects of the campaign was the small number of people who indicated they were willing to work in the campaign headquarters. Only about nine percent of all the volunteers checked this category on their volunteer cards. When the campaign drew a twenty-five-mile radius for the Los Angeles office (located in downtown Los Angeles) and a twenty-mile radius for the Oakland office, the number of potential headquarters volunteers was around one percent of the total. Subtracting the number of people who worked and were unable to help, the campaign found it difficult to get enough volunteers even to help fill the daily literature requests in the office.

Two types of lists were ordered to help solve this problem. First, a list of headquarters volunteers in the radius mentioned was produced, saving the campaign dozens of hours sorting through either volunteer cards or a massive list of all volunteers. These volunteers were called by the field reps, which produced a few daytime volunteers. When this list was exhausted, the campaign produced a second list of all the volunteers in the commuting radius who had volunteered for any type of activity indicating they would actively help, such as getting out the vote or passing out literature. Volunteers who had just offered to put a bumper sticker on their car or to let the campaign use their names were not included in this group. This list eventually produced enough volunteers. It also made it easy for the office phoner to call the volunteers, since the printout included a list of all the volunteer categories each person had previously agreed to help on, and listed his or her name, address, and occupation. The occupation category was a big help, because a phoner could assume that an engineer or an office secretary was working during the day and might not have any free time, while someone retired or self-employed might be more willing or able to come in during the daytime and help the campaign. The lists were split up by pages for calling, and they proved easier to work with than volunteer cards. In order to update the lists, every few weeks another list was printed of new campaign volunteers.

Filling bumper sticker and yard sign requests

The computer produced mailing labels for all requests for a single bumper sticker and yard sign, which helped speed up the mailing of these items. This was important because, to the volunteers, a significant indication of how good a job the campaign committee was doing in trying to win the election was whether or not they received the bumper sticker they had requested. These volunteers not only had an insatiable demand for bumper stickers, but they actually put them on their cars. The campaign printed and distributed nearly 400,000 bumper stickers, and the NRA printed and mailed an additional 250,000, sending one to each of their members. Another million could easily have been printed and distributed, though how many additional cars would have actually displayed a bumper sticker is debatable. During the volunteer meetings in August, for example, each of the volunteers would grab ten to fifteen bumper stickers if no one watched them. Even with rationing, at least half of the volunteer meetings was held without any bumper stickers being distributed.

Since a typical volunteer would wait usually no more than two weeks before calling one of the offices and complaining that he or she hadn't received a bumper sticker, it became imperative to quickly send one to each of the volunteers who requested it on his or her volunteer card.

The procedure in the campaign was to order every week a set of mailing labels of all new volunteers who had requested bumper stickers. The labels were sent to a mailing house, along with envelopes, letters, contribution envelopes, and bumper stickers. During the first month this system was in operation, when the incoming mail was still relatively light, the office noticed that the number of contributions usually picked up considerably for a few days after each mailing, indicating the volunteers would show their appreciation for the bumper sticker by returning a contribution. Several contributors even told the campaign that this was the reason they were sending in a contribution.

Yard sign distribution also could have been a problem for the campaign. Nearly 8,000 people requested yard signs, far more than was expected for the minimal effort on the campaign's part to promote them. Mailing the signs individually so that they would not be destroyed in the mail would have cost approximately $3.50 each. Once the large number of requests and the cost of shipping were realized, it was easy to solve the distribution problem by sending a letter to the volunteers who had requested a yard sign telling them that they could pick them up at one of the campaign's thirteen offices. The response was an immediate flood of people going to pick up the yard signs at the offices, and the operation went very smoothly.

Local projects by field reps

The computer system was a tremendous aid in helping the campaign's field representatives locate and contact volunteers for projects confined to a small geographical area. One of the field reps' responsibilities was to make certain that every gun show and exhibition was attended by a representative of the campaign and that literature was distributed to everyone interested in fighting the initiative. As soon as a field rep decided that volunteers were needed, he or she would ask for a list of all the volunteers in that area from the computer, and within two days the list was produced. This was especially valuable in northern California, where there were lots of small communities with gun shows or shooting events, each located so far apart that volunteers in one community were not likely to help at another show some distance away. The local lists were used for several purposes besides recruiting volunteers for gun shows, such as finding volunteers to distribute literature at swap meets, attend debates, work on special projects, attend fundraisers, and find local speakers for speaking events. The ease in producing lists of local volunteers saved the field reps a great amount of time in finding volunteers for these local events.

The field reps were generally asked to produce zip code lists along with town names when ordering a list. Ordering volunteer names by city name only would have missed many volunteers, since many of the volunteers' handwriting was so bad that town names were commonly misspelled on the computer list. Unless all the spelling variations were given to the computer operator when a list was ordered, many volunteers would not have been included on the list. Early in the campaign it was also discovered that the post office assigns a sequence of zip codes to each geographical area. Using a range of zip codes for an area, 93110 to 93156, for example, would solve the problem of missing nearby neighboring towns and problems caused by the zip code directory not listing all zip codes in use by each city. The zip code ranges could easily be determined by looking at the back two or three pages of the post office's zip code directory which lists the zip codes in numerical order and shows the city or area assigned to it. Using the area zip code method made

certain that all local volunteers were included in the printed lists.

Precinct literature distribution by volunteers

The largest volunteer effort in the campaign was the distribution of over two million pieces of literature by 21,000 volunteers to registered voters in the volunteers' neighborhoods. In early September, it was estimated that there would be about 18,000 volunteers in the computer system at the time names were to be selected from the computer for the precinct literature distribution. In addition, the campaign staff estimated that about 4,500 more packets should be produced to give to new volunteers who joined the campaign after the cutoff date for producing mailing labels to generate volunteers, which was September 15th. When the computer selected all of the volunteers on the list except those who only offered to let the campaign use their name, there were only about 17,000 volunteer names, because there were more duplicate volunteer cards turned in than had been expected. In order to find another 1,000 recipients of the precinct packets, the computer also selected 1,000 of the small contributors to receive a precinct packet.

Each of the people selected was coded as a precinct walker, and a computer tape of the volunteers with their names and addresses was produced. This computer tape was then given to another computer firm to match with 125 registered voters in each volunteer's precinct. The registered voters were chosen by using a predetermined formula to select conservative precincts and mostly Republican and undecided voters. In a large number of cases it was discovered that several volunteers resided in the same precinct, and many volunteers were also in precincts with a very high number of liberal Democrats. Confining the selection of registered voters to a person's own precinct or those immediately neighboring the volunteer's precinct would have given some volunteers only a few registered voters to contact, thus failing to make full use of hundreds, if not a few thousand of the volunteers. Consequently, the selection method was changed to pick out 125 registered voters within a precinct walker's zip code. Even with this method, though, some volunteers, more often than not people located in rural areas, received names of registered voters several miles away from their homes.

Once a volunteer was matched with 125 registered voters, the mailing house printed the names of the registered voters directly onto the literature, packaged the literature with a letter and instruction sheet, and printed a mailing label for the volunteer assigned to contact those registered voters. The completed packets were sent by UPS to the volunteers in early October. The total cost of matching volunteers with registered voters and producing and mailing the package was approximately $100,000, not including the separate cost of printing 2.8 million pieces of literature.

The precinct walkers were asked to personally deliver the literature sent to them to each of the voters. If the volunteers were unable to deliver the literature, they were asked to mail it, since the voter's name and address were printed on the literature. It turned out that the literature was longer and wider than is allowed by the post office for a first class piece of mail. The campaign had been sending the same size literature by bulk mail to the volunteers, and no one realized that there might be a problem sending the literature first class. This problem was discovered after 11,000 of the packets had been sent out. To assure postal delivery of the literature, the solution was for the volunteer to put 29 cents on the literature instead of 20 cents if they choose to mail it instead of walking the assigned precinct. A supplemental notice was included in the remaining 7,000 packets, and a letter was mailed to all 18,000 of the volunteers telling them of the problem and the solution. Since the computer firm had coded the 18,000 people who were to receive the packets (the list now had about 24,000

volunteers), producing mailing labels for the precinct walkers only took about two hours. Thanks to the computer list of the precinct walkers, a letter was in the mail to all of the volunteers within 24 hours of discovery of the problem, and it got to most of them in time.

The most interesting aspect of this problem was the reaction of the 7,000 volunteers who received this letter telling them of the postage problem before they actually received their precinct packets of literature. During the week after the letter was mailed, the Los Angeles office alone received between 1,000 and 2,000 phone calls from people demanding that they be sent another packet of literature to deliver because they hadn't received theirs. Once the volunteers received their literature, they were in no position to later complain that they didn't want to deliver it. This probably increased the actual number of pieces of literature delivered directly to the voters by the precinct workers.

Phone banks

The computer system was also the basis for most of the phone bank operations. Each of the phone banks began with a paid coordinator, and it was up to them to recruit volunteers. To help them in this task, they were given a complete list of the volunteers in their area from which to recruit phone bank volunteers. As the volunteers started coming in to the offices, they called more volunteers to work in the phone banks. Approximately 2,000 volunteers worked in the eleven phone bank offices during the last month, with the Anaheim and San Fernando Valley offices having more than 500 total volunteers, with over a hundred working in each of those offices every day.

Once the offices had a steady flow of volunteers, the volunteers began phoning each of the 18,000 precinct workers to help motivate them to distribute the literature. The list of 18,000 was divided up among the eleven phone banks for calling based on their geographical locations. The lists were slightly realigned according to the number of telephones available and the expected level of volunteers at each phone bank.

The phone call dialogue to the precinct walkers included questions asking the volunteers if they would be able to deliver the literature, if they had any questions on how to distribute the literature, and if they would be able to help in the phone bank headquarters. By October 21st, over 11,000 of the precinct walkers had been contacted, with seventy-eight percent of them saying they would or had delivered the literature, and an additional fifteen percent saying they would try to deliver it. There was a general feeling among most of the phone bank volunteers and coordinators that the calls helped to motivate the precinct walkers and make them feel that someone cared if they delivered the literature. Reinforcing this viewpoint was the receipt of over 1,200 letters from these volunteers informing the campaign that they had delivered the literature.

Every phone bank has a problem in finding telephone numbers for the forty percent of the people who don't put their phone number on the volunteer cards, or who contact the office by mail and don't include a phone number in their letters. As the campaign progressed, the computer firm periodically printed a list of all of the volunteers who did not have a phone number listed on the computer. This list was printed in alphabetical order by city, and within each city the volunteers were listed in alphabetical order. The volunteers then took a page or two of volunteers in a city and looked them up in the phone book. As phone numbers were found, the volunteers wrote them on the computer sheets and they were returned to the computer firm. The computer firm took the updated sheets and entered either the phone number or a letter "T" for those whose number had been looked up and not found. The next printing of the volunteers without phone numbers would not include anyone with a letter "T" in the phone number fields. Between looking up phone numbers and

calling directory assistance, the number of phone numbers for volunteers, contributors and supporters on the computer went up from about sixty percent to eighty-five percent.

As the phone banks finished calling the precinct walkers, they turned to calling an additional 4,300 new volunteers and asking them if they would be able to deliver literature. This list was produced by the computer from new volunteers since September 15th, when the original list of precinct walkers was printed. Those who said "yes" were given packets of unaddressed literature and asked to walk their neighborhoods. Between these phone calls and volunteers coming in off the street for literature, another 4,000 packets were given to the volunteers.

As the phone banks completed their calls to the volunteers, they began calling registered voters from a registered voter list of a conservative congressional district in their area. The phone pitch included a comment that Proposition 15 was opposed by most law enforcement officers in California, which the campaign's polls indicated was an important issue to undecided voters.

The final operation of the phone banks was the get-out-the-vote calling. The computer produced a list of all volunteer, supporter, and contributor households for each of the phone banks' geographical sections of the state. Just before and during Election Day, these people were called to remind them to vote, followed by calls to the registered voters who had expressed opposition to the initiative. Because of the strong sentiment generated on this issue, the calls to the known supporters from the campaign's computer list were generally not necessary, since only one or two people out of every hundred needed to be reminded that Tuesday was Election Day. But the campaign didn't take any chances on their key supporters forgetting to vote.

One other volunteer project is worth mentioning. The weekend before Election Day the campaign planned to have volunteers distribute literature at shopping malls and large grocery and discount stores. Since this project was generally confined to the major population areas, a printout of volunteers by city in each area was helpful for this project. There were thousands of volunteers to choose from in both Southern California and the Bay area, and the list by cities allowed the field reps to call down the list of people in every city with a shopping mall until they found enough volunteers. This made their job in finding volunteers very easy.

Research

Another innovative use for the computer list of volunteers was in the area of campaign research. The initiative was thirty-three pages long and very complex, and the ramifications of exactly what would happen if it were passed were unclear. It was estimated that there were about fifty major potential issues in the campaign. With each side well armed with statistics, it became important to find answers quickly every time a new issue came up. Among other things, the "No on 15" researchers were trying to prove that crime would not go down if the initiative passed. There were also several legal questions about the constitutionality of the initiative.

One of the problems the campaign had was finding people who might know the answers to some of these issues. In order to facilitate the research, the computer selected three lists from the occupations the volunteers and contributors had listed on their volunteer cards. One list was of anyone in a police-related field, the second was for people in the legal profession, and the third list was made up of people in news-related fields. The hundred-plus police officers and investigators provided a ready-made list of people who might know favorable crime statistics or examples of where the pro-proposition arguments were incorrect. The legal profession list also proved immensely valuable. It was discovered that some of the attorney-volunteers had written articles or handled law cases on obscure but important

issues relevant to the campaign. The news-related list helped recruit volunteers with experience in interviewing and writing, to help supplement the research staff as well as to provide a list of crime reporters who could help with the crime statistics. This was truly a case of using the experience and expertise of the volunteers to aid the campaign. The best feature of the list was that all of these people were already volunteers in the campaign, and they were quite willing to help.

Fundraising, press, and campaign reports

The computer lists were used for a variety of fundraising purposes, some of which have already been mentioned. The volunteers and past contributors were solicited by direct mail, and they were invited to fundraising events and dinners in their areas throughout the campaign. The computer allowed the campaign to sort the list easily by geographic area so that the people in Southern California were invited to the Los Angeles fundraisers and not the San Francisco fundraisers. The lists of gun businesses were also used to solicit money, and the list of potential large contributors was used as a starting point for the large fundraising dinners. The fact that these lists had been found and put on the computer earlier in the campaign made it easy to retrieve them when needed for fundraising.

One of the categories on the volunteer card was for people who wanted to help on fundraisers. This list of a few hundred people provided a good base of volunteers to help sell tickets and to assist in setting up the fundraisers. This was especially useful when a local organization wanted to hold a small fundraiser in an area some distance away from the location of the fundraising staff.

The computer also contained a California press list for mailing news releases and notifying them about press conferences. The list was coded by priority, with the major press outlets being coded as a priority one and the smallest weekly and monthly newspapers and magazines coded as priority three. Several sets of this list's mailing labels were printed early in the campaign, both of the entire list and some of the different priority categories. Each set of labels was put on envelopes and stored separately. Whenever the press department needed to get a mailing out quickly, they just picked out an appropriate set of pre-addressed envelopes and mailed the news releases.

As previously mentioned, the Sacramento computer firm handling the contributor names produced the contributor sections for the campaign finance reports. The computer balanced deposits daily, which helped the campaign know how much it could spend, and it gave the campaign a set of computer-printed reports that were added to the rest of the campaign finance report for the state reports. This was probably the least expensive way the contributor reports could have been done, considering the expense in time and money it would have cost to handle them manually.

Without the computer operation, most of the volunteer portion of the campaign would have been either impossible or much less effective. Although the cost seems high, using computers in campaigns actually reduces overall costs and increases the effectiveness of other campaign operations.

How They Whipped "Whoops" in Washington State

David D. Schmidt

The previous case study of an initiative campaign demonstrated how the generous application of money and campaign technology can sometimes turn an electoral tide. This case study of a very different initiative proves quite the opposite: Cash and campaign technology are not always enough to produce a victory. Strategic use of limited resources and clever tactical skill can overcome intimidating odds, as the managers of Washington State's 1981 initiative on power plants showed. This initiative required the Washington Public Power Supply System (known derisively as "Whoops" because of cost overruns and alleged mismanagement) to let voters decide whether bonds should be issued for the construction of major power plants. Despite strong and well-funded opposition from industry, Wall Street, and many policy-makers, the initiative's leaders were able to stretch their meager war chest by capitalizing on public anger at "Whoops" and by engaging in effective forms of media-oriented guerrilla warfare, as David Schmidt explains.

Success in initiative politics is heavily dependent on public support for the issue and the organizational savvy of initiative proponents. Washington State's Initiative 394 campaign in 1981 is an outstanding example of initiative proponents capitalizing on these two assets to overcome their inferior financial status (relative to opponents) and winning big on Election Day. Initiative 394 was opposed by an array of financial giants: the nuclear power industry, Wall Street investment firms, labor unions, even the state government. Yet initiative proponents defeated these Goliaths in a landslide electoral victory.

The issue involved a state agency known

as "Whoops," which is the derisive pronunciation of the acronym WPPSS, the Washington Public Power Supply System. As early as 1973, when WPPSS began construction on a series of five planned nuclear power plants, local environmentalists pointed to the irony of an agency nicknamed "Whoops" building power plants with a potential for catastrophic accidents. Later, as cost overruns on the project mounted, the name "Whoops" acquired additional ironic meaning.

Washington State environmentalists first used the initiative process in an attempt to stymie WPPSS when they collected the 123,711 petition signatures of registered voters that were required to put the "Nuclear Safeguards Initiative" on the state's November 1976 state ballot. At this time the benefits of nuclear

David D. Schmidt is editor of the Washington, D.C.-based Initiative News Report, *a biweekly newsletter.*

power were widely believed to outweigh the costs (and risks, which had been much less publicized). The initiative, which would have imposed severe safety standards on nuclear power, was defeated by a two-to-one margin of voters. Six similar initiatives in other states, including California, went down to similarly overwhelming defeats that same year.

The Washington State "Safeguards" proponents, discouraged by the nationwide pattern of losses, disbanded their organization after the 1976 election. For one activist, however, the campaign was merely an initiation into a new brand of political action. He was Steve Zemke, who later became founder and leader of the group that sponsored Initiative 394. By 1978 Zemke was a biology graduate student at the University of Washington who interrupted his studies to organize a petition drive to put a "Bottle Bill" initiative on the state ballot. This proposal, which qualified for the November 1979 ballot, would have imposed a five cent deposit on beer and soft drink containers, as an incentive to encourage recycling and reduce litter. Even though a "Bottle Bill" had been in effect for seven years in neighboring Oregon and proved quite popular there, the Washington State initiative shared the fate of the 1976 nuclear initiative: The major industries (in the case of the "Bottle Bill," bottlers, canners, brewers, soft drink makers) opposing the initiative sponsored an expensive "Vote No" ad campaign, breaking the state's previous record for initiative campaign spending. The initiative was defeated, with fifty-seven percent voting against it.

Zemke's main problem in that campaign was that the opposition spent thirteen times as much as his side. But that was only part of it. The opposition used the money on a smart campaign, utilizing every conceivable avenue of communication to persuade the electorate to "Vote No." These included billboards, television, radio, and newspaper ads; grocery bags in most major food stores bearing the "Vote No" logo; stickers on cans, bottles, six-packs, and cases of drinks; mass mailings to voters; signs on the interior and exterior of buses; letters to the editors of newspapers; and speakers at public forums and debates. They even organized workers in the affected industries to participate as volunteers, distributing "Vote No" literature to friends and relatives.

Even as the ill-fated "Bottle Bill" campaign was in progress, however, antinuclear power activists began discussing plans for a new initiative. The nuclear accident at Three-Mile Island near Harrisburg, Pennsylvania, in late March 1979 had just sensitized the nation to problems with the safety of nuclear power. And now a second factor was changing public perception of the cost of nuclear plants: The WPPSS price tag had mushroomed from $4.1 billion in 1973 to $15.9 billion in 1979. The WPPSS nuclear construction program was to become the most costly state-sponsored construction venture in the nation.

Framing the issues

The activists believed public opposition to nuclear power could be mobilized by two issues: First, the fact that nuclear waste from Pennsylvania and many other states was being dumped in Washington; and second, the costly mismanagement of WPPSS. Two proposals were advanced. One faction argued for an initiative to ban importation of nuclear waste into the state. The other faction, led by Olympia attorney Chuck Caldart and economist Jim Lazar, argued for an initiative requiring public approval, by referendum vote, for bond issues to finance WPPSS's nuclear projects. The latter approach, which provided the basis for Initiative 394, had several advantages: First, the concept of voter approval for government bonds was already familiar to voters and was an accepted part of state and local government procedures. Second, an initiative to require referendum approval for nuclear plants had passed in 1978 in Montana, proving the popularity of the voter-approval concept. And third, because the proposal focused on the popular and understandable aspects of cost control, rather than the complex technical issues of nuclear power safety, a confusing technical debate could be avoided during the campaign.

But this approach did not appeal to the hard-line antinuke activists, who sided with the nuclear waste ban faction. Caldart and Lazar tried, without success, to convince them that such an initiative would have no effect. Even if it were approved by the voters, Caldart and Lazar contended, it would be voided by the courts as violating the interstate commerce clause of the U.S. Constitution, which gives the federal government sole power to regulate interstate commerce. But the antiwaste faction wouldn't budge, even though both sides knew that if their efforts were divided, each side would be less likely to get their proposal on the ballot. Caldart and Lazar rejected a proposal to circulate both petitions, for fear of fostering public perception of their cost-control initiative as a hard-line "antinuke" measure.

While leaders of these groups refused to cooperate, they made no attempt to stop any of their followers who chose to circulate both petitions in the spring of 1980. One of these was Steve Zemke. The never-say-die Zemke was not discouraged by his losses in 1976 and 1979; rather, he believed he was on the right track with his initiative campaigns if his opponents were forced to spend record sums of money to beat him. Zemke's folding petition table, which could be observed on weekends at shopping malls, was plastered with petitions not only for the two nuclear initiatives, but for two other initiatives supported by liberals and environmentalists.

If the leaders of these groups had been as willing to cooperate as Zemke, all four proposals might have qualified for the ballot. But split into four factions competing for volunteers, their prospects were dim. And prospects grew dimmer when Mount St. Helens exploded on May 18, 1980, covering the eastern half of the state with a blanket of volcanic ash and clouds so thick that street lights had to be kept on all day. Although

the heavily populated Seattle area was unaffected, petition circulators' morale throughout the state sagged. They knew their own signature quotas would have to be raised to make up for the shortfall in ash-covered areas where petitions could not be circulated.

Meanwhile, in the state legislature in Olympia, backers of both antinuclear initiatives lobbied legislators to pass their proposals, but to no avail. The antinuclear waste measure passed the state House of Representatives but was stymied in the state Senate, where nuclear industry lobbyists stalled it. The legislature ended its session in May without favorable final action on either proposal.

Throughout the spring petition circulation season, Zemke served as an unpaid advisor to the four groups sponsoring the initiatives he supported. Having served as petition coordinator and campaign manager in the 1979 "Bottle Bill" battle, his advice was respected. In mid-June, with only two weeks remaining before the petition filing deadline, Zemke met with Caldart and Lazar's group to assess their chances of qualifying for the ballot. Since they only had about one-third the necessary number of signatures, Zemke urged them to drop their own proposal and help with the antinuclear waste petition (the "Don't Waste Washington" initiative, as it was labeled by proponents). The latter faction had twice as many signatures and thus had a better chance to qualify. But if the groups refused to cooperate, both initiatives would surely fail, Zemke warned.

To their credit, the Caldart–Lazar group abandoned their petition and joined the "Don't Waste Washington" effort. But that initiative was still in jeopardy. Five days before the deadline, Zemke attended a meeting of the proponents' committee. Since they had collected 4,000 signatures in excess of the required number, the leader announced, they were finished. Zemke, amazed at their naivete, spoke up at this point. "I hate to throw cold water on your victory celebration, but you need at least 25,000 more signatures, and you'd better start figuring out how to get them." On initiative petitions, he explained, ten to twenty percent of the names are invalid when checked by state officials: Some signatures are illegible, some aren't registered voters, others are duplicate signatures.

The unmanned table

Due to Zemke's foresight, a potentially fatal blunder was narrowly averted. But the task of getting the extra signatures remained. Volunteers were assigned to set up petition tables in shopping malls for a final push. But Zemke thought their efforts might not be enough. With a nine-to-five job, however, he could devote only two hours a day to petition circulation. The solution? A Zemke innovation: the unstaffed petition table. Having personally asked thousands of voters to sign initiative petitions over the previous several years, Zemke noticed that some people were repelled by petition circulators soliciting passersby. He thought there might be thousands of people who had avoided signing simply because they didn't like the high-pressure approach. Acting on this insight, he tried an experiment. The next day, Zemke and another Seattle initiative veteran, Bill Harrington, set up folding tables all over town, each with petitions taped securely on top. At the end of the day, they drove around to retrieve the tables. In five days, they collected 1,500 signatures in this manner. The petitions were turned in, and the Secretary of State released the official count a month later. It was close: only 1,100 signatures over the minimum of 123,711 valid voter names required.

To the surprise of initiative proponents, the nuclear industry mounted only token opposition to the initiative, and it passed with seventy-four percent voting in favor. But it was a hollow victory. As Lazar and Caldart predicted, the measure was voided as unconstitutional by a federal court before it was to go into effect. Even as a publicity effort the initiative was only slightly successful, since the lack of opposition ensured that it attained minimal public visibility.[1]

As the November 1980 vote on the "Don't Waste Washington" initiative neared, Caldart and Lazar's people tried to regroup for another attempt at their WPPSS proposal. In October 1980, they conducted a poll to determine the level of voter support, which is an essential first step in any initiative campaign. The results showed voters even more willing to support controls on WPPSS' spending than their overwhelming backing for the "Don't Waste Washington" proposal. But leaders of the group were suffering from burnout. The director, Joe Ryan, was exhausted by the year's work and quit in November 1980. The remainder talked of canceling plans for the 1981 initiative.

The reorganization of forces

Until then, Zemke had stayed on the sidelines, encouraging the group members to keep going, reminding them that WPPSS's cost overruns were piling up ever higher. But at this crisis stage, Zemke knew it was essential for someone to take charge immediately. In early December 1980, he called a meeting of the twelve most active veterans of the abortive spring petition drive and told them, "I'm going to work to put an initiative on the ballot in 1981, and the only question for each of you is to decide whether you're going to be part of the campaign."

Zemke took over as chairman and campaign manager. He named the group "Don't Bankrupt Washington," in an attempt to capitalize on the popularity of the "Don't Waste Washington" initiative. His second act as chairman was to send a questionnaire to about 300 state activists, including legislators and other public officials. They were asked to comment on the 1980 version of the measure and to suggest changes. As a result, the intitiative's spending control provisions were extended to include cities, counties, and Public Utility Districts, as well as Joint Operating Agencies such as WPPSS that were included originally. New criteria for evaluating energy projects were added, including the require-

David D. Schmidt

ment that a cost-effectiveness study be done on each power plant. Amazingly, WPPSS had never done a study on any of its five nuclear plants to determine whether the projects were economically viable.

The final version retained the essential feature of Lazar and Caldart's proposal: It would require voter approval before bonds could be issued by public agencies to build major power plants. "Major" plants were defined as those designed to generate 250 megawatts or more—about enough to supply 250,000 homes. That number was chosen because plants of this size were already required to get siting approval from the state. Since each of WPPSS's five nuclear dynamos was to generate about 1,000 megawatts, all would come under the restrictions of the initiative.

In February 1981 the Secretary of State affixed its official descriptive summary, title, and number to the proposal. The "Don't Bankrupt Washington" Committee kicked off their petition drive in early March, after the legislature failed to enact a bill similar to the initiative. During the same session, the legislature released a study that blamed WPPSS's rising costs on mismanagement and raised the price tag for the five nuclear plants to $17.3 billion. After the legislature adjourned, however, WPPSS released its own new cost estimate: A horrendous $23.9 billion (the state budget for two years was only $12 billion). These news items, which received extensive coverage in the Washington State media, aided the petitioners by keeping the WPPSS issue in the public eye and gave voters added incentive to sign and circulate the petition. And whenever initiative proponents were interviewed for news stories, they never failed to hammer away at the fact that the newest cost estimate was "a 600% increase over 1973."

The spring season that year was exceptionally rainy, even for a state where T-shirts jokingly advertise the "Seattle Rain Festival: September–June." This hindered petition circulators, who were restricted to indoor shopping malls. By the first week of May, they had collected only 40,000 signatures toward a goal of 170,000. More signatures were needed than in the previous year's "Don't Waste Washington" drive, because petition requirements are based on a percentage of the people who turn out to vote in the most recent gubernatorial election. Since more people voted in 1980 than in 1976, the minimum number of signatures needed to put an initiative on the ballot rose by almost 15,000.

At this point, Zemke set up a phone bank to activate more petition circulators. Volunteers staffed an array of telephones and called everyone on the mailing lists of supporters of previous environmental initiative campaigns. People were asked to complete the petitions that had already been mailed, donate money, and volunteer time to staff petition tables. The magnitude of the effort is indicated by the size of Zemke's mailing list of supporters: By the end of the campaign, it grew to 10,000 names, more than double the number of members in the state's largest ecology group, the Sierra Club.

In early June the rain finally let up, and citizens of Washington State emerged into the sunlight to find Initiative 394 petition circulators in malls and on street corners across the state. Volunteers urged passersby to sign and "put a lid on WPPSS's spending." Zemke publicized his own calculation, using WPPSS' latest cost estimates, that WPPSS's debt amounted to $30,000 for each household in the state. By the petition deadline in the first week of July, "Don't Bankrupt Washington" collected 186,000 signatures—enough to ensure qualifying for the November ballot.

The opposition

The interests that were profiting from WPPSS's cost overruns were not about to sit idle while their multi-billion dollar Golden Goose was killed by the state's taxpayers. While WPPSS itself, as a government agency, could not spend money on an initiative campaign, the contractors building WPPSS's nuclear plants were under no such restriction. For them, spending a million dollars to save $24 billion worth of contracts was a small investment. Nuclear industry leaders began to map out strategy for an opposition campaign and began raising funds, under the aegis of the Western Environmental Trade Association. This industry group, although sporting the green ecology "e" symbol on its letterhead, is actually an alliance made up of most of the state's biggest businesses: Weyerhauser, Georgia Pacific, Seattle First National Bank, Alcoa, Kaiser Aluminum, etc.

Initiative opponents' first move was to hire Winner/Wagner Associates of Los Angeles to manage their campaign. Charles Winner and Ethan Wagner had impressed utility industry executives for the first time in 1976, when they ran the nuclear industry's successful campaign against California's antinuclear power initiative. In the years that followed, Winner/Wagner developed a specialty in defeating utility-regulation initiatives placed on state ballots by citizens petition. It was a lucrative business, since individual utility companies were willing to spend as much as a million dollars to save a nuclear plant from the threat of shutdown.[2] Although Winner/Wagner had never lost a campaign on a utility issue, the firm was by no means invulnerable. Opponents of California's tax-cutting "Proposition 13" had hired Winner/Wagner in 1978, and crusty old antitax crusaders Howard Jarvis and Paul Gann gave them a thorough basting when "13" passed by a two-to-one margin.

One reason for Winner/Wagner's string of successes in defeating utility initiatives was their overwhelming funding advantage in every case. Environmentalists supporting the initiatives were typically outspent by factors of ten to one or greater. Mr. Winner's motivation for campaign work is not merely monetary, however: Opposition to initiatives is an important tenet of his political philosophy. He has been involved in more than fifty ballot measure campaigns in thirteen states, working almost exclusively in opposition to proposed initiatives. He equates initiatives with "mob rule" and characterizes the upsurge in their use as a "dangerous trend" that "may strike at the very heart of representative democracy."[3]

What's in a name?—a lot

The opposition's next task, after hiring Winner/Wagner, was to choose a name for the "No on 394" committee. The function of the name is not necessarily to describe the committee, as one might expect, but to help create a favorable public attitude toward the anti-initiative cause. Proponents of an initiative, of course, do the same. Thus, an initiative to restrict nuclear power plants was typically supported by a committee with a name like "Citizens for Safe Power," and opposed by a committee with a name like "Citizens for Jobs and Energy." What voter could be against "Safe Power" or "Jobs and Energy"? The assumptions used by committees to justify these names are more questionable: The environmentalists believe the only "safe" power is nonnuclear, while the nuclear industry contends that nuclear power is essential to provide jobs and energy. Campaign management firms like Winner/Wagner spend thousands of dollars on public opinion polls to test the appeal of various names for a committee.

No one was more aware of the importance of a name than Steve Zemke, who now became campaign manager of the "Yes on 394" side. His campaign retained the name, "Don't Bankrupt Washington" and thus had a commanding lead in the name recognition competition. But Zemke had an impish inspiration to harass the opposition in this regard by legally stealing their name. In late July, when they announced that the "No on 394" committee would be called "Citizens for an Adequate Energy Supply," they neglected to rush someone to the state capitol in Olympia to officially register the name (as required by law before any money can be spent). When they did, they learned that someone from the pro-initiative side had already been there and filed the same name, so they hurriedly came up with another one. They held a press

David D. Schmidt

conference the next day, calling themselves the "Committee Against Shutdown of Energy." But Zemke's people noted that the acronym "CASE" was already on file in Olympia. Finally, the anti-initiative forces got wise and sent someone to Olympia to file their next name before announcing it: "Citizens Against Unfair Taxes, the No on 394 Committee."

Zemke explained, after the election campaign was over, that the skirmish over names was more than just a clever way to frustrate the opposition and make them spend more money. The unusual succession of name changes helped focus media attention on the "No on 394" side before it had developed a unified theme for the campaign, which resulted in their making conflicting statements about the effects of the initiative. This lowered their credibility. "We flushed them out before they were ready to fight," he said.[4]

In mid-August, the "No on 394" Committee further weakened its credibility by accepting a loan of $200,000, plus a contribution of $25,000, from Morrison-Knudsen, Inc., a mammoth engineering contractor involved in building the WPPSS nuclear plants. The company's interest was obvious: If voters approved the initiative, Morrison-Knudsen's profits from numerous cost overruns might be cut. While legal, the loan transaction smelled of scandal to the news media and they made it a major news story. It was the largest sum of money ever to change hands in a Washington State political campaign, and it became a major issue. Second, according to the legislature's report, Morrison-Knudsen was one of the worst offenders among WPPSS contractors: Their cement-pouring contract, originally for $40 million, had skyrocketed in eight years to $214 million. Once the media watchdogs tasted blood with the Morrison-Knudsen story, they continued hounding the "No on 394" Committee with other stories about WPPSS contractors who were contributing to the anti-initiative campaign. One newspaper story listed each contractor, along with the contribution it made and the exact amount of cost overrun attributable to that contractor. The news stories also played up the underdog financial status of the "Don't Bankrupt Washington" Committee. By September 10, 1981, the State Public Disclosure Commission records showed that the "No on 394" side had spent $403,675, almost ten times as much as "Don't Bankrupt Washington."

Paid vs. free media

Not everyone watches, listens to, or reads the news—but everyone definitely got the "Vote No" advertising message. While the "No on 394" money couldn't buy favorable news coverage, its financial advantage allowed the "Vote No" message to be aired on paid media. In most initiative campaigns, both sides concentrate their advertising in the final weeks of the campaign, when it's supposed to have the most effect. But the "No on 394" Committee couldn't afford to wait until the end of the campaign, because their polls showed their side trailing badly. Since funding was no problem, they *could* afford extra weeks of advertising. They opened their advertising deluge in the last week of August and continued flooding the air waves for nine weeks of constant radio and television ads.

The anti-initiative ads attacked "394" because of its alleged high cost to taxpayers. The announcer's voice told listeners that the initiative would require bond referendum elections every six weeks to approve spending for WPPSS's nuclear construction. The elections alone would cost "millions," would cause construction delays costing "hundreds of millions," and would finally cause cancellation of needed power plants, at a cost of "billions." Although these claims did have a real, though flimsy, factual basis, their purpose appears to have been to fool voters into believing they could stop further WPPSS cost overruns and delays by voting against the initiative. The truth was completely the opposite.

One result of the anti-initiative ad campaign was to further reduce the "No on 394" Committee's already tarnished credibility with the news media. "The opponents of Initiative

394 have run a campaign of disinformation . . . a sleazy campaign," chided *Seattle Post-Intelligencer* editorialist Shelby Scates. He continued in a similarly caustic vein:

The anti's are . . . having you think we have an expensive excess of democracy in the Northwest. Maybe that's the case in Beverly Hills, whence these hired guns will crawl when they've collected their fee for the hit. Not here. What's expensive is WPPSS. It's not pronounced "Whoops!" without feeling. What else is expensive is the $100,000 shelled out, mainly by WPPSS contractors, to the firm of Winner/Wagner. . . .[5]

If Scates' comments bothered anyone on the "No on 394" Committee, they didn't show it. Their next move, about halfway through the nine-week campaign, was to add a new anti-initiative message to their ads. This featured a narrator reading the definition of "cost effectiveness" as defined by the initiative. The narrator talked about how difficult it was to understand the initiative and urged voters to reject it on that basis. Proponents responded to this ad with press releases justifying the "cost effectiveness" provisions: The wording had been lifted verbatim from the "Northwest Power Bill" passed by Congress the previous year. The anti-initiative forces continued to run the ad, however, since they knew that their ads would reach many more voters than the pro-initiative press release.

Earlier in the campaign, Winner/Wagner had tried another staple from their bag of campaign tricks: a mass mailing designed to produce the appearance of popular support for the "No on 394" Committee, in the form of a paper citizens' group composed of anyone who would sign and return a post card indicating they opposed the initiative. The mailing was massive and indiscriminate. Even Zemke, a bachelor, received a mailer addressed to "The Zemke Family" from the "No on 394" Comittee.

The mailing strategy, used by Winner/Wagner in several initiative campaigns the previous year, was this: First the mailing was sent to several hundred thousand voters early in the campaign, before most people knew anything about the initiative. Within a couple of weeks, 10,000 or so had returned the post cards, which required no postage. Winner/Wagner then prepared a full-page anti-initiative newspaper ad proclaiming that the "Citizens Committee of 10,000" urges voters to reject the initiative. If there was enough space, all the names were printed. The ads were run in the state's major newspapers, simultaneously with another mailing to several hundred thousand more voters. Two weeks later, the same newspaper ad appeared, this time backed by the "Citizens Committee of 20,000." And so it went, every two weeks up to the election, with constantly growing numbers of supporters. These appeals don't ask for money or volunteers, since Winner/Wagner's anti-initiative campaigns were amply funded, mainly by large corporations.

As soon as Zemke received his mailer from the "No on 394" Committee, he realized what they were up to. He had seen them use the tactic in Oregon the previous year. To counteract it, Zemke added the title "Yes on 394, the Committee of 186,000" to the name of the "Don't Bankrupt Washington" group. The new title was used by workers answering phones in the campaign office, as well as printed on press releases. The opposition protested, complaining that petition signers, who numbered 186,000, were not really active supporters of the initiative. Zemke tossed the charge back in their faces, saying that their own "Committee of 10,000" was a sham. After a week or two, the "No on 394" Committee dropped the subject, since its leaders realized they could never get 186,000 citizens to sign and return their cards.

Zemke had outsmarted the opposition once again. But these victories were minor compared to the most important battle in any initiative campaign: the battle for radio and television advertising. In this crucial arena, the opposition's finances gave them a lopsided advantage. Winner and Wagner knew that no matter how much bad press their side got, persistent broadcast advertising could close the

David D. Schmidt

gap between their trailing poll status and victory on Election Day. "Come-from-behind" victories typified Winner/Wagner's previous anti-initiative campaigns.

Winning with dollars

For initiative proponents facing a well-funded Winner/Wagner anti-initiative effort, the cost of advertising all too often proved to be their downfall. Television and radio ads can cost tens of thousands of dollars to produce, and tens of thousands more to broadcast in prime-time often enough to reach voters effectively. In the last week of September, the "Don't Bankrupt Washington" Committee did not seem capable of mounting such a media campaign, based on their accounting records filed with the State Public Disclosure Commission. The group had spent all but $12,000 of the $53,000 they raised. The opposition, by contrast, had by this time raised three quarters of a million dollars and spent half of it.

Poorly funded initiative proponents caught in such a bind usually produce their own ads at the lowest possible cost, then try to convince television and radio station managers to broadcast the ads free of charge as a means of fulfilling the station's obligation to provide balanced coverage of controversial issues. The problem with this approach is that station managers would rather meet this responsibility through news coverage and broadcasting unpaid ads on the late, late show, rather than lose money by running unpaid ads in prime time.

Madison Avenue works

Zemke realized that if the "Yes on 394" media campaign followed this pattern, the election might be lost. "If we're going to beat them, we have to fight them on their own turf," he remarked. "If Madison Avenue ad firms are working for the opposition, we'll hire our own to work for us." He started by commissioning a nationally known New York polling firm

headed by Dick Dresner to design a poll to assess public perception of the issue and determine which pro-initiative arguments were strongest in the minds of the voters. The poll was completed by the first week of September.

The next step was to produce ads that presented the case for the initiative in the clearest, simplest, strongest manner. In late September, Zemke and Seattle campaign consultant Blair Butterworth embarked for New York to work with ad man Tony Schwartz to produce radio and television ads. Since Schwartz personally supported the initiative, he gave the "Don't Bankrupt Washington" Committee a special discount: $15,000, plus production costs. That was one-third his normal fee. The next task was to raise the money necessary to pay for broadcasting the ads. Zemke estimated that $100,000 would be sufficient. While in New York, they met with potential supporters, like Alida Rockefeller Dayton, who made the largest single contribution to the campaign: $45,000 worth of broadcast time slots on Washington State stations. In Washington, D.C., Zemke and Butterworth met with leaders of national environmental groups to plead their cause. Only a couple of groups gave money, but others helped Zemke by introducing him to philanthropists who were their own groups' biggest contributors. The East Coast fundraising tour netted $65,500 for the pro-initiative forces.

The Dayton contribution was by far the largest contribution ever made to an anti-nuclear power initiative campaign, and it must have raised a few eyebrows in the "No on 394" camp when it was reported to the Public Disclosure Commission. But they didn't dare criticize proponents for taking money from a Rockefeller, when their own contributions came from special interests with a financial stake in WPPSS's cost overruns. In addition to the Morrison-Knudsen loan mentioned earlier, they received a $50,000 contribution from Babcock and Wilcox of Lynchburg, Virginia. (This was the same firm that designed the nuclear plant at Three Mile Island.) The committee also received hefty sums from Wall

Street brokerage firms that made money selling WPPSS's tax-free revenue bonds to investors. Merrill, Lynch was bullish against the initiative to the tune of $20,000; Goldman, Sachs and Salomon Brothers each kicked in $15,000; Paine, Webber and Kidder, Peabody each gave $10,000.

Meanwhile, back in Seattle, the "No on 394" Committee was airing yet another deceptive ad. This one showed a businessman finding out about the allegedly frequent bond referendum elections that would be required if Initiative 394 were approved, and exclaiming "How much is it going to cost!?" Of all the opposition claims, this one had the thinnest factual basis. Since the initiative did not specify how often bond elections would have to be held, the opposition construed the measure to mean that there would have to be an election every time WPPSS sold bonds—as often as every six weeks in 1981 as WPPSS's financial crisis deepened. Naturally, the ads didn't mention WPPSS, for the same reason that the shipping company that owned the Titanic didn't feature that boat on its travel posters after it sank. "Whoops," which was by now the nation's largest issuer of tax-exempt bonds, was sinking fast. In October, WPPSS ran out of money to continue construction of two of its five nuclear plants, and construction was suspended.

In an attempt to discredit the "election every six weeks" opposition claim, the "Don't Bankrupt Washington" Committee asked the state's attorney general to issue an official opinion refuting the claim, but to no avail. The deputy attorney general complied, but it was little more than a moral victory for pro-initiative forces, since the opposition continued to broadcast the ad, and proponents did not have the money to broadcast a rebuttal. They were saving their media funds for the end of the campaign.

The opposition broke the state record for initiative campaign fundraising by October 22, when the "No on 394" Committee reported to the Public Disclosure Commission it had passed the $1 million mark. Among the late contributors were out-of-state utility companies with nuclear power plants, such as Consolidated Edison of New York, Baltimore Gas and Electric of Maryland, and Southern California Edison ($5,000 each); oil companies such as Union Oil of California ($10,000), Mobil, Chevron, and Exxon Nuclear ($5,000 each); and last but by no means least, aluminum companies, which are massive users of electricity (Reynolds, Kaiser, Alcoa, Intalco, and Anaconda each gave at least $30,000).

Fundraising

While the "No on 394" forces were spending their money on advertising as fast as it came in, "Yes on 394" campaign manager Zemke put into effect his plans to raise the bulk of his funds from local supporters. In late September, the "Don't Bankrupt Washington" Committee started an aggressive phone bank operation to complement their previous direct-mail fundraising effort. The phone bank, Zemke said later, proved to be a cost-effective way both to bring in money before the election and to keep the organization going throughout the following year. The method was to first send a fundraising letter to each person on the I-394 supporters' list, which numbered over 10,000. Then, "Yes on 394" volunteers or paid staffers would call each person, within days after they had received the letter. Respondents were asked to contribute any way they could: If they couldn't give money, would they volunteer their time, or sell tickets for the "free drawing"? This latter technique was another successful fundraising gimmick. Supporters of the initiative "sold" tickets to friends for a dollar "donation" apiece, making them eligible to win a trip to Hawaii, or other prizes donated by local merchants. It was the oldest fundraising trick in the book and one of the most effective: The sale of "drawing" tickets brought in $50,000. State records showed that between September 25 and

October 22, the "Yes on 394" side raised a total of $110,000.

A simple message

On October 18, the "Yes on 394" media counterattack opened with radio ads, which were augmented a week later by television ads. The pro-394 committee spent $40,000 for a two-week radio ad campaign and $50,000 for one week of television broadcasts. The message was simple and direct, yet clever in its use of the universally recognized pronunciation "Whoops" for the acronym WPPSS. In thirty seconds, the main "pro-394" ad recounted the sorry history of the agency, identified the ads' sponsors, and urged a "Yes" vote:

You know when WPPSS announced they were going to build new power plants, they said they would cost 4 billion dollars, then whoops—they went up to 8 billion—whoops to 14 billion—whoops to 20 billion and now whoops 24 billion dollars. The WPPSS contractors say you should vote no on Initiative 394. We're the "Don't Bankrupt Washington" Committee, we paid for this ad, and we say let's just vote yes on Initiative 394 to let the voters decide if a new power plant should be built. Sorry about that, WPPSS.

In the television version, the same sound track was used, with the added visual element of a photograph of nuclear power plant cooling towers, plus a changing printout of prices corresponding to the announcer's litany of WPPSS's changing cost estimates. Another ad

answered the opposition's "costly elections" argument by explaining Initiative 394, then concluding with the rhetorical question, "Which costs more—voting or building a nuclear plant? Vote Yes on 394."

More than a year after the campaign, media consultant Schwartz said that Initiative 394 was one of his most successful campaigns, out of hundreds he has worked on. He praised the measure's sponsors, when asked what suggestions he had for poorly funded campaign organizations: "They have to learn the importance of getting their act together and raising money from their supporters. . . . In Washington State, they've learned this lesson. In most cases, you find that the people in favor of an initiative spend the money the wrong way, or don't recognize that they could raise the money needed for proper use of media." Schwartz also recommended that financially pressed groups refrain from "filmmaking" to keep costs down:

The most important part of the ad is the spoken message. The visual is just material to support and not interfere with the listener hearing the message. This type of ad [the WPPSS ad quoted in full above] is very inexpensive. There's the cost of the announcer, then no more than seven or eight hundred dollars of production costs. The purpose of the ad is communication, not filmmaking. You can make a statement . . . and it can work like gangbusters, and you don't need a million dollars worth of equipment to do it.[6]

Since the "Don't Bankrupt Washington"

Committee could not afford the additional expense of tracking polls, pro-394 forces had to wait until Election Day to gauge the effectiveness of their ads. The only polling data made public by the eve of the election was a mid-October poll that showed support had dwindled from the midsummer peak of three to one, down to forty-nine percent in favor, forty-six percent opposed, and five percent undecided. The opposition's media campaign had proven effective, so long as it remained unchallenged. A trend of declining voter support was evident, the type of trend that almost invariably has led to defeat of initiatives in California, the only state where systematic polling data on initiatives is available to the public (courtesy of San Francisco's Field Institute and pollster Mervin Field).

A skillful final push

In any tight political race, there is the temptation for campaign managers to launch a final advertising "broadside" just before Election Day, by placing ads containing claims they well know are half truths, distortions, or even blatant falsehoods, in the hope that there won't be time for the other side to make its rebuttal. This is perfectly legal in Washington State and in most other states, since the First Amendment right of "freedom of speech" has discouraged passage of laws against lying in political campaigns. Zemke, aware of the possibility of a last-minute "broadside" from the opposition, checked financial disclosure records filed with the Secretary of State a week before the election to analyze the "No on 394" Committee's latest expenditures. Sure enough, they had paid for full-page ads in Sunday newspapers around the state. On Saturday before the election, Zemke made a point of getting an early edition of a Sunday Seattle paper. The "No on 394" Committee had proven unable to resist the temptation. "Initiative 394 will shut down power plants we've already paid for!" screamed their ad.

It was too late for pro-394 forces to produce and place rebuttal ads, even if money was available to pay for them—and it wasn't. Quickly, Zemke called the editorial departments of all the state's major newspapers, asking them to either confirm the truth of the opposition's ads, or not run them. He reminded them that in a similar situation a few years before, they had refused to print a political ad until its sponsor documented its claims. In that instance, a candidate opposing former Washington Governor Dixy Lee Ray had attributed several quotes to Ray that were so outrageous editors couldn't believe she had uttered them; they wound up printing the ad after the opposing candidate proved the quotes were accurate.

Although none of the editors agreed to stop the "No on 394" ads, they did give front-page coverage to the dispute over the ads' veracity. Zemke also called several radio and television commentators to inform them of the controversy, his prompt action resulting in many broadcast news items and a few editorials warning voters to beware of the opposition's latest ad. One television station manager went so far as to hold up a copy of the ad while making a televised editorial and told viewers "This ad contains lies!"

As the ad dispute raged in the state's media, the "Don't Barnkrupt Washington" Committee's "get-out-the-vote" effort was in full swing. Starting ten days before the election, "Yes on 394" phone bank workers began reminding supporters to vote on Election Day, in addition to asking for a contribution and for volunteer effort. The Election Day push set volunteers to distributing leaflets at bus stops and shopping areas, as well as holding large "Yes on 394" signs at major freeway exits in urban areas of the state.

When the polls closed, Zemke and the other I-394 campaign organizers were satisfied that they had run the best campaign their limited financial resources had allowed, and they sat back to await the results. With the combined forces of Wall Street, WPPSS, and the nuclear industry arrayed against them, it would be no great shock to lose. Their opponents had spent over seven times as much money on their campaign, running up a record-breaking total of $1.25 million. Even so, the pro-394 campaign had been a fundraising success, bringing in more money than any previous initiative campaign group lacking substantial corporate or labor union backing. They had spent $204,000, and run up an additional campaign debt of $20,000. If they lost, it would be difficult to raise the money to pay it off. But they never had to worry about that, because when the returns were counted, fifty-eight percent of the votes were in the "Yes" column. The voters had shown that their anger over WPPSS mismanagement could not be deflected by an expensive ad campaign.

Endnotes

1. *Initiative News Report*, Volume I, Nos. 1, 2, 7 (1980); Volume II, Nos. 7, 10, 12 (1981).
2. *Initiative News Report*, Volume I, Nos. 3 & 6 (Sept. 22 and Nov. 3, 1980).
3. Charles Winner, quoted in Larry J. Sabato, *The Rise of Political Consultants*, New York: Basic Books, Inc., 1981, p. 27.
4. Steve Zemke, interviews with the author, July 9–10, 1982.
5. Shelby Scates, "Initiative Is Common Cents Measure," *Seattle Post-Intelligencer*, September 27, 1981.
6. Tony Schwartz, interviewed in *Initiative News Report*, Volume 4, No. 11, July 1, 1983.

PACs on the Warpath:

How Independent Efforts Helped Reelect Jesse Helms

Lisa De Maio Brewer

There has never been a U.S. Senate race quite like North Carolina's 1984 contest between Republican incumbent Jesse Helms, a hero to conservatives, and Democratic Governor Jim Hunt, a rising star in his party's firmament. Not only was it one of the most vicious and bitter elections in modern times, but a combined total of more than $26 million was spent by the two candidates—a national record for a Senate seat.

The candidates were not alone in their spending. A number of political action committees (PACs) and organizations, mostly on the ideological right and in support of Helms, expended additional hundreds of thousands of dollars for media advertising, direct mail, and voter registration and turnout efforts. This is permitted under federal election law if it is done independently of the campaigns and candidates, without any coordination or consultation. Independent spending is a controversial phenomenon because, while some regard it as a First Amendment extension of "free speech," others believe that it is often not truly independent and evades the spirit of the election laws. Questionable or not, independent spending has played a significant role in many recent American elections, and Lisa De Maio Brewer examines its impact on North Carolina's 1984 Senate prizefight.

Northorth Carolinians are basically parochial and don't like outsiders telling them how to vote. But with North Carolina's senior U.S. Senator Jesse Helms appearing as much on national news programs as on local, it was to be expected that the 1984 North Carolina race for the U.S. Senate would attract national interest.

A former North Carolina newspaper reporter, Lisa De Maio Brewer served as director of press and public relations for the Fund for a Conservative Majority during the 1984 elections.

Helms, long a champion of the conservative right, had twice won election to the Senate from a state where registered Democrats outnumber Republicans three to one. His Democratic opponent was popular two-term Governor Jim Hunt, who was perceived as everything from a "progressive conservative" to a "Walter Mondale liberal."

Although espousing different political philosophies, the two statesmen had worked reasonably well together over the previous four years. But by early 1983, the relationship had begun to erode under the weight of negative advertising funded by independently organized supporters of both men—principally the National Congressional Club (pro-Helms) and the North Carolina Campaign Fund (pro-Hunt).

The battle of the left and right had begun.

"I think it was the biggest Senate race ever of national interest," says Charles R. Black, Jr., the chief political strategist for the Helms for Senate campaign and senior partner in the consulting firm of Black, Manafort, Stone, and Atwater. "Helms is the strongest conservative leader who has drawn opposition from liberals national in scope. Jim Hunt is regarded as an up-and-coming liberal of national scope. Hunt had a strong record of winning elections."

Political organizations around the country began to watch the developments in North Carolina with a careful eye. Many began to plan their independent expenditure efforts eighteen months in advance of the election.

Ideologues find power in positive thinking

"We put our first white paper together in October, 1983—even though Governor Hunt didn't announce his candidacy until February 4, 1984," says Robert C. Heckman, Chairman of the Fund for a Conservative Majority (FCM), the nation's second-largest political action committee. "Our donors from all around the country had expressed such a strong interest in the race, which we knew to be a politically strategic one, that we wanted to be involved in a big way. That decreed something more substantial than the maximum contribution of $10,000."

Heckman's group conducted the largest independent expenditure campaign of the race: a project that spent over half a million dollars advocating Senator Helms' reelection. "We did everything," Heckman relates. "We retained Lance Tarrance of Houston to do our polling, to see where the 'soft' or undecided voters were. We clipped the North Carolina papers. We formed a Steering Committee composed entirely of North Carolina residents. We tested fundraising packages. We tested ads.

We knew there were already a lot of negative ads running in all branches of the media, and we decided not to do any. It is our policy, and it was also thought to be most effective, to keep our advertising on a positive level, so that's what we did."

The independent effort, called "Friends of Jesse Helms," featured two waves of television commercials produced by Bill Lee of Fernstrom and Associates in Washington, D.C. The spots proved to be surprisingly free of the negativism that had characterized previous FCM campaigns and starred moderate Republican Congressman James T. Broyhill in the role of honorary Chairman.

The choice of Broyhill was a revealing one. A twenty-two year House veteran and heir to a fortune that had made the state renowned for its furniture, the courtly, low-keyed lawmaker projected "Establishment" respectability. His public image was a stark contrast with that of Helms, whose combativeness had become legendary.

Traditionally, independent efforts by ideological PACs such as FCM have swung the battle-axe for their "above-it-all" favorites. Pragmatism dictated a different approach for North Carolina, even though the Helms campaign was not squeamish about wielding its own axe and had already taken a hard-right ideological stance. FCM polls by Lance Tarrance of Houston indicated the Helms strategy was making headway with conservative Tidewater Democrats but was threatening to undermine the traditional Republican base in the Appalachian foothills, where voters are of a more moderate stripe. Governor Hunt had a positive image in these parts, and the Democrats' gubernatorial nominee, Rufus Edmisten, was a native of the region.

Heckman wisely calculated that his group would be most effectively utilized guarding the flank of the hard-charging Helms. He carefully concentrated his media around the foothills and let Tarrance's data choose his spokesman: No one had a higher credibility rating in the region than James T. Broyhill.

Broyhill and Heckman unveiled the new

spots during a June 15, 1984, tour of the Tarheel state. The three-city blitz included press conferences in Raleigh, Charlotte, and Greensboro—three of the four North Carolina media markets where the first wave of commercials would be airing. Hunt press secretary Will Marshall attended the 8:30 A.M. Raleigh conference and immediately reported the surprising results to the Hunt camp.

"Do not believe for one moment that the positive spot this committee showed to the press this morning accurately predicts the kind of advertising on which they will spend their million dollars," Hunt spokesman Gary Pearce told a 10 A.M. news briefing. "Their track record is one of negative, attack advertising. This ad is the proverbial wolf in sheep's clothing."

Heckman termed the Hunt response "a bald-face lie" at the Greensboro press conference a few hours later. Privately, he was chortling: "We were delighted to get that kind of reaction from the Hunt camp," he reflects. "We had no intention of conducting a negative campaign of any kind whatsoever, and we lived up to that. But their visible concern over our role in the race actually increased our press coverage, and unfortunately for them, we were able to have the last word."

With the first wave of pro-Helms ads running in the early summer, FCM pumped $41,000 in TV buys into the state. A second wave of commercials would run in late October, costing $66,400. In all, over $114,000 was spent by the PAC in television production and buys alone. (The remaining three-quarters of FCM expenditures were primarily invested in voter-contact phone banks and direct mail fundraising.)

Helms campaign strategist Black watched the independent activity with interest: "When we saw what FCM was doing with Congressman Broyhill, we tested in our next survey and saw that Broyhill had tremendous name I.D. and credibility—especially in the markets in the western part of the state where Helms had trouble. Up there the people are not really philosophically motivated. I think the Broyhill commercials helped a great deal on that."

Heckman points to additional research which indicated that Helms' victory exceeded the expectations of his campaign's projections in the western mountain region, while falling behind projections in the east. Such figures suggest FCM's carefully tailored media and message may have had a significant, if not decisive, impact on the outcome.

Helms for Senate press secretary Claude Allen, now with the Senate Committee on Foreign Relations, is quick to refute any speculation of coordination between the Helms and FCM forces—a violation of federal election law. Any information about the FCM project came unsolicited from reporters or Helms supporters who were not involved, he says. That account is echoed by Grace Wiegers, liaison between FCM's Washington headquarters and its North Carolina unit. Now political director of the conservative PAC, Wiegers recalls the painstaking care with which consultants and staffers were screened to avoid employing anyone with connections to Helms, a precaution taken after being "burned by the Federal Election Commission" for having been less assiduous with their associations in 1982. Something else practiced by FCM that year that won't be repeated, according to Wiegers, is negative advertising. Tarrance's figures indicate the electorate will no longer tolerate it coming from an independent source, a finding seemingly confirmed by FCM's much-improved results in 1984.

Interest groups muster their membership

While the FCM media campaign illustrates how ideological PACs can achieve success today without negativism, grassroots tactics by interest group organizations and PACs in the Helms race are equally instructive. These PACs almost invariably sought to motivate their own membership to support Helms through highly targeted media, usually direct mail, space advertising, bumperstickers, and the like.

"We did not use any television," says Wayne LaPierre, who directed the National Rifle

Lisa De Maio Brewer

National Rifle Association bumpersticker distributed in North Carolina.

Association's $250,000 effort to secure Helms' reelection. "I am skeptical of TV for an independent expenditure. I felt it wasn't suitable for what we wanted to achieve, in terms of resource allocation . . . It's not as easy to control, not as easy to target your audience."

The targeted audience for the NRA included the hunting and firearms community. The organization boasts a huge computer list of firearm owners and NRA members, as well as those who purchase hunting licenses, subscribe to wildlife magazines, and are members of gun and hunting clubs. Rather than using television advertising, NRA began its campaign by distributing a message to its "natural base" via written communications.

"We went in with direct mail [stating] why we felt the race was important, why people should get out and help organize," says LaPierre. "We felt this would lay the groundwork for media and radio so people wouldn't come along later and say, 'Why is NRA doing that?'" The organization mailed twice to its membership in North Carolina and once to 75,000 hunters, for 200,000 pieces overall.

LaPierre also expresses a belief that the NRA targeted mailings in behalf of Helms spilled over by word-of-mouth to influence other voters, usually in a positive way. "In a [rural] state like North Carolina," he explains, "the people are, for the most part, pro-firearm ownership and pro-hunting."

The NRA's media campaign consisted of a series of newspaper ads placed in North Carolina's small city dailies and rural weeklies. Copy asked, "Who will stand with sportsmen in the U.S. Senate to protect traditional North Carolina freedoms?" and "Who did North Carolina hunters and gun owners turn to in the U.S. Senate?" A substantial radio advertising campaign was also launched. "Primarily, we aired one spot," says LaPierre, "focusing on leadership, saying that Jesse Helms gets out front, he doesn't compromise, and that's something to be proud of. So let's back Jesse Helms: our freedom was not won by compromise."

Proponents of Governor Hunt argued that he too was a friend to the North Carolina sportsmen, and wondered why the NRA had chosen sides. "Governor Hunt was good on our issues," LaPierre admits, "We even said that in our mailings. But . . . we have a PAC policy: If someone is in office and they stand out front for us, we stick with them at election time. With Helms, there wasn't much choice — he had been so far out front for us—he even went against his own party sometimes. That principle took us into the race. If it had been an open seat, and both candidates were equally good on the issues, we would have stayed out."

The Helms camp was pleased to have the extra support. Press secretary Allen notes that the bumpersticker campaign was especially visible, and strategist Black agrees. "The NRA got a tremendous amount of reaction. They hit everything at once—and consequently, it had a measurable impact we could feel. They had a major operation underway."

LaPierre is certain that the independent campaign achieved its goal of swinging nominally Democratic sportsmen Helms' way: "The majority of our membership in North Carolina—as in most of the Southern states—

is probably Democratic . . . we keep telling the Democrats who are choosing the national party leadership (that) the Democrat constituency is overwhelmingly for our issues, but the Democrats keep selecting national leaders who speak out for gun control. I think in our independent expenditure for Helms, we were able to win votes over who might have voted Democratic otherwise."

The registration tug-of-war

While the Fund for a Conservative Majority and the National Rifle Association undertook the most expensive independent expenditures in the nation's most expensive Senate race, the lion's share of press attention was captured by a frugally financed voter registration drive. Spokesmen from both the Helms and Hunt camps agree that the Moral Majority's get-out-the-vote program was a highly effective one.

Hunt press secretary Will Marshall claims it had the greatest impact of any factor in the election "in sheer electoral numbers . . . Jerry Falwell boasted that they had registered 125,000 fundamentalists—well, it's impossible to say." He observes, however, that Helms rolled up his biggest majorities in those counties where the Hunt campaign had detected Moral Majority activity.

Recent black-oriented registration drives in the state—spearheaded by the Rev. Jesse Jackson—had devastated Helms' allies at the polls in 1982. Claude Allen echoes popular white perceptions that may have fueled a church-led backlash in 1984: "You had the liberals saying, 'You can't do this, and you can't do that.' We proved they were hypocrites. I mean, you had Jesse Jackson passing the bucket in church to raise money for his campaign! . . . Jackson focused on one issue: race. This [Moral Majority drive] focused on conservative churches. The Christian community was an untapped source of support."

And Moral Majority tapped it. Allen adds that not only did the Moral Majority independent effort succeed in registering thousands of

voters, it also successfully brought Helms voters to the polls on Election Day.

Ecclesiastical electioneering

Not all of the credit for activating the conservative religious movement can be given to Moral Majority. Less ballyhooed independent projects had a significant impact as well, such as those sponsored by the American Coalition for Traditional Values (ACTV) and the National Right to Life Committees.

David Osteen, executive director of the National Right to Life Committee, claims Jim Hunt's strong pro-abortion record promoted his group's involvement in the race, which consisted of distributing Helms pro-life literature. The distribution effort was reported as an in-kind contribution to Helms, valued at just under $5,000.

Democrats also credited the voter registration drive conducted by the American Coalition for Traditional Values as having an influence on the Helms/Hunt race. For instance, the campaign manager for defeated North Carolina Democrat Congressman James Clarke charged, "There's a hot place in hell reserved for those folks [for politicizing the churches]."

Just what did ACTV do? According to spokesman Matt Smyth, it contributed approximately $9,000 directly to the Helms campaign but also conducted a registration and get-out-the-vote drive that proved successful in registering 150,000 new fundamentalist voters and turning virtually all of them out on Election Day. But the groups greatest impact was felt not in registration of voters, but in their education.

ACTV and its affiliated organizations printed and distributed over 200,000 "report cards" to Tarheel voters, providing information on key moral and family issues. In an educational, nonpartisan manner, Helms's and Hunt's positions on abortion, school prayer, the ERA, church schools, national defense, and taxes were contrasted. In addition, information was

Lisa De Maio Brewer

presented contrasting the issue positions of the Democratic and Republican national tickets.

Owing to the apparently apolitical construction of the "report cards," pastors who were previously reluctant to involve themselves could now feel free to distribute the tabloids to their congregations as an "educational service." Other volunteer groups, including students, pro-lifers, Republicans, women's clubs, and other Christian organizations, helped distribute the handouts at churches, shopping malls, and meetings.

The volunteer networks used to distribute the literature were utilized as well for the get-out-the-vote (GOTV) program. Pastors and lay leaders, understandably hesitant to give their church lists of members and their phone numbers to outsiders, allowed ACTV to assign one member in each church to head a phone bank contacting only members of that particular church. Phone banks were used on election eve and Election Day to ensure that members voted. Smyth estimates that ACTV spent under $5,000 on the GOTV project and was successful in getting approximately ninety percent of the newly registered voters out to the polls for Senator Helms on Election Day.

Is it any wonder that North Carolina had the greatest increase in voter turnout of any state in 1984?

Going independent

Current federal election law restricts not only the amount of money individuals may contribute directly to campaigns ($1,000 per election), but also the amount that can be contributed by political action committees ($5,000 per election). "Five thousand dollars doesn't really do anything for the candidate or for the people we would like to reach," says the NRA's Wayne LaPierre.

Many groups, such as those discussed in this article, opt to exceed these constraints by conducting independent expenditures. There are no limits on the amount of money to be spent in such a project, as long as all activities remain truly "independent" from official campaigns.

A frequently heard complaint about independent expenditures is that they are often not truly "independent." The Federal Election Campaign Act of 1971 stipulates that any such independent payments must be made "without consultation, cooperation or consent, and not at the request or suggestion of a candidate, agent, or authorized committee." Will Marshall insists that was not always the case during the North Carolina Senate race, citing a John Birch Society flyer critical of Hunt as coming "straight from the Helms campaign. My qualms are that the 'independent' campaigns are not always independent. . . ."

It was, in fact, difficult to find any independent expenditure activities that were conducted on behalf of Governor Hunt. A few negative, anti-Helms advertisements were placed in North Carolina papers as paid political advertisements by the North Carolina Rail Labor and Management Coalition, and the North Carolina Central America Network. (A search through directory assistance offered no telephone listings. Neither campaign press spokesman had heard of the groups, but assumed that students or single individuals were behind the projects.) The Sierra Club, a liberal-oriented organization concerned with ecology and conservation, conducted early mailings and literature drops on behalf of Hunt's campaign, and the National Organization of Women contributed its largest sum for a male candidate, $5,250, to the governor's campaign.

Why the lack of independent efforts for Hunt?

"The right is better organized," explains Rob Christensen of the *Raleigh News and Observer*, a veteran North Carolina reporter. "Beyond that, Senator Helms was more of a national figure than Jim Hunt. Conservative groups, especially those associated with the New Right, were intensely interested in seeing Senator Helms re-elected." According to Christensen, the Hunt campaign even made it clear that they did not welcome independent expenditures, fearing independent expenditures by labor unions or "liberal" groups could backfire politically in what was an essentially conservative state.

The *Charlotte Observer's* chief political correspondent, Ken Eudy, offered another explanation for the vastly superior independent support of Helms:

"[Helms claims] Jim Hunt gets millions of dollars worth of free—either neutral or laudatory—news media coverage . . . that the coverage he [Helms] gets is slanted and biased against him to the extent that he needs to pay millions of dollars to get his message through. And I think conservatives believe that, by and large."

Helms spokesman Claude Allen couldn't agree more. He even considers the so-called "biased" news coverage to be an independent expenditure in its own right. "It's a multimillion dollar industry in North Carolina," Allen explains. "One paper can give more free advertising critical of Senator Helms than the two campaigns combined [will buy]."

And which of the independent efforts do the pundits feel had the most impact? Eudy gives the nod to the FCM television spots for helping bridge the gap between the conservative and moderate Republicans, a split that he has seen in North Carolina since 1972. "If there were any doubt, particularly among the western, mountain Republicans, who to vote for, I think Broyhill helped them stay with Helms," he observes, adding that voter groups targeted by the NRA and Christian organizations were "pretty well staked out beforehand."

Running a Registration Drive:
New Voters Recast Chicago Politics

Michael Cordts

One of the most dramatic and memorable elections in recent U.S. history was the mayoral victory of Harold Washington in Chicago. In becoming Chicago's first black mayor in 1983, Washington first scored a come-from-behind primary win over the incumbent woman mayor (Jane Byrne) and the son of the founder of the city's Democratic Machine (Richard Daley), and then narrowly defeated a well-funded Republican candidate in the general election. These historic events were not chance occurrences. As journalist Michael Cordts makes clear in this analysis, Washington's triumph was produced by a massive registration drive of black voters who were determined to make the city more responsive to their needs.

The results of the organizers' efforts continue to be demonstrated in Chicago, by the way. Additional registration drives helped to fuel Washington's difficult but successful reelection bid in 1987, for which he had a rematch with Jane Byrne in the Democratic primary. Washington's second term was an abbreviated one, cut short by his sudden death from a heart attack in late 1987.

Ed Gardner had never met Harold Washington. But the millionaire president of Chicago-based Soft Sheen hair products was convinced by Chicago black activist and former policeman Renault Robinson to chip in $50,000 and the services of Soft Sheen's advertising department to produce radio spots urging people to register to vote and to "Come Alive October 5"—the registration deadline for the November general election.

Registration groups soon began meeting at Gardner's gleaming factory. Representatives from The Woodlawn Association; Rev. Jesse Jackson's Operation PUSH; the People's Movement for Voter Registration; and from

People Organized for Welfare and Employment Rights (POWER) met for weekly "skull sessions." Those who had joined forces to protect what they saw as continuing decay of civil and economic rights for blacks and other minorities were soon convinced by Robinson, journalist Lu Palmer from the People's Movement, and POWER's grass roots organizer Slim Coleman that a massive registration drive could possibly bring a black to the mayoral office. It did. How did it happen?

Mayor Byrne politics

Early in Jane Byrne's administration, she had scored points with blacks when she and her newly acquired newspaperman-husband and political strategy advisor, Jim McMullen,

---

Michael Cordts is a news reporter for the Chicago Sun Times.

moved into the gang-ravaged Cabrini Green housing project for a short time in March 1981.

But she passed over a black as interim school superintendent; replaced two black school board members with two white women opposed to desegregation; passed over a highly qualified black for superintendent of police; oversaw a gerrymandering of aldermanic districts that hurt blacks; and attempted to unseat a black alderman who proclaimed his independence from the dominant city Democratic Machine.

The clincher was appointing three whites to the Chicago Housing Authority board that serves a nearly all-black clientele. When blacks protested the appointment, the mayor made sure no blacks could disrupt the City Council approval meeting by packing the gallery with city workers.

A caller to a radio talk show suggested blacks strike back by boycotting ChicagoFest, a pet project of Mayor Byrne's. Rev. Jesse Jackson took up the idea, and it unified most of the black community. All of this generated deep distrust in Byrne's black constituency that, rightfully, claimed to have put her in office in the first place.

"You come to a point and you say, 'That's it.' The last appointment (to the Chicago Housing Authority) was it," said Nancy Jefferson, executive director of a West Side community council and a member of Byrne's transition task force.

The black registration drive

Harold Washington was the two-term U.S. representative from Illinois's First District, the most stable and longest-lived black community in the United States. In the spring of 1982, he was not completely convinced a black could be elected mayor of Chicago.

Washington demanded hard evidence that the "movement" was more than just an arithmetical possibility. Even though he won his last election by the widest margin in the country, he would not be a sacrificial lamb in a mayoral race. But he gave the opposition hope.

He had told supporters in June to register 50,000 new black voters by October 5 (the last day of registration in Chicago's 2,914 precincts for the November 2 election), "and then maybe I'll run."

"I handed him 50,000 names before the deadline and said, 'Now you run,'" said Coleman. And, as Washington watched in amazement, that registration drive became a crusade.

Said one black ward committeeman in early October, "If you're not registered in *my* neighborhood now, you stand to be humiliated."

These were the elements of this remarkable registration drive:

- More than one hundred community groups united under an umbrella organization called People's Movement for Voter Registration, including Nancy Jefferson's heavyweight organization. People's Movement concentrated on seventeen of the city's fifty wards that are predominantly black, with special emphasis on public housing residents still enraged at the mayor. Registration tables were set up at supermarkets, parks, picnics, and special events in the black community.

- One of the city's legendary street gangs, the El Rukns, formerly known as the Black Peace Stone Nation, escorted more than one hundred people to City Hall to register in late August.

- The Mount Pisgah Church, which had been feeding thousands of families weekly, refused to give out bags of groceries to anyone who could not present a registration card.

- The influential Rev. George Clements, pastor of Holy Angels parish who had touched Chicago by adopting a son, refused to admit pupils whose parents were not registered. He preached of the "sin" of failing to vote that "cries out for vengeance from the heavens."

- More than seventy-five black ministers who had backed Byrne in 1979 launched a registration drive from the pulpit in early August. They were joined by another one hundred ministers a few days later.

People

Nothing and no one embodied the success of the registration drive more than People Organized for Welfare and Employment Rights (POWER), which was glued together by "radical" Slim Coleman. Coleman, 39, came to Chicago in 1969 from Cleveland where he worked as a union organizer for the Iron-workers. Before that, he organized hospital workers in Boston, having dropped out of Harvard a few courses short of a degree in philosophy, history, and government.

He set up shop among the Appalachian whites in Uptown Chicago forming the "Heart of Uptown Coalition" and backing a series of unsuccessful radical aldermanic candidates, including José "Cha Cha" Jimenez, a street-gang leader.

POWER, a coalition that eventually grew to thirty-one welfare rights and community groups, was organized in December 1981 to protest cuts in the general assistance program. After a series of lawsuits, clashes with the Republican governor, and a lack of commitment from Mayor Byrne, POWER turned to the massive voter registration drive "to make sure they would listen to us."

Coming together for the first time under Coleman were diverse community groups well known to each other, historically separated by different areas of concern, and now united by the times. "We'd been trying for years to get such a coalition together," said Roger Fox, research director of the Chicago Urban League. "The time was right. Their interest and involvement was a manifestation of what people were prepared to do on their own. You didn't have to talk people into registering. They wanted to."

The key to POWER and, some would argue, to the election, were brainstorming sessions. "We were asking each other how to tap the class issue, how to get to these people," Coleman said. "Then somebody said, 'We all know one place they go every month.'" POWER had found in a survey of 1,800 public aid recipients that all were angry but that only thirty percent were registered. That's when POWER joined the community-based Outreach program, run by the Board of Elections, and the voter registration began. In August, the Board of Elections agreed to allow registration for the first time at twenty-four public aid and six unemployment offices.

Asserting it was nonpartisan, POWER secured funding for themselves from both Republicans and Democrats, but only the Democratic candidate for Governor, Adlai Stevenson III, gave money ($10,000, a gift from which he would clearly benefit many times over). Incumbent Republican Governor Jim Thompson refused to allow registration in state office buildings, by contrast.

The registration program won the support of some Machine-connected officers. The newly elected chairman of the local Democratic party, Alderman Edward R. (Fast Eddie) Vrdolyak, needed to prove he knew how to crank votes out of the Machine in November. It also was no secret that Byrne favored a Washington candidacy in hopes of splitting the anti-Byrne vote between Washington and another candidate also in the race.

Coleman, who now admits there was heavy electioneering for Washington during registration at public aid and unemployment offices, gloats that Vrdolyak "fell right into our trap, took the bait hook, line and sinker. . . ." The Machine's acquiescence in the registration drive proved costly indeed.

An overwhelming response

There was an overwhelming response from the "captive" audience. The Outreach program registered 102,444 voters, more than seventy percent of them black. Of the 102,444, 42,000 registered in front of public aid and unemployment offices.

By dusk October 5, the Outreach program had added an incredible 250,249 new voters. Michael E. Lavelle, chairman of the Chicago Board of Elections, called the results "tremendous." The reluctant but stirred Washington, however, stayed out, pointing to a 1979 study by the Chicago Urban League that indicated it may be easier to get Chicago blacks to register than to vote.

The Thompson debacle

The gubernatorial race between Republican Governor Jim Thompson and former U.S. Senator Adlai Stevenson III left little doubt that black Chicago was ready to flex newfound muscle. Thompson went into Election Day with a cushy 400,000 vote lead in the polls. He won by 5,074 votes. It was the closest gubernatorial race in the state's history. This definitely showed that registration drives could pull newly registered voters to the polls.

Washington's decision

On November 10, eight days after being reelected to Congress by the widest margin in the nation, Washington announced his candidacy for mayor. He had to be dragged into the fray, and he was reminded of the ingredients that had elected blacks as big-city mayors: a losing effort that brought widespread name recognition, a surge in voter registration during the second run, a high turnout, a huge black plurality and at least ten percent of the white vote, and two white candidates in the race.

Washington had been in the 1977 mayoral primary, gathering only eleven percent of the vote in a city forty percent black. Two whites were now in the Democratic mayoralty primary race, Mayor Jane M. Byrne and Cook County State's Attorney Richard M. Daley, son of the late, great Chicago Machine boss, Richard J. Daley.

The numbers

Winning ninety-five percent of the black vote in Machine Chicago (as other successful black mayor candidates had in other cities) was iffy at best. Also unknown was the size of Washington's power base in fragmented and fractious black Chicago. The Washington formula for success was "80-80," a black turnout of eighty percent with eighty percent of those voting for him.

Like a teacher prodding a promising but undisciplined student, Harold Washington preached long and hard that the political pie would never be fairly divided in racially divided, Machine-controlled Chicago. The sermon was always the same: Winning would require a color-blind coming together of the disenfranchised and the angry, coupled with a resolve to take control. Most of all, the leadership to bring it all about would have to come from the community. All was possible under the right political circumstances, said Washington.

The campaign

The contest unfolded Chicago-style, ugly and rough-and-tumble and with zest: A three-way race between a black and two white Irish Catholics—a woman incumbent and a challenger named Daley—wrestling for control of the Chicago Machine that proved in November it could still get the vote and, in some cases, with imagination. (U.S. attorneys were again forced to compare cemetery and voter lists.)

By the day of the Democratic mayoral primary, there were an estimated 615,000 registered blacks, up almost 160,000 since the massive registration drive began. In a postmortem of Washington's win, the black turnout was estimated at 473,000 votes. Using the yardstick of needing eighty percent of the black vote to win, Washington collected 378,840 black votes, about eighty-nine percent of his total 424,146. A crucial ten to eleven percent of his total came from whites and Hispanics.

The 10 Wards in Chicago with the Largest Net Increase in New Registrants Between the 1983 Mayoral Primary and the April 12 Mayoral General Elections

Ward	Percentage Black	New Registrants	Percent Increase	Total Voters
21	98.4%	1,256	3.2%	40,456
9	89.1	1,237	4.0	32,335
16	98.5	1,131	3.5	33,269
17	99.0	1,111	3.1	36,933
34	96.9	1,065	3.0	36,341
29	87.6	1,028	3.8	27,940
6	98.3	1,002	2.4	43,117
28	96.6	1,000	3.4	30,365
8	96.1	932	2.4	38,984
23	96.1	888	2.4	38,513

When the dust of the Democratic mayoral primary cleared, 1,235,324 of Chicago's 1,594,253 eligible voters had gone to the polls—a 77.5 percent turnout—which put Washington within general election victory of becoming Chicago's first black mayor. The results of the primary were:

- Washington, 60, a state legislator for sixteen years and a rising star on Capitol Hill, received 424,146 votes, 36.5 percent.
- Jane M. Byrne, 48, the city's first woman mayor who had amassed a staggering $10 million campaign fund, received 388,259 votes, 33.4 percent; and
- Cook County State's Attorney Richard M. Daley, 40-year-old son of the legend, received 344,721 votes, 29.6 percent.

The battle was not yet over, however. Many Chicagoans, including the chairman of the Cook County Democratic party, were unhappy with Washington's primary win in a city that has been called the most segregated in the nation, and precinct captains retched at Washington's promise to end the patronage that fuels the Machine. Many supported little-known GOP candidate Bernard Epton, and the national Republican party helped to finance his campaign. Washington, D.C.-based media consultant John Deardourff was retained and support came from all directions.

The Democratic reaction

National Democratic Party Chairman Charles T. Manatt came to Chicago in early March and begged for unity, calling the election of Washington in the general election the national party's "top priority." "We have a job to do in 1984," he warned Cook County Democrats who balked at singing Washington's praises. "His election is important to the future of the party."

Voter registration continued to amaze the experts. The number of registered jumped another 31,536, the biggest registration increase ever between a Chicago mayoral primary and a mayoral election. By the March 14 deadline for the general election, 1,625,786 voters were registered—a sixteen year high. Washington's winning total in the April 12 general election, 656,727 votes (a plurality of 39,568 over Epton) reflects one of the most awesome displays of bloc voting that America has ever seen.

Running an effective registration drive is a tactic that neither party can afford to ignore. With presidential year voter turnout figures down to around fifty-four percent, campaign professionals understand the growing importance of registration drives coupled with get-out-the-vote efforts. The Washington victory in Chicago proved the point beyond doubt.

The Navajo Nation Elects a Chairman:

The *Real* Americans and the *Realpolitik*

Jean M. Westwood

All American elections are alike in some ways and different in other important respects. However, few are as distinct as a campaign for chief of the Navajo Nation. This vital post among Native Americans became the focal point of an intense battle in 1982 between Peter MacDonald, the longtime tribal chairman, and Peterson Zah, an insurgent reformer. One of Zah's backers was former Democratic National Committee Chair Jean Westwood, and in this article Westwood describes the evolution of an untraditional campaign in a supremely traditional setting. Despite the unfamiliar trappings of a Navajo contest, readers will recognize certain modern-day political essentials: voter registration drives, absentee voting efforts, radio advertising, and even pork barrel politics by the incumbent.

How would *you* win against an incumbent who had served three four-year terms and was considered unbeatable by both knowledgeable politicians and the press?

The area you must carry is about the size of West Virginia. It's spread over parts of three states and involves many aspects of local and state politics. In addition, pockets of eligible voters are concentrated in the Oakland–San Francisco area; from Salt Lake City to Provo, Utah; in Denver, Colorado; in Albuquerque, New Mexico; and in Phoenix, Arizona.

To make matters worse, the incumbent has almost complete control of government funds, the election laws, the only (weekly) newspaper,

and the legislative process. Indeed, one reason you are running is that over the years he has gained control of most legislative and judicial powers, and destroyed the separation of powers you believe to be the basis of good government.

The last estimate of the total population is 160,000 with a median age of 18.1—so there are about 80,000 potential qualified voters. Most of the area is rural although there are seven larger communities, but none over 10,000. Most roads are unpaved clay, which can turn into slick bogs when it rains or snows.

Unemployment ranges from thirty to seventy-five percent—depending on how and whom you count—and the majority of those with jobs are in government service (so that many of your potential supporters cannot openly work for you without the risk of losing

Jean M. Westwood is a former chair of the Democratic National Committee and a resident of Arizona.

their jobs). The incumbent has a large say in who holds even the supposedly safe federal positions.

Peterson Zah was trying to decide if he should take on the odds and run against Peter MacDonald, the incumbent chief of the Navajo Nation—the "state" described above. Zah's campaign experience included getting elected to a school board (serving eventually as president); working in county and state legislative races; and running as a Democratic National Convention delegate in 1972—a race he lost when the Arizona state chairman bent the rules to help a party powerhouse.

Zah was considering taking on MacDonald in the nonpartisan race when John Lewis of the Arizona Intertribal Council asked me to

A triumphant Peterson Zah with his son on the Navajo Nation Inauguration Day.

meet with the Zahs to discuss campaign plans. Was there a way to win this "impossible" race? That was what Peterson Zah asked me in the fall of 1981.

Basic issues and support groups

I had known Zah since 1972, and I had watched his career with DNA (the Navajo acronym for the federally funded Navajo Peoples Legal Services), of which he was now director. He had used that office to teach consumers how to deal with their problems and how to keep out of court if possible. DNA had local representatives, Navajos elected from their own chapters (local tribal units), who then composed a board within each of the five geographic agencies (or districts) and also chose representatives to sit on the overall DNA board. The local people established their priorities under the budget each year. This is how Zah thought government should be run. It became a main campaign theme.

Background

Zah had long been involved with reservation issues. Six years ago he participated in a march protesting the corruption of the Navajo government. But no strong opposition candidate had emerged. MacDonald easily won this 1978 race against his perennial opponent, Raymond Nakai, tribal chairman before MacDonald first won in 1970.

Navajos agreed on some basics any opposition candidate needed. He must be honest. He must be smart. People had to know him. He must have the stable family so important in Navajo culture. He must have clout and show ability to deal with Navajo issues off the reservation. (This was what MacDonald claimed *he* did best.) But he also needed to have credibility at home, to show that he cared passionately about what was happening to the ordinary Navajo and would know the direction government should take.

There was support for Zah—people from the anti-corruption march, people who had

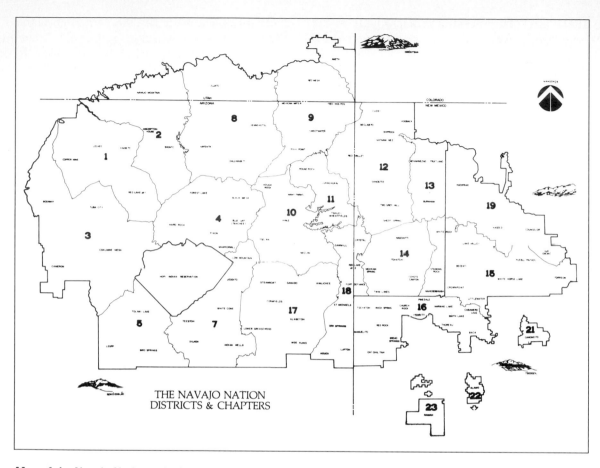

Map of the Navajo Nation, which spans three states.

worked with him in DNA, people from schools and social agencies who felt the problems they had to deal with got worse each year under MacDonald, and people who especially resented the chairman's support of President Reagan.

There were those who felt MacDonald was trying too hard to make the tribe over in the white man's image and to downgrade the old Navajo traditions. The educated, mostly younger, members of the tribe felt MacDonald had never wanted them and instead hired either sycophants or outsiders—indeed they thought control of the tribe now rested with a small group of outside advisors and MacDonald. Others simply were tired of MacDonald and felt Zah was the only person

capable of mounting a successful campaign against him.

Peterson had consulted with his family members, as any Navajo would have before making an important decision. They were apprehensive but reluctantly agreed that he was the only one with a chance.

Now Zah wanted some help. He wanted me to put together a training document and then run a campaign seminar for a group who wanted to help but had little hands-on campaign knowledge or experience.

I put together a manual that contained all the basics of campaigning. It included control flow charts and minimum and maximum budget planning plus overall campaign, headquarters, field, and local organization

Jean M. Westwood

structures, planning for full- and part-time workers (in this case they were all volunteers, and there were *no* paid workers) for scheduling and advance, master calendars, issue development, advertising and press, canvassing and voter registration, election laws, absentee balloting, get-out-the-vote, Election Day sample forms, even the thank-you materials. I made up twenty-five looseleaf copies of the manual and organized them in sections by function so any part could be taken out, abridged, or modified and given to local committees, press, schedulers, etc. I conducted the seminar on basic campaign skills at Window Rock in November 1981.

Peterson had access to a trailer that could be set up near his DNA office. One person at the seminar, Michael Benson, was free to work full time. So he became the first campaign coordinator. Others volunteered in the evenings and on weekends.

One of Zah's coworkers at DNA, Norman Ration, acted as treasurer and fundraising chairman. According to the Navajo election code, it is unlawful for any corporation or nonmember of the Navajo Tribe to contribute money or anything of value for the purpose of influencing a Navajo election. (Only radio or TV stations were exempted.) The limit a candidate could spend was 50 cents per voter, but part way through the campaign this was changed to one dollar per registered voter. Candidates need not report personal, traveling, or subsistence expenses. This was reportedly used in the past to take money from outsiders. The Zah campaign decided not to solicit or use such funds.

March against Chairman MacDonald in 1977.

Phase One—decision and beginning

There were four phases to the campaign organization:

1. Testing of Zah's candidacy and announcement.
2. Part-time campaigning until late spring.
3. Full-time campaigning from late spring until the primary on the second Tuesday in August, aiming for Zah to be one of the two candidates to emerge from the run-off for final election.
4. The final fall campaign, which had to include conversion of those who had worked and voted for the other six primary candidates.

The first phase was a tryout—with Zah making as many appearances as possible in the first couple of months where he could talk about the issues, get the greatest possible exposure and press, and appear in many places on the sprawling reservation.

At the same time, he was trying to line up support in the various geographic tribal areas. He found workers who could use the basic campaign materials and manuals to put an organization together. Each was asked to recruit others. A calendar was assembled with regular chapter meetings to which Zah would try to get a sponsor to invite him. Those in agencies who could not help openly could still schedule him for speeches to their groups. He went during this time to each major nonreservation area (like Oakland, California) where Navajos lived, to try to create a bona fide organization in each. When stationery was printed, it could include these committees and could show widespread support for his candidacy.

If all went well with this phase, he would announce in February at his home chapter, Low Mountain, Arizona. One phrase he used extensively was picked up by the press: "I'm walking from now to Christmas. From then through January I'll be trotting, then if all goes well, I'll be running hard."

A campaign theme

All did go well. He came up with a campaign theme, "Change for a Better Tomorrow." He put together organizations in Oakland, Phoenix, Albuquerque, and the Winslow–Flagstaff area in time for the first stationery. (Later, groups were formed in Denver and Salt Lake City.) He got good press coverage. Local organizations were formed whose first task was to get people to the official announcement on February 13.

But before that announcement he was asked to be the speaker at a Christmas dinner at the Shiprock chapter house. A thousand people attended. There he informally said he had decided to run. The following Tuesday the Low Mountain Chapter voted 127–0 to endorse him for tribal chairman.

Announcement day

Fifteen hundred people traveled fourteen miles of off-pavement down a rutted muddy road to sit in chairs, lean against fences, sit on top of pick-ups—in biting cold with snow on the ground—to hear Peterson announce his candidacy from a platform beside Low Mountain's log chapter-house building. The platform was covered by a traditional ramada—a brush-roofed shelter. A large grey, red, and black Navajo rug woven by Peterson's mother formed a backdrop. Everyone was served the traditional noon meal of mutton stew, roast beef, beans, and fry bread—donated, prepared and served by Zah supporters. The speeches were all in Navajo—the custom for official gatherings. Throughout the campaign Zah spoke in English only when off-reservation and at dinners where the attendance was mixed Anglo-Indian.

People came from all over the reservation, including thirteen present or former tribal council members. Endorsements or speeches were made by someone from each of the five agencies. From outside the reservation, the new Hopi Indian chairman, Ivan Sidney, was a prominent guest. One of Peterson's main platform pledges was to try to solve some of the Hopi–Navajo problems with friendly discussions instead of using outside lawyers.

Help from everywhere

Dr. Annie Wauneka, the first woman to serve on the Tribal Council and leader of the more active tribal women, called for placing or electing more Navajo women in decision-making positions. She also called for a return to the old autonomy of the Tribal Council. The first Navajo woman attorney, Claudeen Arthur, addressed the need for opportunities for Navajo professionals to work at home and to help their people. (She had been removed the day before from her position as the second-highest ranking Navajo in a federal job on the reservation—field solicitor for the Department of the Interior. The notice said it was because the chairman of the Navajo tribe, Peter MacDonald, had lost confidence in her. The unstated reason was that she did not support many of MacDonald's policies.)

Kenneth Cody, president of the Navajo Nation Council on Aging, stressed the unmet needs of the Navajo elderly; Henry Curley, the needs of the Navajo youth; and Raymond Smith, a former councilman, the need for economic and business development. Nevy Jenson of Cameron, Arizona, offered the traditional blessing. Medicineman Miller Nez spoke. Ambrose Shepherd, president of the Board of Supervisors of Apache County, Arizona, which is partly on the reservation, spoke of Zah's upbringing and his belief in the old Navajo ways.

Zah then told his people to look around them. "We are a nation rich in the resources necessary to build a prosperous nation. Why do so many live in poverty? We have abundant lumber, coal, oil, gas and first rights to water but they all flow off to serve Anglo-Americans first." He stressed that this must change, that Navajo resources should meet Navajo needs first. To do this, tribal government must move back into the hands of those affected by the decisions and into the Tribal Council, in the old way. Finally, he talked of his love for the

old traditions, how they should be respected and interwoven with the new learning needed to cope with the world of today.

The announcement set the tone for the whole campaign, just the way it was planned— the use of local volunteers, the use of endorsements by respected Navajos. The event was staged in traditional Navajo fashion instead of aping the Anglo ways. The major issues on which the campaign would focus were clearly laid out. It was a good beginning.

Phase Two—the part-time campaign

The campaign did not always run as well as the announcement. Zah made all the appearances and events he could manage and still keep his job. In a typical week he spoke at the Red Lake Chapter, met with supporters forming an organization in Tuba City, attended a DNA Board meeting back in Window Rock, and then spoke at a banquet sponsored by Navajo Peabody Coal workers in Kayenta the same night.

It was a killing schedule. His wife Rosalind had not been enthused about the campaign at all, but soon began to chauffeur Peterson in their small Volkswagen. There was no one else. Besides, any candidate was judged partly by how stable and supportive his family was. Her presence helped.

Organizing

One of the largest efforts during this time was to get a coordinating committee set up in each of the five agencies of the Navajo Nation, the natural geographic divisions around which to organize a campaign. The five were: Tuba City (Western), Chinle (Central), Fort Defiance, Shiprock (Northern), and Crownpoint (Eastern). There were twenty-three subdistricts under the agencies, and below these eighty-eight election communities containing 109 polling places. Two larger towns, Kayenta and Gallup, in isolated areas were also asked to organize. A coordinating committee for each agency was asked to have two parts. One was to be political—to contact people on the Tribal Council, chapter officers, land boards, etc. The other was to organize the structure and strategy for their agencies' overall campaign for Zah. The campaign had a central advisory committee with representatives from each agency.

A typical case was that of the Tuba City committee. At a March meeting its members were asked to fill out their coordinating committee, elect officers, obtain office space and supplies, find speaking and event dates, appoint workers from outlying communities, line up such fundraisers as car washes, softball tourneys, and cake walks, and set up books and keep track of the money. They were taught how to keep lists of volunteers and of supporters, how to make contact by phone and in person, and how to make index cards of every household of registered voters and identify "maybe" and "sure" people.

Claudeen Arthur was trying to identify voting segments by geographical areas and past voting trends and to set goals—in the Tuba City area sixty-eight percent had voted for MacDonald last time—so the aim was to contact the 11,000 out of 18,000 who did not vote then and get them to vote for Peterson. The basic structure was being set up in each agency, and under that in the larger and then the smaller chapters.

To give the campaign more visibility, they held an "official opening" of their trailer headquarters in mid-March. At this point Michael Benson was overseeing registration, distributing organization manuals, detailing duties of the committees, and acting in general command. Kenneth Begay and Miller Nez were scouting for commitments by individuals or groups and scheduling special events and dinner meetings. Norman was doing the

Peterson Zah greeting local volunteers.

Jean M. Westwood

fundraising as planned, but it was coming in dribs and drabs. Gloria Showalter and Casey Watchman were making preliminary budgets for materials, advertising, billboards, and publicity. Nancy Evans was preparing chapter profiles and formats for canvassers, and assembling materials for canvassing.

Claudeen was trying to get the election laws clarified. New regulations were being proposed. Even the date of the general election was not set. They felt that the Navajo Election Commission should finalize their proposals so the Tribal Council could vote on the law for this election.

They were also pushing the Commission to appoint new voting registrars both on and off the reservation so an effective voter registration program could be implemented. Eventually, general registration and new registrars were permitted by the Tribal Election Commission (which had extensive power to change or interpret election laws). But the efforts to look at past candidate financial records, allowed by law, dragged on from March through July. Harry Wero, the director, was a MacDonald appointee and cooperated as little as possible.

A few bumps along the road

Not everything was going smoothly. First Alberta Tippeconnic and Eugene Price of the Phoenix committee asked me to review their attempts to organize their local efforts better. Then they asked me to meet with Peterson and a group he would bring down there. But the problems were those typical for the beginning of a campaign. They needed some personnel shifts, some tightening of procedures, and more experience.

There were scheduling foul-ups—they were sure someone from other primary campaigns had called to ask for and make engagements in Zah's name. Also, Michael Benson was proving not willing enough to delegate authority. As a result some of the local committees did not get the materials or answers they needed. Luckily, the members turned out to be self-starters. When the

campaign got going full speed, they were almost all autonomous units.

Scheduling

The central coordinating committee decided that only one person should do the scheduling and that no one should make a final agreement on any appearance until it was cleared with that one person. Rosalind was the best one for this job. This prevailed for the rest of the campaign. A master calendar was kept in the office. Events were tentative until she approved them.

A poster was put together that could be used by any chapter or group. It consisted of a picture of Peterson with a large white area on which the notice of an event could be printed. These would be posted at the chapter house, the nearby trading posts, schools, and agencies, wherever possible. An American flag was already raised outside the chapter house when an event was in progress. This was a customary practice that told those passing in their pickups an open meeting was going on.

A local group would put on an event, usually at the chapter house. Sometimes they could get the chapter to sponsor it and sometimes the supporters themselves put it on. The place could be a small log chapter house warmed by a wood stove, without electricity or running water, or a large modern building with the crowds ranging from seventy-five or one hundred up to as many as one thousand people. But at every event a traditional meal was served. This is part of the Navajo way. You feed whoever comes to your house. The local supporters provided the meal even in the most poverty-stricken areas. (This was not true of the MacDonald campaign. In many places he or the Tribe put up the money for the food.)

At these events Peterson would speak. Others would also make speeches on his behalf or about the issues. He would urge all who were willing either to work in his campaign or to vote for him to sign on the proper sheets. The campaign told people who could not work actively how to become registrars. The goal

Navajo woman cooking one of the bi-weekly lunches.

was to register as many voters as possible.

Zah would end by answering questions. Because so many people wanted to ask questions and Peterson wanted to listen and answer, he was always late to the next meeting. Finally, Rosalind decided they would simply have to cut back to two events a day.

Fundraising

Fundraising was a nickel-and-dime affair. The pattern that evolved out of necessity and that worked amazingly well was this: Someone in the audience would end up passing the hat, literally, to raise extra money. The local units were expected to be self-supporting except for materials. If they could, they were also expected to help the overall campaign.

Almost from the beginning, buttons were sold except to those who could not afford them. One of the best fundraisers turned out to be T-shirts with campaign slogans. Bumper stickers were added to the list of saleable items as the campaign progressed.

MacDonald tactics

MacDonald held back his announcement as long as he could. He finally announced at a rally at Teec Nos Pos that was extensively advertised on radio and newspaper. He said that he only promised *himself*—"a candidate the outside world knows and respects, with allies in many places; a candidate who knows how the government and Council work, who will give stability and leadership."

A furor arose over the numbers present at MacDonald's announcement. The count by reporters showed 1,000 to 1,500 in attendance. His staff insisted there were 4,000 and that the *Navajo Times*, the tribal-owned paper, must so report it. The privately owned *Gallup Independent* reported that MacDonald's staff had also tried to get them to retract their count and use the larger figure. The next week, *Times* editor Duane Beyal ran a story stating that the leadership of the tribe had informed him the *Navajo Times* was essentially a newsletter promoting the Navajo tribal government. In all honesty, he felt he must so inform the public. Beyal was then placed on a ten-day suspension. When he went back there was tighter control.

This gave the Zah campaign more ammunition in their charges of highhandedness by MacDonald, but it also added to the fear tactic MacDonald was using to keep those in tribal jobs from helping Zah. His people were coming to Zah appearances and making a note of those present or taking pictures of the crowd.

Phase Three—the full-time campaign until the primary

It was now time for the Zah campaign to go all out. At the end of May, Peterson left his job. Norman Ration left the campaign to help administer DNA, and Michael Benson also left. Gloria Showalter became overall coordinator. Kay Rogers took charge of headquarters

224

operations, Kenneth Begay became field coordinator, and Wilfred Yazzie took over fundraising. Legal counsel was John Chapela. Elsa Friedenburg became voter registration chair. Many students helped as volunteers during the summer months.

Issues and few answers

Issues papers were being developed by asking the best authority to write a preliminary draft, then having the advisory committee and Peterson check it over. One new issue developed because Zah got questioned about it at so many meetings. The Tribal Council had greatly increased the salaries of the chairman, vice chairman, and themselves in 1979. Recently they had increased it again by a large amount. They had also awarded the chairman and vice chairman a pension of 6.25 percent for each year of service, and themselves a pension of ten percent for each year of service, all to be paid for life.

It did not sit well with the poverty-stricken reservation. Zah promised to rescind them all if he won. He never brought this up himself. He didn't have to. Someone in the crowd would always ask about it.

The campaign pace really accelerated when Zah quit his job. The emphasis remained the same: talk to your neighbor, line up a local group, organize an event for Zah, keep track of those who will support or vote for him, raise what money you can, and most important, register those who aren't registered.

A routine evolved at headquarters. One of the best fundraisers was lunch served for $2.00 (later $2.50) on Tuesdays and Thursdays just outside the headquarters under a protecting ramada. Once in a while the staff had to supply a missing item, but most of the food was donated, as were the chairs and tables they used.

The deadline at the *Navajo Times* was noon Monday for the Wednesday paper, so Monday morning was frantic. Peterson and Rosalind usually got back very late Sunday from their weekend stops and Claudeen had to wake them up to put a story together about what had happened and where. Most stories were also sent to papers in the surrounding and metro areas.

Money and "style"

During the preprimary period, the Zah campaign spent only $4,600, although with a last-minute spurt they raised a total of $6,581. They reported all they took in or spent. MacDonald, on the other hand, often managed to combine tribal business with free campaigning. He did not report anything until the time he filed, taking the position that he was not an official candidate until then. He reported spending nearly $13,000 during the primary.

Where did the differences in money and campaign-style show up? In large billboards vs. homemade lawn signs. In arrivals at events by the MacDonald forces in limousines, planes, or helicopters. And by the Zahs in a loaned pickup or an economy car a little bigger than their Volkswagen. MacDonald sometimes wore tribal dress but his wife wore high heels and Anglo dresses, his aides three-piece suits. The Zahs came in their normal reservation dress. Those who thought a leader should be better than the people liked the MacDonald style. But others were insulted because the chairman came in, made a speech, left before the meal, and didn't answer questions. Zah stayed to listen, so they could relate more to him.

Because many older Navajos do not read or write, or speak English, all ballots on the reservation must carry pictures of the candidates. But almost every family has a radio at home and listens to the Navajo language programs broadcast by most stations surrounding the reservation. So radio was the best means of advertising. Zah could afford very little of it before the primary, while this was the major area of expenditure for MacDonald. Peterson was scheduling every appearance possible to offset this. He noticed tape recorders at his speeches and encouraged the owners to bring them up front, get a good recording, and then play it again for family and groups of neighbors.

The central committee decided on an all-day reservation-wide rally the 24th of July at

Wheatfield Lake, where people could camp out. They had sports and games, a 10 kilometer run, speeches by Zah and supporters interspersed with entertainment and prizes, and volunteers training for the final two-week push. A barbeque lunch was served to everyone. Each agency committee and some single chapters brought one item of food. One supporter donated a steer. It was a huge success.

Primary day, the second Tuesday in August, finally came. The Zahs had a last-minute scramble to fill in poll-watchers. The volunteer in charge of that was one of the few who fell down on the job. But when it was all over the two remaining candidates were Zah with 19,301 and MacDonald with 20,176. MacDonald was first but by fewer than 900 voters out of a total of 48,729.

Phase Four—the final campaign

The MacDonald forces were stunned. They would put every resource they had into the fall campaign. But the momentum would be going Zah's way. Zah immediately called the primary losers to arrange meetings with them and their main supporters. By Thursday three had announced their support.

There was a more immediate problem. The Navajo Tribal Code required that the primary winners choose and file their running mates within five days. MacDonald's present vice chairman would remain. But Zah had to choose. Traditionally if one was from Arizona, the other should be from New Mexico (Utah was a much smaller part of the reservation). Peterson had decided his choice should be made just as he would run the government—beginning with the people involved.

He had sent a request to his New Mexico campaign helpers to prepare a list of people, considering criteria Zah thought the candidate should meet. Then the New Mexicans should meet, talk about the personalities, and narrow down the list. Right after the primary Zah called a meeting of the special advisory committee,

open to anyone else who wanted to come. The list got narrowed down again. Finally, a small group interviewed each of those remaining. Edward T. Begay was chosen. He had been a chapter president, a three-term Tribal Council member, a member of his school board, and also chairman of the McKinley County, New Mexico, Board of Commissioners. He was a Christian, to offset Zah's traditional Navajo religion.

Fall planning

The Zah forces decided to make very few appearances in August, but instead, to get ready for the fall campaign. They once more reorganized the headquarters, agency, and local committee structures, incorporating many who had come over to their side. Many campaign workers had become so devoted they were neglecting home and family to get the necessary campaign chores done.

Each agency coordinating committee was asked to have a meeting with representatives from all the chapters where they had people, to elect officers for the fall, to plan their fall event or events as assigned, to get local speakers on their major local issues lined up, to plan registration and voter outreach efforts.

They hoped money would start flowing their way now, and they were right. They made plans to buy full-page ad space (including the back page) in the *Navajo Times* for the last several weeks before the election; to buy up radio time on the Gallup, Farmington, Tuba City, Holbrook, and the privately owned reservation stations. Wilbert Willie, one of the losing primary candidates, took over the making of the tapes and their distribution. MacDonald had already paid for huge blocks of radio time, but time was bought where it was available backwards from election day as quickly as donations allowed.

Several campaign newsletters and one three-fold brochure were mailed out. Other basic handout brochures were produced with simple pictures of the candidates, a little biographical material, a listing of the issues—all designed to be read easily.

Each agency group was asked to send in suggestions for events. The Zahs were determined now to *plan* events, instead of just taking those offered. The committee used the primary figures, broken down by agency and chapter, to see where they had done well, poorly, or were close, and to determine where efforts should be concentrated.

Each weekend of the campaign was set up to cover an important area or event on the reservation. Each agency was asked to sponsor one or two rallies. The more isolated districts were also asked to do rallies or meetings. The two biggest events of the fall were the annual tribal fair at Window Rock in September and the Shiprock parade and fair the first weekend of October. Plans were made for all of these.

It was decided to kick off the fall campaign with a send off "dinner" for Ed Begay, sponsored by his home Church Rock Chapter on September 2nd. Time was set aside in the middle of the last two September weekends to go back to Denver, Salt Lake–Provo, and Albuquerque, then to San Francisco–Oakland, Los Angeles–Barstow, and to Phoenix.

An intensive voter registration campaign was planned to meet the October 2nd deadline. Finally, it was decided to mail instructions on how to apply for and use absentee ballots to all possible off-reservation names. The intensive planning paid off. The fall campaign went much more smoothly than the primary. The $37,000 in donations certainly helped. MacDonald spent $70,000. (After it was over, the reports showed MacDonald used $20,000 of his own money, borrowed another $25,000 and had unpaid debts of $8,000, so he actually received less than Zah in donations.)

The Zah–Begay float for the tribal fair was made by volunteers who worked on it for many days. It was followed by a traditional family wagon in which the two families rode with their children. Ed and Peterson took turns driving the team. At the Shiprock fair the families again rode the wagon. Begay and Zah

wore satin shirts made by one of their admirers in their campaign colors of white and blue, their names embroidered on the back.

MacDonald's campaign

The Zah campaign did not expect a special MacDonald ploy that actually began the month before the primary. Between then and the general election, the chairman sponsored legislation in the Tribal Council that added $30 million in tribal trust money to the $46 million yearly budget already voted on.

Two million dollars set up an office of Veterans Affairs and gave grants of money to veterans and families. In addition MacDonald had a program to honor the Navajo veterans, bringing in generals to give away medals. This served to cement the veterans' vote and to show how he could call on the outside world for help.

An $18 million Tribal Economic Recovery Act was announced to combat the recession. Of this, $1.8 million went to the Tribal Arts and Crafts program. Each chapter was allocated $20,000 to be used to create jobs for the next ninety days. Then there was a loan program (to get your money you had to fill out a form showing you were behind with house or car payments, etc., and to listen to a MacDonald campaign talk). There were food giveaways in some areas—while MacDonald was there, of course.

MacDonald even laughingly referred to his $18 million *recovery reelection* fund. The Zah campaign estimated that $10 million went to projects which would really benefit local people, but that all of it was an effort to "buy" votes by showing what MacDonald could do (but with the Navajos' own money).

The Zah forces just kept plowing ahead. The campaign concentrated on registering new voters. Zah and Begay kept traveling and speaking. They always introduced themselves by their clan names. (Navajo culture is a matriarchy. Your clan is your mother's family and her mother's family. You name your own clan [your mother's] and then say "I was born for" to name the clan into which you are married, as well as your father's side.) Particularly the older people know each other by their clan names and can then relate to you. Since Peterson's and Edward T.'s clans have always led the Navajo people, this also fit the traditions. So they would introduce themselves, speak, eat the good food, listen, answer questions, and ask for help and votes.

When election day came they had done all they knew how to do. They even took the last blow—a ballot that had Peterson Zah's picture almost blacked out—in stride. Campaign workers traveled to their home chapters to vote, although someone was always at headquarters to man the phones. Zah supporters were invited to come into headquarters and speak live on paid radio time to urge Zah voters to go to the polls.

They had a large potluck planned that night at the trailer ramada whether they won or not.

Poll watchers were to call in their results so the campaign could maintain a count. The polls closed at seven P.M., and by ten o'clock Zah was 1,000 votes ahead and the crowd celebrated. There would be only 5,000 more total votes November 2nd than in the primary but Zah picked up 10,000 votes and MacDonald less than 5,000. No matter what the outside world had thought about their chances, Zah's supporters had known it was time for the incumbent to leave and that he could be ousted. They had won the "impossible campaign."

[Editor's Note: In politics as in the rest of life, what goes around often comes around. Just four years after he was ousted as tribal chairman, Peter MacDonald waged a successful comeback battle, and he was reelected chief of the Navajo Nation in 1986, defeating Peterson Zah's bid for a second term by a narrow margin.]

Jean M. Westwood

26

The First Media Campaign

Keith Melder

The last case study is a delightful if sordid tale of a campaign that encompasses all the ills brought on by the new technologies and mass communications. Indeed, it is a veritable roll call of dishonor: Substance was subsumed by style, many important issues were avoided, negativism and smears were rampant, the news media were manipulated, the voters were dazzled and distracted by hoopla, and novel political techniques reigned supreme. However, the election occurred not in modern times but in 1840, and "the first media campaign," as Keith Melder terms it, was not between two blow-dried specimens of the television era but between two lesser political lights of an earlier age, Martin Van Buren and William Henry Harrison.

This trip back in time is a fitting way to end a reader on the glittering technologies of contemporary election campaigns because it reminds us yet one more time that the essence of politics in America is the same in many vital respects as it was in the nineteenth century.

Political buffs and collectors agree with historians that the great log-cabin and hard-cider campaign of 1840 was one of the most spectacular political events in American history. They do not always agree about the results of this event, however. Political collectors love the 1840 campaign because of the profusion and variety of campaign techniques and gimmicks it produced. Many historians are more skeptical about the campaign, arguing that its methods were questionable, appealing to nonrational, emotional motives of the voters. Convinced that politics ought to be characterized by reasonable deliberation and concern about substantive issues, these scholars complain that the demagoguery, irrelevancies, and the

Keith Melder is a curator in the Division of Political History in the National Museum of American History of the Smithsonian Institution.

"senseless mummery" of the campaign misled the electorate.

Without taking sides in disagreements among scholars, it may be possible to understand and appreciate the political circus that took place during the presidential contest of 1840. In the course of this nation's political history the log-cabin and hard-cider campaign was a watershed event, the first classic and fully developed expression of the "hurrah" campaign, the typical enthusiastic struggle for America's highest office.

Setting the stage

For both Democrats and Whigs, the campaign began with the election of 1836, won by Martin Van Buren over William Henry Harrison and three other regionalized Whig candidates. As the incumbent in 1840, President Van Buren naturally succeeded to the Democratic nomination. For the Whigs, who had not yet won a presidential election, the choice of a candidate was more complicated. Long-time politicians Henry Clay and Daniel Webster were both very much in contention for the nomination. As the most prominent of all Whigs, Clay was the man to beat, although he had made many enemies during his long years in politics. Harrison, the Whig front-runner in 1836, remained in the running between 1836 and 1839 by cultivating party leaders in the states. Another crucial fact of this period was the economic depression of 1837, which brought severe hardships to business and working people alike. Still felt in 1840, the effects of this depression threatened to have an impact on the election.

The very first Whig national nominating convention met in December 1839, setting several precedents. Thurlow Weed, Whig leader from New York state, and Thaddeus Stevens of Pennsylvania led in organizing this convention to defeat Clay, who—they believed—could not win the presidency. By rigging the rules so that each state delegation would cast its whole vote for a single nominee, the convention eliminated many votes for Clay and ensured a vigorous floor fight. Using modern procedures and shrewd machinations, the Whig leadership united behind William Henry Harrison of Ohio. John Tyler was added to the ticket as vice-presidential nominee, almost as an afterthought, to balance the ticket with a Virginian. As a precaution the convention issued no Whig election platform; the party was not sufficiently united to risk taking a stand on basic issues. Instead, a colorful campaign would represent Harrison to the voters.

Before the convention's end, Whig leaders called for a winning campaign of exciting displays and mass participation. Through a remarkable coincidence, Harrison's principal campaign image was suggested by a Demo-

TIPPECANOE PROCESSION.

A highlight of the Harrison campaign was the use of giant, wood-framed leather balls, ten feet in diameter and emblazoned with partisan slogans. About six of these were rolled from town to town in various regions, where they became the focal point of campaign rallies.

Keith Melder

cratic newspaper, the Baltimore *Republican*. Sneering at "Old Granny" Harrison, the paper declared, "Give him [Harrison] a barrel of hard cider, and settle a pension of two thousand a year on him, and my word for it, he will sit the remainder of his days in his log cabin. . . ." The Whigs gleefully took this sarcastic estimate of their candidate and converted it into the central theme of their campaign. Harrison was far from having a log-cabin nativity, however. He was born on a great Virginia plantation, the son of Benjamin Harrison V, a signer of the Declaration of Independence. He belonged to the early American elite.

Creating an image

Political organizers designed Harrison's campaign around the log-cabin and hard-cider image. His own ample residence at North Bend, Ohio, was identified as a log cabin (the original structure had been built of logs) and the candidate was endowed with the rural simplicity and virtue of the frontier cabin-dweller and farmer. The "Farmer of North Bend" became one of his many identities. Campaign events and devices celebrated the log cabin endlessly. It was featured on thousands of novelties and devices such as ribbons, ceramics, sheet music, and banners. "Cabin raisings" took place in hundreds of communities where cabins were built to serve as local Whig party headquarters. Miniature cabins were carried in parades and full-sized cabins were constructed on campaign parade floats. Campaign organizers distributed draughts from actual barrels of hard cider carried on floats or located at their headquarters. Sign painters by the hundreds were recruited to paint banners associating the Hero of Tippecanoe with cabins, cider, and the simple, rustic life.

What followed can be likened to a series of explosions taking place around the country. First there were numerous ratification meetings in the states. Then came George Washington's Birthday, which Whigs in many places made

into a great partisan celebration and the first major Harrison rally of the year. Some of the flavor of these occasions is picked up in a contemporary description of the Ohio State Convention, February 21–22, 1840:

The grand procession on the 22nd surpassed in enthusiasm anything ever before or since in the history of Ohio. The people had been gathering . . . and from all the counties of the State they had come together. From the banks of the Scioto . . . and every river and creek between Lake Erie and the Ohio, every log cabin seemed to have contributed its stalwart Buckeye boys to make the great crowd to set "the ball a rolling on for Tippecanoe and Tyler too." It was an army with banners moving through streets whose walls were hung with flags, streamers and decorations to honor a brave old patriot and pioneer . . . who had settled down in a log cabin to spend his days as a humble farmer at North Bend. . . .

A forerunner to the modern campaign button was the Harrison ribbon. This example trades on the log-cabin and hard-cider theme while still portraying the candidate as a dashing military figure.

The Favorite Whig Songs of 1840

The Great Commotion

To the tune of "Little Pig's Tail"

What has caused the great commotion,
  motion, motion,
    Our country through?
    It is the ball a rolling on, on.

Chorus
For Tippecanoe and Tyler too—Tippecanoe
  and Tyler too,
And with them we'll beat little Van, Van,
Van,
Van is a used up man,
And with them we'll beat little Van.

Like the rushing of mighty waters, waters,
  waters,
    On it will go,
    And in its course will clear the way
    For Tippecanoe [rest of chorus]
See the loco standard tottering, tottering,
  tottering,
    Down it must go,
    And in its place we'll rear the flag
      Of Tippecanoe, etc.
Don't you hear from every quarter, quarter,
  quarter,
    Good news and true,
    That swift the ball is rolling on
      For Tippecanoe, etc.
Now you hear the Van Jacks talking, talking,
  talking,
    Things look quite blue,
    For all the world seems turning around,
      For Tippecanoe, etc.
Let them talk about hard cider, cider, cider,
    And log cabins too,
    'T'will only help to speed the ball
      For Tippecanoe, etc.

[And on for many more verses]

THE HARD CIDER QUICK STEP

Composed & Respectfully Dedicated to the

DELEGATES OF THE

GREAT WHIG CONVENTION

Held at Baltimore May 4 1840

By

L. B. S.

Published by S. CARUSI Baltimore.

Tyler and Tippecanoe

To the tune of "Rosin the Bow"

Now the Whigs at the coming election
  Shall carry their candidates through.
They've made the judicious selection
  Of Tyler and Tippecanoe.

They say that he lives in a cabin
  And that he drinks hard cider too!
Well, what if he does? I am certain
  He's the hero of Tippecanoe!
And pray who is Martin Van Buren?
  What wonders did *he* ever do?
Was he at the battle of Horseshoe
  Bend, Thames or at Tippecanoe?
Oh no, he had no taste for fighting—
  Such rough work he never could do.
He shirked it off onto brave Jackson
  And the hero of Tippecanoe!

[And on for numerous verses]

Similar scenes were enacted hundreds, perhaps thousands of times during the political season between February and November. Great leather "campaign balls" ten feet in diameter were rolled from place to place around the country.

Mobilizing the media

As he had done in the New York state campaign of 1838, Thurlow Weed hired Horace Greeley to edit the principal campaign newspaper. Even before "Old Tip's" nomination, Greeley

Keith Melder

began planning a network of Whig newspapers led by his own weekly, appropriately named the *Log Cabin*.

The *Cabin* reinforced all the campaign imagery depicted during rallies and processions. From May to November it carried endless sentimental stories of Tip's heroism, his kindness to the troops who fought under him, and his generosity to visitors at his North Bend cabin/mansion. Battle stories from the War of 1812 and Harrison's Indian fights endowed the Old General with a heroic, mythic, larger-than-life image similar to that assigned to Andrew Jackson in the campaign of 1828.

The *Log Cabin* featured texts of speeches by the great Whig orators—Clay, Webster, the Old Hero himself, and others. Although many of these orations were dull and pointless, some of them focused on real issues in the campaign, such as the economic hard times and abuses of executive power. Greeley also printed scurrilous attacks on the Democrats and their policies, especially those of President Van Buren. An infamous speech by Rep. Charles Ogle, and a favorite for reprinting by Greeley and other Whig editors, accused Van Buren of profligate waste of public funds in decorating the White House. It was one of the most offensive and effective of the Whig campaign smears.

Most *Log Cabin*s included campaign music, poetry (generally dreadful doggerel), and advertisements for campaign gadgets and devices deemed "essential" for loyal Harrisonians. Reaching a circulation of 80,000 copies per week (Greeley believed it would have topped 100,000 had he been able to print that number), the *Log Cabin* was a vivid, highly effective promotional device for the campaign.

The campaign rollicked along through the spring and summer with huge regional Whig Convocations being held throughout the country. At Baltimore in May, on the day set for the Democratic nominating convention in that city, the Harrisonians staged a "Young Men's Whig National Convention" that completely eclipsed the gathering of their rivals. Typically, they convened "immense" delegations with bands, banners, and floats and paraded through Baltimore, much to the discomfort of the awed Democrats. In June the Whigs of Illinois and other Western states gathered for three days at Springfield for a rally attended by an estimated 20,000 souls, including old soldiers of the Revolution and a young Whig named Abraham Lincoln. In August at Nashville, not far from Andrew Jackson's own plantation, Whigs of the great Southwest assembled for a regional celebration.

Probably more important in generating Whig enthusiasm were the local and state festivities that took place with great frequency, encouraging the participation of masses of local people heretofore uninterested in partisan politics. Every edition of the *Log Cabin* included lengthy descriptions of such rallies, "cabin raisings," and celebrations to illustrate the progress of the Whig cause, its popularity, and the general enthusiasm it aroused. Typical of these was an account of a New York state rally in August:

This has been the proudest—brightest day of my life! Never—no never, have I before seen the People in their majesty! Never were the foundations of popular sentiment so broken up! The scene, from early dawn to sunset, has been one of continued, increasing, bewildering enthusiasm. The hearts of TWENTY-FIVE THOUSAND FREEMEN have been overflowing with gratitude and gladness and joy. It has been a day of Jubilee—an era of Deliverance for CENTRAL NEW-YORK. The people in Waves have poured in from the Valleys and rushed in torrents down from the Mountains. The City has been vocal with Eloquence, with Music, and with Acclamations. Demonstrations of strength and Emblems of Victory and harbingers of Prosperity are all around us, cheering and animating a People who are finally and effectively aroused.

Reading such descriptions, who could doubt the campaign's success? One novel feature of some Whig gatherings was the enlistment of women as participants in parades, makers of banners, and numerous members of the audience.

Democrats were baffled, dazzled, and dispirited by the contagious enthusiasm of the log-cabin and hard-cider campaign and the magnitude of the Whig organization. Again and again in writing to President Van Buren, Democratic politicians expressed skepticism and surprise at the hi-jinks and popularity of their opponents. They voiced contempt for such "silly devices" as log cabins and complained about the "zeal" and "fanaticism" of ciderite crusading. For months Democratic leaders could not believe they were being outmaneuvered. They tried to respond with tactics and devices of their own, but Democratic resources could not match those of the Whigs. The special party newspaper, the *Extra Globe*, edited by Amos Kendall, circulated nearly as widely as the *Log Cabin*, but it lacked the latter's spirit and imagination. Ultimately the Democrats had to admit they had been "out-fought, out-drunk and out-sung."

Selling the goods

This presidential election included many elements of a latter-day Madison Avenue advertising campaign. Slogans, jingles, and testimonials saturated the communications media. Throughout the campaign, the Whig leadership sought to create good feelings about Harrison through such devices as identifying

A brass snuffbox from the "Tippecanoe" campaign of 1840, replete with log cabin and cider barrel.

his image with that of George Washington. Like Washington, Harrison was a Cincinnatus who left his plough to save his country, serving the people again and again; now he was prepared to make another sacrifice to preserve the nation.

Campaign rallies were positive, uplifting experiences for vast throngs of participants. Whig partisans staged events to make people feel good about themselves and confident about the future—if Harrison were elected. Whether they did it consciously or not, campaigners handled the intangible qualities of their work with extraordinary finesse. All of these factors combined to produce the first thorough presidential *image* campaign.

What else was new about this contest? Most tactics and devices were borrowed from other kinds of public celebrations. Processions and parades had served for centuries as expressions of public attachment to civic and religious institutions. Whig strategists appropriated many elements from Independence Day celebrations until the entire summer took on the character of a giant Fourth of July party. Whig partisans also adapted some of the populist tactics that had served so well in Andrew Jackson's 1828 campaign. Such campaign devices as ribbons, souvenirs, music, and broadsides were not new. But under Whig management and with ample funds raised by Whig leaders, they proliferated as never before. The degree to which they were used and literally saturated the country was unprecedented. Thurlow Weed and other Whig leaders had expanded and perfected their organization to an extent never before seen in a presidential election.

Changing the process

Two significant "firsts" may be attributed to the Whigs in 1840. The log-cabin candidate was the first presidential aspirant to go out on the stump in his own behalf. At a time when candidates for the highest office were supposed to remain aloof from electioneering,

Keith Melder

Harrison made twenty-three speeches, all in his home state of Ohio. As unprecedented efforts to display the candidate to the electorate, they symbolized the democratization of American politics. The electorate was curious and apparently pleased to see and hear their hero in the flesh.

The election of 1840 also produced the first national mass-based advertising campaign of any kind, a circumstance not generally admitted by historians of advertising. For the first time a national "product" was marketed vigorously and imaginatively across the land. Whig managers used every available means of communication to display the Harrison image. People everywhere could visualize the candidate from portraits of Harrison depicted on cloth ribbons, printed ceramics, publications, medals, and other devices. The campaign's events—rallies, processions, conventions—were converted into mass media of communication. A political communications revolution had taken place.

The log cabin and hard-cider campaign also deserves to be remembered for other reasons.

It climaxed the formation of the second American party system. In 1840, for the first time, two nationally organized, nearly equal parties sponsored effective presidential campaigns: Party politics had come of age. The political extravaganza also served as a grand exhibition of popular culture and entertainment.

The log cabin legacy

The campaign of 1840 became the model for presidential contests since its time. It set standards for campaign achievement and established a sequence of campaign events that guided rituals of American politics from the mid-nineteenth century to the present. The campaign developed in a sequence of five distinct stages: first a preconvention period when rival candidates maneuvered for popularity, then the stage of the nominating convention, followed by a period of strategy planning and money raising. Then the campaign itself began with the "senseless mummery" of hundreds of mass rallies and

The Whig campaign employed hundreds of artists in the production of elaborate banners, such as this masterpiece.

celebrations. As the campaign drew to a close, a record number of voters went to the polls on different election days (the federal government would later set a single date for presidential voting).

Did it work? Was the log-cabin and hard-cider campaign successful? At a superficial level, it certainly had the appearance of success, for Harrison won the election, the first Whig candidate to succeed to the presidency. Actually, no observer can say with assurance that the spectacular campaign was Harrison's magic formula for victory, even though Van Buren himself observed he had been "washed out of office by a flood of apple juice!" It could be argued that economic conditions were more important than hard cider in making "Old Tip" president. The lingering economic hard times may have influenced more voters than the endless processions and often senseless electioneering.

At another level the great campaign was certainly successful. Political mass participation and showmanship resulted in the largest turnout of eligible voters in American presidential politics to that time. More than 2,400,000 citizens cast ballots, or nearly eighty percent of those eligible. Only the unprecedented barnstorming of William Jennings Bryan in 1896 produced a similar turnout in the years since; recent elections have seen the figures fall to barely half. Harrison received an electoral vote of 234 to 60 for Van Buren and a popular majority of nearly 150,000.

This important campaign lives on in the thousands of "hurrah" campaigns for the presidency and other offices that have taken place in the years since 1840. To some extent it still lives, even though recent campaigners have substituted new technologies of television, direct mail, and polling for the assembly of thousands of people to participate in campaign rallies. They mash their apples differently today, but the juice tastes the same. That old 1840 flavor seems here to stay.

References

Chambers, William Nisbet. "Election of 1840," in *History of American Presidential Elections 1789-1968*, ed. Arthur Schlesinger, Jr. New York: Chelsea House, 1971.

Chambers, William Nisbet. "Party Development and the American Mainstream," *The American Party Systems: Stages of Political Development*, eds. William Nisbet Chambers and Walter Dean Burnham. 2nd. ed., New York: Oxford University Press, 1975.

Greeley, Horace. *Recollections of a Busy Life*. New York: J. B. Ford & Co., 1868.

Gronbeck, Bruce E. "Functional and Dramaturgical Theories of Presidential Campaigning," *Presidential Studies Quarterly*, vol. 14, Fall 1984, pp. 486-499.

Gunderson, Robert Gray. *The Log-Cabin Campaign*. Lexington: University of Kentucky Press, 1957.

Howe, Daniel Walker. *The Political Culture of the American Whigs*. Chicago: University of Chicago Press, 1979.

McCormick, Richard P. "Political Development and the Second Party System," in *The American Party Systems: Stages of Political Development*, eds. William Nisbet Chambers and Walter Dean Burnham. 2nd ed., New York: Oxford University Press, 1975.

Norton, A. B. *The Great Revolution of 1840: Reminiscences of the Log Cabin and Hard Cider Campaign*. Mt. Vernon, Ohio: A. B. Norton & Co., 1888.

Martin Van Buren Manuscripts, Library of Congress.

The Log Cabin, published simultaneously in New York and Albany, by H. Greeley & Co., May 2, 1840–November 20, 1840.

Keith Melder

Index